# WHAT IS GOD LIKE?

*To a Special Friend Ron*

# WHAT IS GOD LIKE?

IS HE THE ULTIMATE LOVER OF 1 JOHN 4:8;

OR IS HE THE ULTIMATE TERRORIST OF MATTHEW 10:28?

## RALPH H. MATTHEWS

Copyright © 2013 by Ralph H. Matthews.

Library of Congress Control Number:     2013906291
ISBN:          Hardcover                 978-1-4836-2077-0
               Softcover                 978-1-4836-2076-3
               Ebook                     978-1-4836-2078-7

All rights reserved. No part of this book may be reproduced or transmitted in any form or by any means, electronic or mechanical, including photocopying, recording, or by any information storage and retrieval system, without permission in writing from the copyright owner.

This book was printed in the United States of America.

Rev. date: 05/14/2013

**To order additional copies of this book, contact:**
Xlibris Corporation
1-888-795-4274
www.Xlibris.com
Orders@Xlibris.com
128617

# Contents

ACKNOWLEDGEMENTS .................................................................... 13
PREFACE ............................................................................................ 15

1   GOD IS PERSONAL ................................................................... 17
2   GOD KNOWS EVERYTHING ...................................................... 19
3   GOD CONCERNS HIMSELF WITH SMALL DETAILS ................ 26
4   GOD BELIEVES IN PAIN ............................................................ 30
5   GOD HAS A HIGH TOLERANCE FOR PAIN .............................. 37
6   GOD WANTS YOU TO DIE ......................................................... 41
7   GOD MAKES COVENANTS ....................................................... 43
8   GOD INSTIGATED BLOOD COVENANTS ................................. 45
9   GOD DEMANDS REST ............................................................... 48
10  GOD SWEARS OATHS AND ISSUES CURSES ....................... 52
11  GOD IS HOLY ............................................................................. 57
12  GOD IS A BUILDER .................................................................... 65
13  GOD HAS SECRETS .................................................................. 67
14  GOD DEMANDS WORSHIP ....................................................... 69
15  GOD CAN BE PERSUADED ....................................................... 77
16  GOD IS A LAWMAKER ............................................................... 80
17  GOD MADE PECULIAR LAWS ................................................... 88
18  GOD CHANGES LAWS .............................................................. 95
19  GOD INVENTED OLD AGE ........................................................ 99
20  GOD ISSUES WARNINGS ....................................................... 103
21  GOD IS AN ENFORCER ........................................................... 106
22  GOD HAS SPOKEN TO EVERY MAN ..................................... 110
23  GOD IS A GOOD COMMUNICATOR ....................................... 117
24  GOD GIVES AND HE TAKES ................................................... 123
25  GOD CREATED SATAN ........................................................... 125
26  GOD CREATED SATAN CUNNING AND POWERFUL ............ 134
27  GOD PUT HATRED BETWEEN MAN AND SATAN ................. 139
28  GOD USES EVIL SPIRITS ........................................................ 143
29  GOD LIVES ON EARTH ........................................................... 145
30  GOD DOES NOT ALWAYS ANSWER PRAYER ...................... 147

| | | |
|---|---|---|
| 31 | GOD DOES ANSWER PRAYER | 152 |
| 32 | GOD FORGIVES | 156 |
| 33 | GOD WILL NOT ALWAYS FORGIVE | 157 |
| 34 | GOD IS A FAITH HEALER | 160 |
| 35 | GOD MAY ASK YOU QUESTIONS | 165 |
| 36 | GOD IS AN EDUCATOR | 167 |
| 37 | GOD IS KING | 169 |
| 38 | GOD HAS A PROBLEM WITH KNOWLEDGE | 173 |
| 39 | GOD IS A FIGHTER | 175 |
| 40 | GOD IS SILENT | 183 |
| 41 | GOD IS ROMANTIC | 185 |
| 42 | GOD EXPECTS MODERATION | 187 |
| 43 | GOD CREATED PERILS | 189 |
| 44 | GOD DOES NOT LIKE INDEPENDENCE | 194 |
| 45 | GOD IS AN ENVIRONMENTALIST | 197 |
| 46 | GOD IS THE ULTIMATE CREATOR | 202 |
| 47 | GOD CREATED THE HUMAN WILL | 204 |
| 48 | GOD IS INTO REAL ESTATE | 220 |
| 49 | GOD USES WEAPONS OF MASS DESTRUCTION | 223 |
| 50 | GOD IS A JUDGE | 225 |
| 51 | GOD IS NOT SAFE | 228 |
| 52 | GOD IS IMPARTIAL | 232 |
| 53 | GOD GETS ANGRY | 234 |
| 54 | GOD HIDES | 236 |
| 55 | GOD WANTS YOU TO FIND HIM | 239 |
| 56 | GOD DOES NOT NEED A CAUSE | 241 |
| 57 | GOD HAS UNLIMITED POWER | 244 |
| 58 | GOD CREATED MAN AND WOMAN NAKED | 246 |
| 59 | GOD IS DEMANDING | 248 |
| 60 | GOD INVENTED FAITH | 252 |
| 61 | GOD IS TO BE FEARED | 255 |
| 62 | GOD IS THE ULTIMATE TERRORIST | 256 |
| 63 | GOD HAS LIKES AND DISLIKES | 258 |
| 64 | GOD HAS INCREDIBLE PATIENCE | 260 |
| 65 | GOD IS BIG ON SYMBOLS | 262 |
| 66 | GOD DESIRES TO BLESS | 268 |
| 67 | GOD HAS INTENSE EMOTIONS | 270 |
| 68 | GOD LIKES ALTARS | 272 |
| 69 | GOD WILL TEST YOU | 274 |
| 70 | GOD WILL HURT YOU | 280 |
| 71 | GOD LEANS TOWARD MERCY | 284 |
| 72 | GOD WILL ONE DAY SHOW NO MERCY | 287 |

| | |
|---|---|
| 73 GOD IS A GUARDIAN | 289 |
| 74 GOD IS LIGHT | 291 |
| 75 GOD DELEGATES MEN TO LEAD MEN | 293 |
| 76 GOD IS TOUGH | 300 |
| 77 GOD BELIEVES IN CAPITAL PUNISHMENT | 306 |
| 78 GOD IS A MIRACLE WORKER | 310 |
| 79 GOD CAN CREATE MASS CONFUSION | 313 |
| 80 GOD HAND PICKED THE JEWS | 315 |
| 81 GOD IS ROLLING IN WEALTH | 321 |
| 82 GOD IS INTO THE ARTS | 323 |
| 83 GOD CANNOT DO SOME THINGS | 331 |
| 84 GOD WANTS YOUR MONEY | 332 |
| 85 GOD CAN FOOL YOU | 334 |
| 86 GOD USES EVERYTHING HE CREATED | 336 |
| 87 GOD DOES NOT LIKE WIMPS | 338 |
| 88 GOD IS LIKE JESUS | 343 |
| | |
| EPILOGUE | 345 |
| WORKS CITED | 347 |

The majority of Scripture verses are taken from The
Holy Bible, Modern King James Version Copyright ©1962 - 1998
By Jay P. Green, Sr. Used by permission of the copyright holder.


Scriptures taken from the HOLY BIBLE, NEW INTERNATIONAL
VERSION (North American Edition) Copyright 1973 1978. 1984 by
International Bible Society. Used by permission of Zondervan Publishing
House.


Other versions used are: ASV - American Standard Version; BBE - Bible in
Basic English; CEV - Contemporary English Version; GNB - Good News
Bible; GW—God's Word; KJV - King James Version; MSG - Message Bible;
NLT - New Living Translation; NIV - New International Version.


**All Scripture is shown in bold print.**

Author's emphasis noted by underlining.

*This book is dedicated to friends of Jesus:*

*Those who are hungry, thirsty and in need of the basic necessities of life.*

**And the King shall answer and say to them, Truly I say to you, Inasmuch as you did it to one of the least of these My brothers, you have done it to Me.**

*Matthew 25:40*

*All profits from this book will be given directly to them.*

*Jesus will notice.*

# ACKNOWLEDGEMENTS

Here are the special people who helped me write this book. Thanks to Madeline, my wife, for the endless interruptions and her invaluable help with the final edit. Thanks to Stephen, my son, for the numerous times he helped with software problems and kept my computer humming. Thanks to Sarah and Shawna, my daughters, for your very valuable proofreading. Tania Beatty and Jen Wilton thank you for making this book a much better read.

# PREFACE

Our God is truly awesome. Men and angels fall down to worship this God; demons tremble in His presence; He is majestic in power; He is terrible in battle; and yet His most outstanding characteristic is that of a lover. He is full of wisdom, He heals with a word, His grace knows no limit, He is the God of abundance and His greatest desire is to share it all with you.

When we ask the question, "What is God like," it can only be in that form - what is He *like*. No one really knows since no man has ever met Him in His fullness. Our human minds are not capable of fully comprehending God. The best we can do is to try and relate to things about Him that we, as humans, can somewhat grasp.

There are many aspects of Him that we are unable to understand. For example, when we talk about the omnipresence of God—His ability to be everywhere at the same time—we have no practical point of reference as we can only be at one geographical place at any point in time. He is Omnipotent, meaning he has *unlimited* power, while ours is limited, measured and not even worthy of comparison. He is incomprehensible, sinless, and unchanging. We can only weakly imagine what these characteristics might be like. However, there are some of His characteristics that we can identify with. When the Bible says He gets angry, or He experienced joy, or that He judges, we can somewhat understand because we have all felt anger and joy, and know what it's like to judge. In this study we will examine some things about God that we can identify with.

The Bible, His creation and His Holy Spirit teach us many things about God. The best information we have about God comes from His Son, Jesus, who left His Father's home and visited with us for 33 years, allowing us some detailed, eye witness information. This is how Matthew records this visit as an angel spoke to Joseph: "**Behold, the virgin shall conceive in *her* womb, and will bear a son. And they will call His name Emmanuel,"** which being interpreted is, **God with us** (Matthew 1:23). John confirms that God, the Creator, and Jesus, are as One in these verses: **In the beginning was the Word, and the Word was with God, and <u>the Word was God</u>. He was in *the* beginning with God. All things**

**came into being through Him, and without Him not even one *thing* came into being that has come into being** (John 1:1-3). He also wrote to us through His prophets and many of His character traits are made clear to us from His laws.

This book places emphasis on the Word of God. Most often the whole verse of Scripture is presented and not just the references, so you do not have to look them up. After all, it is the Word of God that is authoritative and it has power that can change us.

Of course, it goes without saying, that neither this book nor any other book can adequately describe the greatness of our God. The Apostle John put it best in making this statement about the teachings of Jesus: **There are so many other things Jesus did. If they were all written down, each of them, one by one, I can't imagine a world big enough to hold such a library of books** (John 21:25 MSG).

In the Bible, God is often referred to as a triune being: Father, Son, and Holy Ghost. For our purposes, most references are to God the Father, but since Father, Son and Holy Ghost are *one* in terms of perfect unity, reference to either is applicable to all.

The theme of this book is the love of God, for God is Love. Many other characteristics are listed herein and throughout the Bible that present a fearful picture of Him such as His wrath, His destructive powers, and His judgment, etc. However, all these pale once we understand just a tiny bit of His love. The reason is simple: His love far outweighs all else. He is known to use even His fearsome attributes to bring us sinners back to Himself to lavish love upon us. The theme of this book can be put into proper context when viewed through the words of this old hymn, "The Love Of God" (Lehman, 1919):

*The love of God is greater far*
*Than tongue or pen can ever tell;*
*It goes beyond the highest star,*
*And reaches to the lowest hell;*
*The guilty pair, bowed down with care,*
*God gave His Son to win;*
*His erring child He reconciled,*
*And pardoned from his sin.*

# 1  GOD IS PERSONAL

God is not a nebulous being; He is personal. In fact, He is so very personal that He has created humans so that He can live inside them. It seems that the whole purpose in creating us is to know us personally and enjoy our fellowship:

> **Thou art worthy, O Lord, to receive glory, and honor, and power: for thou hast created all things, and for thy pleasure they are, and were created** (Revelation 4:11 KJV).

This very intimate contact with humans, for those who so desire, is recorded in Ezekiel, and although these verses were spoken directly to the Jewish people, it applies to all of His children:

> **And I will put My Spirit within you and cause you to walk in My statutes, and you shall keep My judgments and do them. And <u>I shall put My Spirit in you</u>, and you shall live, and I will place you in your own land. And you shall know that I Jehovah have spoken and have done it, says Jehovah** (Ezekiel 36:27; 37:14).

Jesus, who is God in the flesh, placed a lot of emphasis on living inside us as seen in the following two passages:

> **He who partakes of My flesh and drinks My blood <u>dwells in Me, and I in him</u>** (John 6:56). This was in reference to sharing the bread and wine commemorating His death.

> **At that day you shall know that I** *am* **in My Father, and you in Me, and <u>I in you</u>** (John 14:20).

The apostle John confirms the same concept:

> **And he who keeps His commandment dwells in Him, and <u>He in him</u>. And by this we know that He <u>abides in us</u>, by the Spirit which He gave to us** (1 John 3:24).

> **By this we know that we dwell in Him, and <u>He in us</u>, because He has given us of His Spirit** (1 John 4:13).

Paul teaches the same in his letter to the Galatians. In order for us to be this personal with God, the flesh (carnal) part of us must die:

> **I have been crucified with Christ, and I live;** *yet* **no longer I, but Christ lives in me. And** *that* **life I now live in the flesh, I live by faith toward the Son of God, who loved me and gave Himself on my behalf** (Galatians 2:20).

If you have difficulty in imagining Great, Big, Almighty God whose front yard is measured in light years, living inside a mere human like us, you are not alone. Max Lucado writes: ". . . Christ moved in. He still does. When grace happens, Christ enters. 'Christ in you the hope of glory' (Colossians 1:27). For many years I missed this truth. I believed all the other prepositions: Christ *for* me, *with* me, *ahead* of me. And I knew I was working *beside* Christ, *under* Christ, *with* Christ. But I never imagined that Christ was *in* me" (Page 9). Try and imagine, if you can, that Jesus, His Son, died trying to get your attention.

Why must our flesh die in order for us to know God personally? God hates sin and He hates what it does to His children. He desires to know us personally but He does not want to control us. Sin (or Satan), on the other hand, wants to control us. Consider what God asked Cain when sin was first mentioned in the Bible: **Why are you so angry? Why do you look so dejected? You will be accepted if you do what is right. But if you refuse to do what is right, then watch out! Sin is crouching at the door, <u>eager to control</u> you. But you must subdue it and be its master** (Genesis 4:6-7 NLT).

# 2 GOD KNOWS EVERYTHING

Here are at least four verses from the Bible that say so:

> **For His eyes *are* on the ways of man, and He sees all his steps** (Job 34:21).

> **Great *is* our LORD, and of great power; *There is* no limit to His understanding** (Psalm 147:5).

> **Don't you know anything? Haven't you been listening? GOD doesn't come and go. God lasts. He's Creator of all you can see or imagine. He doesn't get tired out, doesn't pause to catch his breath. And he knows everything, inside and out** (Isaiah 40:28 MSG).

> **. . . saying, "Blessed be the name of God, forever and ever. He knows all, does all** (Daniel 2:20 MSG).

If we could comprehend a small measure of what the above verses really mean, we would shake in our boots. We feel so private inside our own thoughts; inside our own heads. From there we have the ability to shut out even the closest friend or family member, but we cannot shut Him out. We think that our very existence depends on a measure of privacy and He knows this, because even though He knows everything about us He never interferes, at least not in a way whereby we would be intimated by His great power. God shows great respect for our privacy and will never impose in a way that would make us uncomfortable. He could choose to impose condemnation on us because we are sinners but instead will use the gentle art of convection in a still small voice. But, nevertheless He knows!

There is a very real sense in which He communicates with us by the power of His Holy Spirit but never in the sense of intruding. Omniscience is one of those things about Him that we have no way of understanding. This awesome power is not something He uses to frighten us. Somehow, when He does use this power, He applies it with a measure of great wisdom and compassion and we recognize His communication as a still small voice instead of the mighty roar that it could be. This is exactly how He demonstrated it to Elijah on a day when this man was so discouraged that he was suicidal:

> **And he himself went a day's journey into the wilderness, and came and sat down under a broom tree. And he begged for his life, <u>that he might die</u>. And he said, It is enough. O Jehovah, <u>take away my life</u>. For I *am* no better than my fathers . . . and went in the strength of that food forty days and forty nights to Horeb the mount of God. And he came there to a cave and stayed there. And behold, the Word of Jehovah *came* to him, and He said to him, What *are* you *doing* here, Elijah? And he said, I have been very zealous for Jehovah the God of Hosts. For the sons of Israel have forsaken Your covenant, thrown down Your altars, and have slain Your prophets with the sword. And I, I alone, am left. And they seek to take my life away. And He said, Go forth and stand on the mountain before Jehovah. And, behold, Jehovah passed by, and a great and strong wind tore the mountains, and broke the rocks in pieces before Jehovah. *But* Jehovah *was* not in the wind. And after the wind was an earthquake, *but* Jehovah was not in the earthquake. And after the earthquake was a fire, *but* Jehovah *was* not in the fire. And after the fire *was* a still, small voice** (1 Kings 19:4-12).

We need to listen very carefully for the still, small voice. Our spirit was designed to hear it. Our flesh will want to ignore it. We connect with Him via the small voice and we know in our "knower" that it is Him. Jesus assures us of this with these words: **My sheep hear My voice, and I know them, and they follow Me** (John 10:27). We can be confident that it's His voice when the voice aligns with His Word, the Bible.

There is a sense in which we don't mind if God knows everything going on inside a human mind as long as it's not ours. When *we* contemplate evil thoughts, we would like to think they are very private. While writing this chapter, I received an email regarding a little girl who had been kidnapped from her parents' holiday apartment. I viewed the pictures and read the plea for help in finding this precious child. As I prayed for her safety and was asking God to help the authorities to find her, I realized that God knows exactly where this child is at this very moment. He knows everything! He knows who took her and He knows the horrible pain her parents are going through. He knows the trauma that her abductor has already put her through and He knows what this evil person is planning in the days ahead.

## What is God Like?

Knowing that God has all this inside knowledge, the immediate response from most of us is this: why did He allow it to happen and why does He allow it to continue? If we are to make any attempt to understand God, to know what He is like, we need the answer to these questions. As mentioned earlier we cannot know everything about God with our limited, finite minds. He has, however, given us enough knowledge about Himself that we can get to know Him, have fellowship with Him, and ultimately, worship and adore Him for Who He is.

So, why did God allow the kidnapping of a helpless child? Why does He allow this cowardly, perverted man to continue hiding, and why does He allow such an evil person to even live? Our sense of justice, which He gave us, prompts us to demand safety for the child and punishment for the criminal. When the criminal is not caught, we feel helpless and throw the responsibility for this atrocity on God's shoulders, because He knows where the man is hiding and we do not; because He has the power to stop him and we do not. However, if we apply a reasonable amount of *God's* logic, we would be able to conclude the following: When this man—we'll call him Sam—commits a crime, Sam is exercising his God given right to do whatever he wants. It is called *free will.* Sam can go to work on this particular day and plant some potatoes on his farm or he can abduct some father's child. Sam has the God-given option of treating this child as a precious innocent, or he could use her for his own perverted gratification and sexually abuse her. If he chooses the latter we would all want to come down hard on Sam because he made the wrong choice. We know what he did was wrong: he injured and traumatized a child and caused the parents great pain and anguish, and we know he didn't have to do what he did. In a perfect world, his sexual pleasures could have been satisfied by a God given wife. We would like for God to stop Sam from doing this evil deed, but if God stops Sam, then that line of logic requires that to be fair, He must be consistent and stop the rest of us from committing our sins too.

While the sins we commit may not be as horrible as the one Sam has committed, we would have to acknowledge that they are sins nevertheless and the same principal of law must apply to everyone. So, let's assume that God should put a stop to all sin because it is inherently wrong, and because every sin hurts someone. If we believe that, then we've painted ourselves into a corner. Think about it: while this is our prescribed solution for Sam, we certainly would not want God to be stopping us from committing all the wrongs we have done or will to do. Suppose, for example, you are late for work tomorrow morning and God stops you from breaking the speed limit. At 41 in a 40 mph zone, your guardian angel pulls you over and issues you

21

a ticket—which must be paid on the spot. Suppose you cheat a little on your income tax (just a little), and God orders Gabriel to call the tax department on your behalf. What if a person of the opposite sex flirts with you at work tomorrow and you entertain some sinful thoughts? When would you like God to stop you? Immediately after you conceive the sinful thought or just after the sinful act has been committed? We must not forget that the same rule that applies to Sam will apply to you. After all, God does know and He will stop you. We would soon have to acknowledge that such interference constantly taking place in our lives would interfere with our ability to function as a normal human being. Human life as we know it would cease. We would no longer be free-will creatures. We would be more like robots or, at best, like a group of animals herded in whatever direction the Shepherd chooses. It would be His will only and never ours.

The sad conclusion is that Sam must be allowed to do what he did. Further, we are all just like Sam. God must allow Sam his choices as He must allow you and I our choices, at least for now. The day will come when Sam will be separated from God's kingdom and, unless he repents, will be placed in another kingdom. One more suited to him.

> **And these shall go away into everlasting punishment: but the righteous into life eternal** (Matthew 25:46 KJV).
>
> **And shall come forth; they that have done good, unto the resurrection of life; and they that have done evil, unto the resurrection of damnation** (John 5:29 KJV).
>
> **In flaming fire taking vengeance on them that know not God, and that obey not the gospel of our Lord Jesus Christ: Who shall be punished with everlasting destruction from the presence of the Lord, and from the glory of his power** (2 Thessalonians 1:8-9 KJV).

God's Kingdom will be full of people who exercised their God-given right to repent when they made the wrong choices. When they asked for forgiveness, they came under the covering of the blood of Jesus. He will never refuse any sinner this covering. Even Sam if he is interested:

> **And forgive us our sins; for we also forgive every one that is indebted to us. And lead us not into temptation; but deliver us from evil** (Luke 11:4 KJV).

## What is God Like?

**But if we walk in the light, as He is in the light, we have fellowship with one another, and the blood of Jesus Christ His Son cleanses us from all sin** (1 John 1:7).

We see from the above that God does know everything. We have no way of knowing what it's like to know everything. An all-knowing God is aware of every detail of every sin taking place at any given moment. We have some awareness of what people like Sam are doing in our own small world and sometimes a little of what's happening in our neighborhood, and even this limited awareness is apt to makes us sad and sometimes fearful. However, the memories of the dreadful news of a missing child fade in time, and life goes on as normal. The same is not true of an all-knowing God. He does not forget. Not only does He remember what Sam did to this one little girl, He also knows what all the other murderers, molesters, thieves, liars, adulterers and fornicators have done and are presently doing on any given day. He remembers it all.

We must also keep in mind that He is the Creator of all life. He fathered all of us and He loves us more than our earthly fathers and mothers. His love is so great that He gave the life of His only Son in exchange for ours. Now, with love like that, try and picture what God must be going through when He sees what sinners are up to, and worse, what His children are going through at the hands of sinners like Sam. It is impossible for us to conceive it. We'd blow a fuse! We are limited in our imaginations and limited as to how much pain we can bear. Yet, for God, both the sinner and the innocent victims are His creation. He is their loving Father and He must stand by and allow them to abuse and be abused, all so that every man can exercise his or her right to be human. God bears the brunt of all sin. This is what David meant after committing adultery with Bathsheba and having her husband killed when he penned these words: **Against You, You only, have I sinned, and done evil in Your sight; that You might be justified when You speak, *and* be clear when You judge** (Psalm 51:4). Once we acknowledge this, our questions will go from: "Why did God allow Sam to sin and why does He allow sin to continue?" to: "How can God bear all the pain that accompanies our sins?"

Because He knows everything, no one knows pain like God.

Jesus endured the burden of all sin on the cross, and it means that He is the one who hurts most when sin is committed. He is the one who first recognized the fact that if humans harm one another it is not good. To prevent this He made laws such as, **love your neighbor as yourself** (Leviticus 19:18). He made a law to teach us never to desire anything that belongs to another: **You shall** not covet your neighbor's house. You shall not covet your neighbor's wife, nor his manservant, nor his maidservant, nor his ox, nor his ass, nor anything that *is* your neighbor's** (Exodus 20:17). Because it's His law, He is first to be hurt when it is broken.

God's hurting soul is revealed in the book of Jeremiah as Jehovah expresses anguish over our sin: **Oh that my head were waters, and my eyes a fountain of tears, that I might weep day and night for the slain of the daughter of my people!** (Jeremiah 9:1). Knowing everything means deep hurt and tears in abundance.

God's tolerance toward sin is first recognized in Adam our forefather. Adam sinned and God tolerated his disobedience and even made provision for his reconciliation by slaying an innocent animal to cover Adam's nakedness, which simply symbolized his sin: **And for Adam and his wife Jehovah God made coats of skins, and clothed them** (Genesis 3:21). Further, He issued the first prophetic word in promising a permanent sacrifice for Adam's sin by sending the Seed, Jesus, to cover all sin for every sinner who would choose to accept the sacrifice: **And I will put enmity between you and the woman, and between your seed and her Seed; He will bruise your head, and you shall bruise His heel** (Genesis 3:15). The bruising refers to Satan's attempt to take Jesus out by having Him crucified, which proved to be a wounding of the heel verses a wounding to the head which Jesus will deliver to Satan taking him out permanently.

God is all knowing and has a certain tolerance toward our sin, but He should never be taken for granted. He has made it abundantly clear in this verse that there is a limit to His patience and tolerance: **And Jehovah said, My spirit shall not always strive with man, in his erring; he is flesh. Yet his days shall be a hundred and twenty years** (Genesis 6:3). The 120 years had to do with the great flood in the time of Noah and even though He tolerated man's sin for all these years, He kept His word and destroyed every sinner who ignored His warning and took Him for granted.

God knows everything, and with that knowledge comes great sorrow and pain. The anguish of soul that He willingly endures results from an abundance of compassion and mercy.

> **For the Word of Jehovah *is* right; and all His works *are* in truth. He loves righteousness and judgment; the earth is full of the mercy of Jehovah** (Psalm 33:4-5).

> **For Your mercy *is* great to the heavens, and Your truth to the clouds** (Psalm 57:10).

> **Jehovah *is* merciful and gracious, slow to anger, and rich in mercy** (Psalm 103:8).

Not only does God want to show the sinner mercy and compassion, He is also willing to make provision for the atonement of their sins and grant complete absolution, should they so choose: **Let the wicked forsake his way and the evil man his thoughts. Let him turn to the LORD, and he will have mercy on him, and to our God, for he will freely pardon** (Isaiah 55:7 NIV).

God knows everything. He is the only one who knows certain things. Jesus said that His Father was the only one who knows when the end of heaven and the earth will take place: **The heaven and the earth shall pass away, but My Words shall not pass away. But of that day and hour no one knows, no, not the angels of Heaven, but only My Father** (Matthew 24:35-36). The knowledge and power of our God is awesome. It is awesome how much compassion and mercy He must exercise to hold back judgment for the sin He sees on any given day. It is also clear from the verse above that one day this tolerance will end, and He has already determined what day that will be.

It is strange, in one sense, how we as humans have such difficulty trusting God. When we consider how knowledgeable He is and how little we really know, one wonders why we do not trust Him more than we do. We do not know what the next second will bring, but He does. We don't know how long we will live; if we are going to remain healthy; if we will recover from sickness and trials that we will encounter tomorrow; if our wealth will be sufficient; if poverty will overtake us; or if disaster will strike our city or what will become of our loved ones—but God knows all this and much more. It would be good for us to learn to trust Him.

# 3 GOD CONCERNS HIMSELF WITH SMALL DETAILS

When we read the Bible and then ask the question, "What is God like," it is difficult not to conclude that He is a stickler for detail. At times the details seem minute, insignificant and sometimes downright picky, although with further study, we usually find that there is great meaning and purpose in the details. While the Old Testament is rife with such small details (try reading Leviticus!), the New Testament emphasizes the spiritual rather than the physical. The spiritual is defined by every word that came out of His mouth and He warns us that He is still very particular: **Heaven and the earth shall pass away, but My Words shall not pass away** (Luke 21:33). And we pay particular attention to His words for good reason: **It is the Spirit that makes alive, the flesh profits nothing. The words that I speak to you are spirit and are life** (John 6:63). Let us examine just a few details from the Old Testament that may seem small and insignificant to us, but not to God.

- He cares about clean clothes: **And Jehovah said to Moses, Go to the people and sanctify them today and tomorrow, and let them wash their clothes** (Exodus 19:10).

- In Exodus 39:21, God, the Almighty One, the Creator of the whole universe, concerns Himself with a breast-pocket: **And they bound the breast-pocket by its rings to the rings of the ephod with a lace of blue, so that it might be above the band of the ephod, and so that the breast-pocket might not be loosened from the ephod, even as Jehovah commanded Moses.**

- In verse 23 of the same chapter, He is concerned that the opening in a robe might not rip: **And the opening in the middle of the robe *was* like the opening of a corselet, with a band around the opening, so that it might not tear**. These garments were designed by God Himself, passed on to Moses and no detail was to be ignored.

- In Leviticus 1:11, God concerns Himself that the sacrifice is killed only on the north side of the altar: **And he shall kill it on the side of the altar northward before Jehovah. And the priests, Aaron's sons, shall sprinkle its blood all around on the altar.**

- He selects the right shoulder, not the left, of the sacrifice for a contribution to the priests: **And you shall give the right shoulder to the priest *for* a heave offering of the sacrifices of your peace offerings** (Leviticus 7:32).

- According to His directions given to Moses, blood for the ordination of Aaron and his sons had to be applied to particular parts of their bodies: . . . **And Moses took of the blood of it, and put *it* on the tip of Aaron's right ear, and on the thumb of his right hand, and on the big toe of his right foot. And he brought Aaron's sons, and Moses put the blood on the tip of their right ear, and on the thumbs of their right hands, and on the great toes of their right feet. And Moses sprinkled the blood on the altar all around** (Leviticus 8:23-24).

Sometimes His laws contain seemingly trivial details. However, He has made it abundantly clear to us that He is serious about every detail. Here are just a few examples of details that are obviously important to Him and the dire consequences for ignoring these instructions.

- Eating bread with yeast in it during Passover may seem unimportant to some but God concerns Himself with this as demonstrated here: **You shall eat unleavened *bread* seven days; even the first day you shall put away leaven out of your houses. For whoever eats leavened bread from the first day until the seventh day, that soul shall be cut off from Israel** (Exodus 12:15).

- In Exodus 21:28, God commands that the meat of an animal that kills a human should not be eaten: **If an ox gores a man or woman so that they die, then the ox shall surely be stoned, and his flesh shall not be eaten. But the owner of the ox *shall be* set free.** In verse 29, we find out that it might not always go well for the owner of the offending ox: **But if the ox was apt to gore in time past, and his owner has been told, and he has not kept him in, but that he has killed a man or a woman, the ox shall be stoned, and his owner also shall be put to death.**

- In this command God made it clear—wear the bells or die: **The gold bells and the pomegranates are to alternate around the hem of the robe. Aaron must wear it when he ministers. The sound of the bells will be heard when he enters the Holy Place before the Lord and when he comes out, so that he will not die** (Exodus 28:34-35, NIV).

- God concerned Himself with the formula for the Holy anointing oil in that it should never be used except as He commanded and who it was applied to: **Whoever compounds any like it, or whoever puts *any* of it upon a stranger, shall even be cut off from his people** (Exodus 30:33).

- It was the same concern regarding the specifications for duplicating Holy incense: **Whoever shall make *any* like that, to smell of it, shall even be cut off from his people** (Exodus 30:38).

- He was very particular about the way in which offerings were made and left no doubt that He was serious about the details: **For whoever eats the fat of the beast of which men offer an offering made by fire to Jehovah, even the soul that eats *it* shall be cut off from his people** (Leviticus 7:25).

- When He gave instructions as to where a sacrifice was to be killed, no other place would be tolerated: **Any man of the house of Israel who kills an ox or lamb or goat in the camp, or kills it out of the camp, and does not bring it to the door of the tabernacle of the congregation, to offer as offering to Jehovah before the tabernacle of Jehovah, blood shall be charged to that man; he has shed blood. And that man shall be cut off from among his people** (Leviticus 17:3-4).

- Aaron could lose his life by ignoring a small detail such as approaching the Lord at an inappropriate time: . . . **and Jehovah said to Moses, Speak to Aaron your brother, that he does not come at all times into the sanctuary within the veil before the mercy-seat, which is on the Ark, so that he will not die** . . . (Leviticus 16:2).

In His wisdom, God understands our nature to be such that we react to details and place importance on rituals that include them. His reason for presenting a law to Israel that was rich in detail was to help them (and us) to understand that He is Holy and we need to be Holy. In the following verses He makes it clear that they had to be different from the nations around them and His law would help them recognize and remember this:

> And you shall make a difference between clean animals and unclean, and between unclean fowls and clean. And you shall not defile your souls by beast, or by fowl, or by any kind of living thing that creeps on the ground, which I have separated from you as unclean. And you shall be holy to Me. For I, Jehovah, am holy, and have severed you from the nations, so that you should be Mine (Leviticus 20:25-26).

Under the New Covenant, the writer to the Hebrews reminds us that the Mosaic Law is no longer in effect, as it served its purpose and we now come under the law of grace as initiated by Jesus. We now come under the ultimate blood Sacrifice, the blood of Jesus Christ:

> For it *was* a figure for the time then present, in which were offered both gifts and sacrifices that could not make him who did the service perfect as regards the conscience, *which stood* only in meats and drinks, and different kinds of washings and fleshly ordinances, imposed on them until the time of reformation. But when Christ had become a high priest of good things to come, by a greater and more perfect tabernacle, not made with hands, that is to say, not of this building nor by the blood of goats and calves, **but by *His* own blood** *He* entered once for all into the Holies, having obtained eternal redemption *for us*. For if the blood of bulls and of goats and the ashes of a heifer sprinkling the unclean sanctifies to the purifying of the flesh, how much more shall the blood of Christ (who through *the* eternal Spirit offered Himself without spot to God) purge your conscience from dead works to serve *the* living God? (Hebrews 9:9-14).

Details cause us to listen more carefully and help us pay attention to what is being said. The presence of detail indicates to us that this is not to be done with carelessness, sloppiness or disrespect but it should be considered with the utmost reverence.

# 4 GOD BELIEVES IN PAIN

God believes that pain can be used for a good cause. The first occasion where He used pain was in the Garden of Eden when He administered it to Adam and Eve. His perfect plan did not include pain, but because of sin and disobedience, God placed pain in the life of our forefathers for a purpose: **And to Adam He said, Because you have listened to the voice of your wife and have eaten of the tree, of which I commanded you, saying, You shall not eat *of* it! The ground *is* cursed for your sake. In pain shall you eat of it all the days of your life** (Genesis 3:17). He does not inflict the pain Himself, but He does allow the sin we commit to bring us pain. He allows the evil spirits that we believe and obey to bring us all kinds of pain and sorrow. This is evident in many places in Scripture.

God allowed much pain to be inflicted upon the Israelites, His chosen people, when He permitted the Egyptians to use them as slaves: **And it happened after many days the king of Egypt died. And the sons of Israel sighed because of the bondage, and they cried, and their cry came up to God because of the bondage. And God heard their groaning, and God remembered His covenant with Abraham, with Isaac, and with Jacob** (Exodus 2:23-24). God used this pain to teach His people to trust in Him. In their pain, they sighed and groaned and then cried out to God. He responded and became the greatest miracle worker and deliverer the world has ever seen. He practically destroyed Egypt in order to set His people free.

The Israelites suffered the pain of a plague at the hand of the Lord: **And Jehovah plagued the people because they made the calf, which Aaron made.** The purpose here was to teach them obedience (Exodus 32:35).

Joseph suffered pain at the hands of his own family when they sold him as a slave (Genesis 37). Later, in chapter 39, he experienced imprisonment and the pain of ill-treatment in Egypt. Pain was used to teach Joseph to become a leader and the savior of not only his own nation but the nation of Egypt as well (Genesis 41-50).

## What is God Like?

After Israel had entered the Promised Land that God had given them, they soon forsook the Lord and His laws and became disobedient by worshiping other gods. To bring them back to Himself, God used pain brought on by the enemies who surrounded them: **And the anger of Jehovah glowed against Israel. And He said, Because this nation has transgressed My covenant which I commanded their fathers, and has not listened to My voice, I also from now on will not expel any from before them of the nations that Joshua left when he died; so that by them I may test Israel, whether they are keeping the way of Jehovah, to go in it, as their fathers kept it, or not** (Judges 2:20-22). He used pain to test Israel but always with the purpose of bringing His people back to Himself.

David knew the pain of separation from his family and the pain of being hunted like a dog by King Saul. This affliction served to develop character in David whom God, afterwards, placed as ruler over His people (1 Samuel 16 to 2 Samuel 2).

God called Job a perfect servant, but He used affliction to teach him some lessons: **And Jehovah said to Satan, Have you set your heart against My servant Job, because *there is* none like him in the earth, a perfect and upright man, one who fears God and turns away from evil?** (Job 1:8). He used the pain of losing his children, the pain of losing his wealth and the pain of sickness in his body to bring Job to a place of deeper understanding and trust in Him. God did this so Job would understand "it is not my works but God's goodness that leads to blessing." Job thought his good works were proof against hardship, and thought because he did everything right, he was blameless. At the end, he recognized that while he knew about God, now he had seen Him, and so had a better idea of his place in the scheme of things.

Sometimes God waits until it hurts. God deliberately led the Israelites to a place where there was no water: **And all the congregation of the sons of Israel journeyed from the wilderness of Sin, after their journeys, <u>according to the command of the Lord</u>, and pitched in Rephidim. And there was no water for the people to drink** (Exodus 17:1). The Bible does not say how long He waited before solving the problem, but it was certainly long enough for the Israelites to work up a good thirst and a surly temper. During this hardship, they were ready to turn their back on God and stone Moses. Verse 3 tells us . . . **the people murmured against Moses and said, Why *is* this, *that* You brought us up out of Egypt, to kill us and our sons and our cattle with thirst?** We may ask why God waited so long when He knew that they needed water. The answer is that He knew what was still lurking in their hearts: murmuring, murder, hot tempers, and it needed to be exposed and replaced with patience, love and trust.

But why does God use pain? Why not teaching? Or why not rewards, such as greater wealth for good behavior? The answer is, regrettably, that pain is the only thing that really works. The people of Israel were an example for the rest of us. God presented the Law to the world through the Israelites. He visited this nation and instructed them, with painstaking detail, as to how man should worship and have fellowship with God. The best teaching ever made available to man was given to them first. God Himself was their Teacher. The greatest rewards ever given to any nation were given to them at the onset. They were set free from slavery; their enemies were drowned; they were given the best piece of real-estate on earth (with the promise that it would flow with milk and honey); they were given assurance that God would go before them; they were given His promise that He would drive out all their enemies and then protect them forever. But, being the humans they were, that did not suffice. They were so bent on disobedience that only pain got their attention. Just like us. God's administration of pain is an act of mercy. Isaiah 66:16 confirms this in strong language: **For by fire and by his sword will the Lord plead with all flesh.** He could have administered justice and wiped them, and us, off the face of the earth. Instead, He allows pain to bring us back to Himself when we wander away. And, for some of us, it works.

There are other reasons as to why God uses pain. One is this: pain produces obedience. Not always and not for everyone, but for those who are teachable, pain gets our attention. We can acknowledge that we are on the wrong path, and decide to go in the direction He leads. In moments of pain we will often stop and ask ourselves: "What is wrong here?"

In the Bible, the rod often symbolizes an instrument of pain. David, who had a very teachable spirit, admitted that he found the rod, the instrument of pain, comforting: **Yea, though I walk through the valley of the shadow of death, I will fear no evil; for You *are* with me; Your rod and Your staff, they comfort me** (Psalm 23:4). The staff that God carried was for David's protection, but the rod was for correction, and it was used to administer pain. David had wisdom enough to know that this was for his good, and he willingly submitted.

Pain produced by the rod symbolizes love according to the author of Proverbs 13:24: **He who spares his rod hates his son, but he who loves him chastens him early.** It is the antidote to foolishness in children and produces obedience: **Foolishness *is* bound in the heart of a child; the rod of correction** shall drive it far from him (Proverbs 22:15). The writer to the Hebrews confirms that the pain involved in chastisement is an act of love: ". . . **because the Lord disciplines the one he loves, and he chastens everyone he accepts as his son." Endure hardship as discipline; God is treating you as his children. For what children are not disciplined by their father? If you are not disciplined—and everyone undergoes discipline—then you are not legitimate, not true sons and daughters at all** (Hebrews 12:6-8, NIV).

Psalm 119:67 suggests that suffering kept the author on the straight and narrow: **Before I was afflicted I went astray; but now I have kept Your Word.**

Even Jesus, our great example, experienced pain and suffering, and it produced obedience in Him: **For Jesus, in the days of His flesh, when He had offered up prayers and supplications with strong cryings and tears to Him who was able to save Him from death, and was heard in that He feared, though being a Son, yet <u>He learned obedience</u> by the things which He suffered** (Hebrews 5:7-8). We can see from this Scripture that pain is not administered by God because of His anger or wrath. Jesus had no sin and yet learned to be obedient by the pain of His suffering. If God ever administered pain in anger, no flesh would survive. His love, because He is Love, is the motivator. In my mind, there is a vast difference between discipline and punishment. *Discipline* is administered to young men who are being trained as soldiers. *Punishment* is administered when they refuse to submit to discipline.

Another reason God uses pain is that it produces righteousness. Chastisement (or discipline) involves pain, as the writer to the Hebrews says: **Now chastening for the present does not seem to be joyous, but grievous. Nevertheless afterward it yields the peaceable fruit of righteousness to those who are exercised by it** (Hebrews 12:11). God allows us the pain of afflictions to produce patience, develop experience and strengthen our hope, according to Paul: **We can rejoice, too, when we run into problems and trials, for we know that they help us develop endurance. And endurance develops strength of character, and character strengthens our confident hope of salvation** (Romans 5:3-4 NLT). Job (in chapter 5:17 NLT) said that his pain brought him happiness. According to Revelation 7:14 pain will make a Christian pure (i.e., produce white garments). The only way we humans can ever see any good from pain administered by God is to acknowledge that He dishes it out with a purpose.

The Apostle Paul spoke of a lot of pain that he had experienced in his walk with the Lord. He acknowledged in 2 Corinthians 12:7-9 (MSG) that God had allowed him the pain of a thorn in his flesh to keep him humble: **Because of** the extravagance of those revelations, and so I wouldn't get a big head, I was given the gift of a handicap to keep me in constant touch with my limitations. Satan's angel did his best to get me down; what he in fact did was push me to my knees. No danger then of walking around high and mighty! At first I didn't think of it as a gift, and begged God to remove it. Three times I did that, and then he told me, My grace is enough; it's all you need. My strength comes into its own in your weakness. Once I heard that, I was glad to let it happen. I quit focusing on the handicap and began appreciating the gift. It was a case of Christ's strength moving in on my weakness. Not everyone agrees on what the thorn was but I believe we can all agree that it was painful and that God knowingly permitted Satan to administer the pain. Paul, in his wisdom, understood this and accepted it as being good for him. If the Lord gave this godly man one thorn to help him with the sin of boasting, I wonder if some of us would look like porcupines if our thorns suddenly became visible?**

Whenever we experience pain as humans, we quickly acknowledge our need for help. During the pain brought on by some sickness or disease, we run to the doctor or the druggist for something to fix the pain. Then, sometimes when the sickness is serious, some of us call upon God. During natural disasters people are often known to call upon God for help. Most often, they quickly forget Him when the disaster passes. Israel was often chastened by the pain of war, as they were attacked by their enemies, and during their oppression they called out to God. After He had their attention, He always took them back and forgave them.

Pain moves us from complacency to action. We are often keenly aware of things we should do or of things we ought to quit. Most of us rarely take action on the basis of simply knowing about the problem; however, we carefully consider our sins of omission and commission once pain gets our attention.

Pain often produces a dependency on God. In His mercy and compassion He is always there to receive a submissive heart and to offer His healing touch or to give strength and comfort. In His wisdom, He sometimes just gives grace, and the sick one is helped supernaturally through the trial. Other times, He takes the sick one home. Pain serves its purpose, and the sick one is translated to the healthiest and safest place of all: the arms of God. This is our ultimate destiny anyway.

We have a tendency to think that death is the ultimate pain. But even in death God shows us His caring nature according to this passage: **The righteous perish, and no one ponders it in his heart; devout men are taken** away, and no one understands that the righteous are taken away <u>to be spared from evil</u>. **Those who walk uprightly enter into peace; they find rest as they lie in death** (Isaiah 57:1-2 NIV). It could be that for some, God sees pain and evil in the days ahead for them and knows that they would be better off avoiding it. It could be pain that they could not bear. Therefore, as a compassionate and wise Father, He calls them home.

Pain may play another important part in the life of a human being. It may often be the tool God uses to separate the believer (and sometimes the non-believer) from life itself. We tend to cling to life: it's built into our very nature. The problem with this clinging is that we were not destined to live out eternity in this earthly body. When all is well with us—when we are well fed, have a measure of prosperity and our ambitions are being fulfilled—we have a tendency to satisfy ourselves with the comforts of this world and go no further. However, settling there will mean paying the price that is associated with that kind of living and that price can be summed up with the word *anxiety* (or *worry* in some translations). In Matthew 6:25-33, Jesus instructs us not to worry six times. Jesus tried to teach His disciples to think beyond this life to another kind of living, saying: **Therefore do not be anxious, saying, What shall we eat? or, What shall we drink? or, With what shall we be clothed? For the nations seek after all these things. For your heavenly Father knows that you have need of all these things, but seek first the kingdom of God and His righteousness; and all these things shall be added to you** (verses 31-33). However, as simple as His instructions are, we don't always get it. We continue to practice anxiety. We worry about material possessions, live for earthly pleasures, and not for His kingdom. To salvage our precious soul, our compassionate, wise Father will administer enough pain to pry us loose from earth when nothing else works.

Troubleshooting pain:

1. Check your "hedge." Is it up or down? (remember Job's hedge was removed). If it's down, revisit the book of Job for encouragement. That man came out a winner. If your Heavenly Father has temporarily removed it, He will put it back.

2. Check God's cure for Paul's thorn—Grace (2 Corinthians 12).

3. Check the Word for promises of healing. **Believing-prayer will heal you, and Jesus will put you on your feet. And if you've sinned, you'll be forgiven—healed inside and out** (James 5:15 MSG).

4. Cash in on the Manufacturer's warranty: **The LORD himself goes before you and will be with you; he will never leave you nor forsake you. Do not be afraid; do not be discouraged** (Deuteronomy 31:8 NIV). They, Father Son and Holy Spirit, are prepared to send help.

# 5 GOD HAS A HIGH TOLERANCE FOR PAIN

It would be easy to dismiss the connection between God and pain and conclude that since He is the One who can dish it out, all is well for Him. However, we must not forget that if He is a God of love, matters concerning pain are not that simple. The God of love created all creatures, and He loves all of them. If one loves what one creates, one is joyful when those creatures are joyful, and one suffers when they suffer. A God of love cannot detach Himself from the feelings of those He loves.

As we've reviewed some of the examples given in the Bible, God has instigated and allowed much pain and we have to conclude that, being a God of love, He has felt it all—for long periods of time. He watched His children disobey Him from Adam to Noah, and for about 1600 long years, He tolerated that pain: . . . **He went and preached to the spirits in prison, to disobeying ones, when once the long-suffering of God waited in *the* days of Noah, while the ark was being prepared (in which a few, that is, eight souls were saved through water)** (1 Peter 3:19-20).

God selected a special people for Himself through the seed of Abraham, then sent them into captivity and endured their pain for over 400 years. He then took them out of their captivity and gave them a land of their own. His perfect plan was that they would accept that they could only be happy and content if they obeyed His laws. However, the Israelites did not learn and He had to apply more pain. They still needed the lessons that pain teaches and were subjected to numerous wars and persecutions. He suffered the oppression with them, year after year, because He never stopped loving them. His true feelings are recorded in these words during their fifth captivity: **And they put away the strange gods from among them, and served Jehovah. And His soul was moved by the misery of Israel** (Judges 10:16). The NIV translation puts it this way: **and He could bear Israel's misery no longer.** Then He delivered them again from their oppressors.

To this day God continues to watch His beloved children ignore Him and His ways. He is our Father, and He sees the wickedness of every one of His children, every day. Yet He continues to hold back on judgment, administer love and patience and tolerate pain.

One day, while He was with us on earth, God the Son, broke down and cried, expressing the anguish of His soul as He approached Jerusalem: **And as He drew near, He beheld the city and wept over it, saying, If you had known, even you, even at least in this day of yours, the things for your peace! But now they are hidden from your eyes** (Luke 19:41-42). We cannot begin to imagine such a high tolerance for pain, but His ability to bear it is due to the great love that is the heart of God. This love is summed up in the famous words of John 3:16, brought to earth by God the Son: **For God so loved the world that He gave His only-begotten Son, that whoever believes in Him should not perish but have everlasting life.**

God's tolerance of pain is best observed the day His Son died while on earth. He knew before the foundation of the world that the only payment for sin would be the death of an innocent man. There were no such men on earth and therefore the plan meant that an innocent Man would have to be sent from Heaven: **It is written: "There is none righteous, no not one"** (Romans 3:10). The plan involved taking all the sin of all human beings throughout all of time and laying it on this sinless One. The Bible says Jesus became sin for our sake: **For He has made Him who knew no sin, _to be_ sin for us, that we might become _the_ righteousness of God in Him** (2 Corinthians 5:21). If you have trouble seeing Jesus as sin, Paul teaches that He was also a curse: **Christ redeemed us from that self-defeating, cursed life by absorbing it completely into himself. Do you remember the Scripture that says, "Cursed is everyone who hangs on a tree"? That is what happened when Jesus was nailed to the Cross: He became a curse, and at the same time dissolved the curse** (Galatians 3:13 MSG). For a short, agonizing, period of time this is how the Father treated the Son: as the embodiment of sin and as a curse, so the plan of redemption could be completed.

Since God cannot tolerate sin, it meant that God would have to turn His back on the One who had now acquired all this sin. Isaiah 53:6 explains this happens because, **All we like sheep have gone astray; we have turned, each one to his own way; and Jehovah has laid on Him the iniquity of us all.** Now the hard part: God would have to turn away from His beloved Son, having nothing to do with Him, knowing that Jesus was completely innocent and yet let it all happen. God called out to God in those moments, since Jesus was God in the flesh. They have always and will always be in perfect unity of Spirit.

Jesus was also the son of man, and those words were from His human side: **And about the ninth hour, Jesus cried with a loud voice, saying, Eli, Eli, lama sabachthani? That is, My God, My God, why have You forsaken me?** (Matthew 27:46). No human has ever experienced the agony that God experienced in those moments. The cry from Jesus had little to do with His physical suffering even though He was being tortured beyond comprehension: **Just as there were many who were appalled at him his appearance was so disfigured beyond that of any man and his form marred beyond human likeness** (Isaiah 52:14 NIV). Imagine for a moment what it might be like for you if a mob that you knew you could easily control, slowly beat you to death over a number of hours. Imagine you had what it took—unfathomable grace and meekness—to let them have their way. Obviously, you would not be one who had a problem with fear or pain. Jesus had complete control over His life and His body. He said: **This is why the Father loves me: because I freely lay down my life. And so I am free to take it up again. No one takes it from me. I lay it down of my own free will. I have the right to lay it down; I also have the right to take it up again. I received this authority personally from my Father** (John 10:17-18 MSG).

Jesus proved that He could have flattened His tormentors when He identified Himself to the soldiers: **Then as soon as He had said to them, I AM, they went backward and fell to the ground** (John 18:6). If He had power to do this, He could have also paralyzed them. However, if He had, Jesus would not have been able to complete the purpose for which He had come. Therefore, blow by blow, He allowed them to take His strength and spill His blood.

No human ever suffered like this, or will ever suffer like this again. Many men and women have been beaten and tortured by others but all were helpless in the hands of their tormentors. Whether brave or cowardly, they had no choice but to receive what was being handed out. If they could have escaped, they would have. But Jesus, with all kinds of power at His disposal—His Father's, His own, and that of warrior angels—stayed and took the beating. He explained His reason for staying to endure the suffering: **Don't you realize that I could ask my Father for thousands of angels to protect us, and he would send them instantly? But if I did, how would the Scriptures be fulfilled that describe what must happen now?** (Mat 26:53-54 NLT).

The cry He uttered had to do with the impending separation from His loving Father that he was about to suffer. Human comprehension ends there because we know nothing of such perfect unity between two beings and what it would be like to have such oneness broken. The Father and the Son did know, and they experienced the full impact of its horror and pain.

If we could comprehend anything about what happened that day, we would see the Father and His Son willingly enduring pain that could have been avoided; but instead of avoiding it, they counted the cost and concluded that His creation was worth the price of saving. How thankful we should be! He could have scrapped us like a lump of bad clay and started over!

# 6 GOD WANTS YOU TO DIE

God wants at least a part of you to die: the carnal you. When God created us in the beginning, we were perfect in body, soul and spirit. When we succumbed to Satan's scheme, we took on a new selfish and sinful nature the Bible calls *the flesh,* the *carnal man,* or the *outward man.* God says this must die. He even demonstrated this death for us by the kind of death His Son suffered. The Cross is an instrument of death. Anyone put on it was put there to die. Jesus confirms that we must follow Him to this instrument of death in Matthew 10:38 and Luke 14:27:

> **And he who does not take up his cross and follow Me is not worthy of Me.**
>
> **And whoever does not bear his cross and come after Me, he cannot be My disciple.**

Our carnal man is possessive and greedy and loves the material things of this world. All too often *things* become our god. We labor for them and allow them to take time and energy, and we spend much effort in trying to enjoy the pleasures they provide. In this process of dying, Jesus demands we give them up: **So then, every one of you who does not forsake all his possessions, he cannot be My disciple** (Luke 14:33).

This does not mean there is no enjoyment in this life for those who follow Him; it simply means true enjoyment is not found in material things. His desire and plan is for us to find joy that bubbles up from inside the inner man. On one occasion, Jesus sent a group of His followers out to do some Kingdom work and they came back full of delight in what they had just experienced. He had taught them to go out into the neighborhood and set people free from the bondage of Satan. They obeyed and were overjoyed when they understood that His power flowed through them and they were actually able to set men and women free because of the power of His Word: **And the seventy returned again with joy, saying, Lord, even the demons are subject to us through Your name** (Luke 10:17). Not only did they produce joy in themselves, they produced it in Heaven as well: **In that hour Jesus** rejoiced in Spirit and said, **I thank You, Father, Lord of Heaven and earth, that You have hidden these things from the sophisticated and cunning, and have revealed them to babes. Yes, Father, for so it was pleasing before You** (Luke 10:21). And it did not cost anyone a dime!

As dreadful and agonizing as it may sound, giving up one's carnal life on the symbolic cross is not to be feared. We have it on the authority of one who did it. This is Paul's testimony: **But no, rather, I also count all things to be loss for the excellency of the knowledge of Christ Jesus my Lord, for whose sake I have suffered the loss of all things, and count them** *to be* **dung, so that I may win Christ** (Philippians 3:8). According to Paul, it was both attainable and worth attaining.

# 7 GOD MAKES COVENANTS

A covenant is a solemn agreement, a contract or an agreement held to be the basis of a relationship. Covenants can only be made when at least two are involved, and consists of an 'If you, then I . . ."  type of statement (these are different from laws, which are more like 'Do this or else . . . .'). God's first covenant was with Noah: **But I will establish My covenant with you. And you shall come into the ark, you and your sons and your wife and your sons' wives . . . to keep them alive with you** (Genesis 6:18-19).

The second covenant was also with Noah: **And I will establish my covenant with you; neither shall all flesh be cut off any more by the waters of a flood; neither shall there anymore be a flood to destroy the earth** (Genesis 9:11). A symbol was designed for the second covenant and set in the sky to be displayed at various times to remind us of the promise: **I do set my bow in the cloud, and it shall be for a token of a covenant between me and the earth** (Genesis 9:13).

His third covenant was with Abraham concerning a land deed: **In the same day the LORD made a covenant with Abram, saying, Unto thy seed have I given this land, from the river of Egypt unto the great river, the river Euphrates** (Genesis 15:18).

The fourth covenant was also with Abraham to give him hordes of children to live on the land: **And I will make my covenant between me and thee, and will multiply thee exceedingly** (Genesis 17:2).

The fifth covenant, also with Abraham, was marked by blood: **This [is] my covenant, which ye shall keep, between me and you and thy seed after thee; every male child among you shall be circumcised** (Genesis 17:10). The removal of the foreskin, in a male, symbolized purity and sanctification (being set apart) unto God. It was God's mark. There is no suggestion here that the foreskin was impure or unclean because it was quite acceptable from Adam to Abraham and in the beginning everything that God made was good (see chapter 65, *God is Big on Symbols*). God ordered man to cut his body to seal this covenant. In no uncertain terms He demanded that blood be part of the covenant, that it be a permanent mark on their body, the cut be performed when the child was eight days old, and every male was to be included. The covenant is detailed in the following verses:

> **This is My covenant, which you shall keep, between Me and you and your seed after you. Every male child among you shall be circumcised. And you shall circumcise the flesh of your foreskin. And it shall be a token of the covenant between Me and you. And a son of eight days shall be circumcised among you, every male child in your generations; he that is born in the house, or bought with silver of any stranger who *is* not of your seed. He that is born in your house, and he that is bought with your silver, must be circumcised. And My covenant shall be in your flesh for an everlasting covenant** (Genesis 17:10-13).

The consequences for breaking the agreement is seen in this verse: **And the uncircumcised male child whose flesh of his foreskin is not circumcised, that soul shall be cut off from his people; he has broken My covenant** (Genesis 17:14).

The sixth covenant was with Isaac: **And God said, Sarah thy wife shall bear thee a son indeed; and thou shalt call his name Isaac: and I will establish my covenant with him for an everlasting covenant,** *and* **with his seed after him** (Genesis 17:19).

The seventh covenant was with children of Israel: **And he took the book of the covenant, and read in the audience of the people: and they said, All that the LORD hath said will we do, and be obedient** (Exodus 24:7). It, too, was marked by blood: **Moses then took the blood, sprinkled it on the people and said, "This is the blood of the covenant that the LORD has made with you in accordance with all these words"** (Exodus 24:8 NIV).

The eighth covenant was with Israel and was marked and symbolized by the Sabbath. **Therefore the sons of Israel shall keep the Sabbath, to observe the Sabbath throughout their generations,** *for* **an everlasting covenant** (Exodus 31:16).

# 8 GOD INSTIGATED BLOOD COVENANTS

The first blood covenant in Scripture is found in Genesis 3:21, and was performed by God Himself. He used blood as part of the covenant between Adam and Eve to take care of their first sin: **And for Adam and his wife Jehovah God made coats of skins, and clothed them**. The animals killed would have been the first physical death to take place on the earth. It took place in the presence of Adam, Eve and God. The lesson would have been obvious: sin equals death. They had never seen death up to this point, and God meant to show them that sin has horrible consequences. He also made it obvious that the self-made covering of fig leaves was inadequate. This practice of spilling blood to cover sin was passed on to the children of Adam and we see that Abel understood and brought a blood sacrifice to atone for his sin but Cain failed to get it. He opted to do it his way: **And in the end of days, it happened, Cain brought to Jehovah an offering of the fruit of the ground. And Abel also brought of the firstlings of his flock and of the fat of it. And Jehovah had respect to Abel and to his offering, but He did not have respect to Cain and to his offering. And Cain glowed with anger, and his face fell** (Genesis 4:3-5).

The practice was continued by Noah:

> **And Noah built an altar to Jehovah. And he took of every clean animal, and of every clean bird, and offered burnt offerings on the altar** (Genesis 8:20).

And by Abraham:

> **And Abraham lifted up his eyes, and looked. And, behold, a ram behind** *him* **was entangled in a thicket by its horns. And Abraham went and took the ram and offered it up for a burnt offering instead of his son** (Genesis 22:13).

And by Job:

> When the parties were over, Job would get up early in the morning and sacrifice a burnt offering for each of his children, thinking, "Maybe one of them sinned by defying God inwardly." Job made a habit of this sacrificial atonement, just in case they'd sinned (Job 1:5 MSG).

When the time arrived for God to introduce mankind to His law, He gave direction to Moses to carry out the same blood covenant: **Speak to all the congregation of Israel, saying, In the tenth of this month they shall take to them each man a lamb for a father's house, a lamb for a house . . . And you shall keep it up until the fourteenth day of the same month. And the whole assembly of the congregation of Israel shall kill it in the evening. And they shall take** *some* **of the blood and strike on the two side posts and upon the upper door post of the houses** *in* **which they shall eat it** (Exodus 12:3, 6-7).

This blood covenant, in which an innocent animal was used, was a temporary measure until the time when God the Son, Jesus, would spill His blood to take away the sin of man once and for all time.

> **For this is My blood of the new covenant, which is shed for many for the remission of sins** (Matthew 26:28).

> *For He* **has delivered us from the power of darkness and has translated** *us* **into the kingdom of His dear Son; in whom we have redemption through His blood, the remission of sins** (Colossians 1:13-14).

> **. . . nor by the blood of goats and calves, but by** *His* **own blood** *He* **entered once for all into the Holies, having obtained eternal redemption** *for us.* **For if the blood of bulls and of goats and the ashes of a heifer sprinkling the unclean sanctifies to the purifying of the flesh, how much more shall the blood of Christ (who through** *the* **eternal Spirit offered Himself without spot to God) purge your conscience from dead works to serve** *the* **living God?** (Hebrews 9:11-14).

Why are covenants associated with blood? The best answer is this: because God Himself ordained it. He was the first to associate blood with sin when He symbolically shed the blood of an animal to cover the sin of Adam and Eve. He used blood again to signify a covenant with Israel that He would spare their lives when the death angel was sent to kill all of the first born sons in Egypt: **And the blood shall be a sign to you upon the houses where you** *are.* **And when I see the blood, I will pass over you. And the plague shall not be upon you for a destruction when I smite in the land of Egypt** (Exodus 12:13). Blood was the element on earth that God picked to symbolize life because He declared: **the life of the flesh** *is* **in the blood** (Leviticus 17:11). God classified blood as sacred when He gave Noah his new menu after the flood, saying: **Every moving thing that lives shall be food for you. I have given you all things, even as the green herb. But you shall not eat of flesh with the life in it, or the blood of it** (Genesis 9:3-4). Later this was reemphasized under the law of Moses: **And I have given [this blood] to you on the altar to make an atonement for your souls. For it** *is* **the blood that makes an atonement for the soul** (Leviticus 17:11).

The shedding of blood under the Old Testament Law, or the Old Covenant, pointed to the New Testament Covenant in that God promised us redemption and sealed that covenant by the blood of His only Son, Jesus. Under the New Covenant, Jesus raised a cup of wine and ordered His disciples to drink it to symbolize the blood that He would soon give up in exchange for our redemption: **For this is My blood of the new covenant, which is shed for many for the remission of sins** (Matthew 26:28). If we ignore the importance of blood as it relates to the saving of our souls, we ignore the importance that God placed on it. Ignore the blood and we cannot be forgiven: **In fact, the law requires that nearly everything be cleansed with blood, and without the shedding of blood there is no forgiveness** (Hebrews 9:22 NIV).

# 9 GOD DEMANDS REST

The first thing God did for Adam after giving him the entire planet, a wife and a job was to make provision for a day off. He did this by simply setting an example for Adam: **And on the seventh day God ended His work which He had made. And He rested on the seventh day from all His work which He had made. And God blessed the seventh day and sanctified it, because in it He had rested from all His work which God created to make** (Genesis 2:2-3). At this point it was not a command or a law. Neither was any reference made to it when God gave Adam his one and only law, "Do not touch that tree." The Word says the Lord took the day off and rested. Chapter 16 mentions the Law of Love in the sense that it could very well be the law that governs Heaven. Since God IS Love it could be that all He ever wanted was for man to do all things out of an act of love rather than be forced to do it by a law. This seems to be what Jesus is explaining to a lawyer who had asked what was God's most important law: **Jesus said to him, You shall love the Lord your God with all your heart, and with all your soul, and with all your mind. This is the first and great commandment. And the second** *is* **like it, You shall love your neighbor as yourself. On these two commandments hang all the Law and the Prophets** (Matthew 22:37- 40). We understand this to mean that if we do this, no other laws are necessary. We could call it the Law of Love. Obey this law and we will have perfect peace and harmony because we are always looking to please our Heavenly Father and our brothers and sisters. James calls it the Royal Law: **If you fulfill the royal Law according to the Scripture, "You shall love your neighbor as yourself," you do well** (James 2:8).

Now, back to Adam and his day off. When Jehovah took the Sabbath off it would stand to reason that Adam would also take the day off, not because he had to but because he wanted to: to be with the One he loved—to spend time with Him. God left it up to Adam to practice the Law of Love out of his own free will. Even if he felt a day of rest wasn't needed after working six days, then Adam should have taken the day of rest just because His Creator took it and He was resting.

The day of rest occurs again in Scripture in the book of Exodus. The Israelites are receiving the Law and this time God *commands* that they keep the Sabbath as a day of rest: **Remember the Sabbath day, to keep it holy. Six days you shall labor and do all your work. But the seventh day *is* the Sabbath of Jehovah your God. You shall not do any work, you, nor your son, nor your daughter, your manservant, nor your maidservant, nor your cattle, nor your stranger within your gates. For *in* six days Jehovah made the heavens and the earth, the sea, and all that *is* in them, and rested the seventh day. Therefore Jehovah blessed the Sabbath day, and sanctified it** (Exodus 20:8-11).

It is not difficult to imagine that from the time of Adam to the time of Moses, a lot of changes had taken place relating to the day off Adam started out with. It is obvious that God thought it was now necessary to command His people to rest after six days of work. It is likely that by the time of Moses, God's people had lost sight of a day of rest - considering who their last "employer" had been. It seems very unlikely that Pharaoh gave them Saturdays off. It is very possible that in His kindness toward His people, now they were under His leadership, that Jehovah ordered them to take one day a week for rest and worship.

For us, and Israel, Egypt symbolizes the world and the world system. In it, we always find things to keep us busy and distracted from having an intimate relationship with our Creator. Satan ruled Egypt through Pharaoh, just as he rules this present day world. A day of rest is what our leisure-hungry and work-addicted culture desperately needs. Here is a verse from a poem by Oswald Chambers written in 1894 (McCasland Page 32). It is likely that this could describe life for the typical Israeli slave and it could just as easily be my city or yours:

> *Busy, driving, rushing Londoners,*
> *Driven, palefaced, wiry blunderers,*
> *Striving ever,*
> *Praying never,*
> *Busy, driving, rushing Londoners.*

Without a command from God, we are not likely to rest. After all, we are very busy people! There is always so much to do. Even as we strive and make some effort to obey His command to rest, our tendency is to be *doing* something. The medical profession constantly reminds us that we are a society of people who are stressed out.

Even though we are no longer under the Law as confirmed by Paul in his writings, God still commands that we rest. It may not necessarily be on a Sabbath or a Sunday as indicated here: **One indeed esteems a day above** *another* day; and *another* esteems every day *alike*. **Let each one be fully assured in his own mind** (Romans 14:5). Regardless of the particular day, it certainly means to cease from work and spend time with Him - out of love.

What would a day of rest be like in God's order of things? Would it mean bowing in front of Him and spending the entire day in worship? Would it mean being in Church all day? Would it mean—as it did in the church I grew up in—no work and no play? How does one spend a day of rest that would make God happy and keep us healthy?

Most of us would find these questions relevant and I believe most of us have had questions regarding the correct way to spend our Sabbath or Sunday, whichever you celebrate. Mark Buchanan writes an excellent book on the subject called, *The Rest of God: Restoring Your Soul by Restoring Sabbath*. Mark teaches that our day of rest, whichever day you pick, is more about a day of worship, celebration, stillness, feasting, fellowship and fun. And yes, he does suggest that God approves of fun! The minute we set rules to try and regulate these activities, we lose the spirit of the true Sabbath. There is only one rule that covers it all and it is the rule of Love. We practice this rule because we love Him and the people around us:

> **Jesus said to him, You shall love the Lord your God with all your heart, and with all your soul, and with all your mind. This is the first and great commandment. And the second** *is* **like it, You shall love your neighbor as yourself** (Matthew 22:37-39).

It may well be that the Israelis had it tough trying to keep the Sabbath under the Law in that it was filled with do's and don'ts. But it may not have been if they had stuck with the spirit of the Law and had not tampered with it by adding their own lengthy rules and regulations. Jesus shattered their concept of the Sabbath when **He said to them, The sabbath came into being for man's sake, and not man for the sabbath's sake** (Mark 2:27).

There is definitely something about these words that brings things into perspective regarding enjoyment and pleasure that ought to take place on our day of rest. We just need to find the right balance between our desire to please God and our drive to please ourselves. The only thing I would like to add here is that to please God and to spend time with Him requires a time and a place—a special time and a special place. The time and place can be any time and any place that you set apart as special, just for you and God. We cannot expect true worship, which He deserves, to take place wherever we might happen to be and during any left over time that we failed to use up in

## What is God Like?

all our busyness and pleasures. He is far too Holy to be treated that way. This is not to say that we cannot have stolen moments with Him in the rush of our days, but He has ordered us to take time off to spend with Him. God is like that.

# 10 GOD SWEARS OATHS AND ISSUES CURSES

One dictionary defines an oath as: *a solemn, formal calling upon God or a witness to the truth of what one says or to witness what one intends to do.*

The Lord used such an oath in speaking to Abraham when He honored him for offering his son, Isaac, as a living sacrifice when he said: . . . **I have sworn by Myself, says Jehovah; because you have done this thing, and have not withheld your son, your only one; that in blessing I will bless you, and in multiplying I will multiply your seed like the stars of the heavens, and as the sand which is upon the seashore. And your Seed shall possess the gate of His enemies** (Genesis 22:16-17). This oath was to seal a promise. Here are some others:

- The following oath was in anger against Israel for disobedience: **And Jehovah heard the voice of your words, and was angry and swore, saying, Surely there shall not one of these men of this evil generation see that good land, which I swore to give to your fathers** (Deuteronomy 1:34-35).

- In Psalm 132:11, He swore one to David: **Jehovah has sworn to David in truth; He will not turn from it; Of the fruit of your body I will set on the throne for you**. Again, the oath was issued to seal a promise.

- Jehovah Himself instructed the Israelites to use oaths in bearing witness: **If a man delivers to his neighbor an ass, or an ox, or a sheep, or any animal to keep, and it dies, or is hurt, or driven away, no one seeing, an oath of Jehovah shall be between them both, that he has not put his hand to his neighbor's goods. And the owner of it shall accept it, and he shall not make *it* good** (Exodus 22:10-11).

- And here He specifically orders the Hebrews to swear by His name: **You shall fear Jehovah your God and serve Him, and shall swear by His name** (Deuteronomy 6:13).

## What is God Like?

It is obvious that it is permissible to swear an oath, as God Himself swore them. Our hesitation comes from the fact that most of us have been taught that swearing is taboo for us as Christians. Further, Jesus had this to say about swearing: **But I say to you, Do not swear at all! Not by Heaven, because it is God's throne; not by the earth, for it is the footstool of His feet; not by Jerusalem, because it is** *the* **city of the great King; nor shall you swear by your head, because you cannot make one hair white or black. But let your word be, Yes, yes; No, no. For whatever is more than these comes from evil** (Matthew 5:34-37). As with most things left to us humans, we have a tendency to mess them up. The Jews of His day had messed up on swearing oaths by using them in flippant, false, blasphemous and frivolous ways. Jesus taught that this kind of everyday, casual, swearing should stop. It seems they were making oaths on everything—Heaven, God's throne, the earth, their head, etc. He was basically saying that a Christian's word ought to be as good as any oath. James confirms the same thought: **But before all things, my brothers, do not swear; neither by the heaven nor by the earth, nor any other oath. But let your yes be yes, and** *your* **no, no, lest you fall into condemnation** (James 5:12).

"Oath" has two accepted definitions (Oxford University Press): 1 *a solemn promise, often invoking a divine witness.* 2 *a profane or offensive expression used to express anger or other strong emotions.* The first is permitted; the second is not. Jesus did not condemn the proper use of an oath and would never have condemned something His Father had done and continues to do. He condemned what they were doing with oaths and commanded them to stop.

Here is why the oaths that God swore are so important to us today. In the New Testament, He reminds us of a very significant oath pertaining to rest that is especially applicable to the generation of today. The original passage containing this oath comes from Psalm 95, in which God reminds that generation, and us, not to repeat the failures of the Israelites during their journey in the wilderness. The writer to the Hebrews puts it this way:

> **For those of us who have belief come into his rest; even as he has said, <u>As I said in my oath when I was angry, They may not come into my rest</u>: though the works were done from the time of the making of the world. For in one place he has said of the seventh day, And God had rest from all his works on the seventh day; And in the same place he says again, They will not come into my rest . . .** (Hebrews 4:3-5 BBE).

Regarding cursing, Oxford defines a curse as: *a solemn utterance intended to invoke a supernatural power to inflict harm or punishment on someone or something.*

God cursed Satan for tempting Eve: **And Jehovah God said to the serpent, Because you have done this you *are* cursed more than all cattle, and more than every animal of the field. You shall go upon your belly, and you shall eat dust all the days of your life** (Genesis 3:14).

The second curse was the very ground on which they stood: **And to Adam He said, Because you have listened to the voice of your wife and have eaten of the tree, of which I commanded you, saying, You shall not eat *of* it! The ground *is* cursed for your sake. In pain shall you eat of it all the days of your life** (Genesis 3:17). It should be noticed that the second curse was not directed at Adam as the first was directed at the serpent; it was directed to Adam's source of livelihood, the ground. That curse still holds for sinners but is broken by the blood of Jesus for those who accept Him as Savior.

The third curse was issued by God against Cain after he had murdered his brother Abel and lied to God about what he had done: **And now you *are* cursed more than the ground which opened its mouth to receive your brother's blood from your hand** (Genesis 4:11).

The next curse recorded in Scripture is issued by Noah to one of his sons and it was upheld by God: Ham had gone into his father's tent and discovered him drunk and naked, but instead of trying to keep his shame a secret, Ham went out and told his two brothers (Genesis 9:22). He gossiped. When Noah sobered up and found out about the snitch, he pronounced a curse on Ham's descendants, saying: **Cursed *be* Canaan. He shall be a servant of servants to his brothers** (Genesis 9:25). The crime committed was failing to respect his father, even though his father did intoxicate himself and had temporarily lost his senses. Shem and Japheth handled the situation differently by walking backwards into the tent with a garment and covered their father's nakedness. Apparently, God honored the curse that Noah issued because we see later that the descendants of Ham were either driven out of the Promised Land where they had settled, or they became servants to the people of Israel. In these conversations with Abraham and Moses, God gives Canaanite land to the children of Israel:

> **And I will give the land to you in which you are a stranger, and to your seed after you, all the land of Canaan, for an everlasting possession. And I will be their God** (Genesis 17:8).
>
> **Go up into Mount Abarim, *to* Mount Nebo in the land of Moab, which is opposite Jericho; and behold the land of Canaan which I am giving to the sons of Israel for a possession** (Deuteronomy 32:49).

## What is God Like?

We don't have all the details regarding the character of Ham and his son Canaan, but we can be sure that God knew them and that He handled the situation justly. Curses can only take effect if they are deserved as Proverbs 26:2 indicates: **Curses cannot hurt you unless you deserve them. They are like birds that fly by and never light** (GNB). According to Psalm 106:37-38, the Canaanites were a wicked people and they led Israel into demon worship and the murdering of their own children: **Yea, they sacrificed their sons and their daughters to demons, and shed innocent blood, even the blood of their sons and of their daughters, whom they sacrificed to the idols of Canaan; and the land was defiled with blood.** No wonder God backed up Noah's curse.

Regarding curses used by Jesus: as stated in the introduction, any characteristic of God is common to both Jesus and Holy Spirit. They are equal in character and holiness. Jesus would never use a curse if His Father disapproved. As far as Jesus was concerned, the kind of cursing that His Father practiced was still effective and certainly could still be practiced. On one occasion He issued a curse on a tree that should have produced fruit but didn't and caused it to shrivel up and die: **And Peter, remembering, said to Him, Rabbi, behold, the fig tree which You cursed has withered away** (Mark 11:21).

If you are thinking of using an oath or a curse, read what Jesus said about them first in Matthew 5:33-48. James 5:12 teaches: **But before all things, my brothers, do not swear; neither by the heaven nor by the earth, nor any other oath. But let your yes be yes, and *your* no, no, lest you fall into condemnation.**

It is not good to be on the wrong side of God. It is not good to offend a friend of His, you may get cursed. In Genesis 12:2-3, God says this about His friend Abraham: **And I will make you a great nation. And I will bless you and make your name great. And you shall be a blessing. And I will bless those that bless you and curse the one who curses you. And in you shall all families of the earth be blessed.**

From the following two Scriptures in Jeremiah and Malachi, we see that God is also capable of cursing people He formerly blessed, when they are in sin and rebellion:

> **I will make them abhorrent and an offense to all the kingdoms of the earth, a reproach and a byword, a curse and an object of ridicule, wherever I banish them** (Jeremiah 24:9 NIV).

> **And now, O priests, this command is for you. If you will not hear, and if you will not set *it* on your heart to give glory to My name, says Jehovah of Hosts, then I will send a curse upon you, and I will curse your blessings. And indeed I have cursed it, because you do not set *it* on *your* heart** (Malachi 2:1-2).

It is apparent that Old Testament men used curses:

> **And Joshua charged *them* at that time, saying, Cursed before Jehovah *is* the man who rises up and builds this city of Jericho. He shall lay the foundation of it in his first-born, and in his youngest *son* he shall set up the gates of it** (Joshua 6:26).

In Galatians 1:8-9, Paul curses anyone teaching false doctrine: **But even if we or an angel from Heaven preach a gospel to you beside what we preached to you, let him be accursed. As we said before, and now I say again, If anyone preaches a gospel to you beside what you have received, let him be accursed.**

We have to assume that because of the great wisdom exhibited by this apostle and his knowledge of Scripture, he knew what he was doing in issuing this curse. However, using a curse is obviously not something Christians should take lightly. Jesus exhorts us in Matthew 5:44 (KJV) that we should only bring blessing down on the heads of others, even our enemies: **But I say unto you, Love your enemies, bless them that curse you, do good to them that hate you, and pray for them which despitefully use you, and persecute you.**

Paul's temperance, and wisdom is further observed in Romans 12:18-19 (NIV): **If it is possible, as far as it depends on you, live at peace with everyone. Do not take revenge, my dear friends, but leave room for God's wrath, for it is written: "It is mine to avenge; I will repay," says the Lord.**

When they are needed, God is able to administer a curse with precision, wisdom and justice. Vengeful cursing should be left to Him. God has at least one more major curse to issue according to Jesus: **Then He also shall say to those on *the* left hand, Depart from Me, you cursed, into everlasting fire prepared for the Devil and his angels** (Matthew 25:41).

Make sure you are on the right hand!

# 11  GOD IS HOLY

Dictionaries define holiness with words such as perfection, majesty, freedom from moral evil, absoluteness, moral and ethical wholeness. As humans we have no concept of the true meaning of any of these words, because we have never experienced anything so lofty. Even though we were created in His image, it is one of His characteristics, not one of ours. God is holy—and then it gets scary—He commands us to be holy.

There are numerous verses that declare He is Holy and commands us to be like Him. Two are:

> **For I *am* Jehovah who brought you up out of the land of Egypt, to be your God. You shall therefore be holy, for I *am* holy** (Leviticus 11:45).

> **But as he which hath called you is holy, so be ye holy in all manner of conversation; Because it is written, Be ye holy; for I am holy** (1 Peter 1:15-16 KJV).

The Holiness of God is not something He made up, or assumed for Himself. He does not have an ego problem. When the Word says He is Holy, He is simply stating a fact. A fact that we cannot fully grasp but we would do well to try and understand what He is commanding. When we make an attempt to approach a Holy God we have a serious problem: We are not holy! We cannot ignore His Holiness and our lack of the same; we cannot bypass the holiness issue. He said, "Ye shall therefore be holy because I am Holy." He always means what He says!

What is it like to be truly holy? One obvious trait would be sinlessness—never sinning and having no desire to sin. We are just the opposite: we sin and desire to sin, because our hearts are **deceitful above all things, and desperately wicked: who can know it?** (Jeremiah 17:9). Prior to our conversion we were separated from God due to our sin. It's only when we come back to Him in a born again experience that we adopt the desire to stop sinning, which is a profound act of our will. Even then, we still live with a sinful, carnal nature that keeps on sinning. This is the dilemma that Paul describes here: **But if I do what I do not desire,** *it is* **no more I working it out, but sin dwelling in me. I find then a law: when I will to do the right, evil is present with me. For I delight in the Law of God according to the inward man; but I see another law in my members, warring against the law of my mind, and bringing me into captivity to the law of sin being in my members** (Romans 7:20-23).

This lack of holiness is solved only by accepting the holiness of God Himself, in the person of Jesus, as Paul teaches and is reflected in these verses:

> **But put on the Lord Jesus Christ, and do not take thought beforehand for the lusts of the flesh** (Romans 13:14).

> **I have been crucified with Christ, and I live;** *yet* **no longer I, but Christ lives in me. And** *that* **life I now live in the flesh, I live by faith toward the Son of God, who loved me and gave Himself on my behalf** (Galatians 2:20).

> **For you ought to put off the old man (according to your way of living before) who is corrupt according to the deceitful lusts, and be renewed in the spirit of your mind. And you should put on the new man, who according to God** *was* **created in righteousness and true holiness** (Ephesians 4:22-24).

As you can see a "new man" is required, and therefore the old one has to die. This can only be done with Christ's help and by the power of God's Holy Spirit. So, while we cannot experience what true Holiness is like at this time, while living with our sinful nature, God has been compassionate and graceful by allowing the holiness of His Son to be ours. His holiness allows us into the presence of a Holy God.

Further, by believing, or having faith in Him and the things He said, God credits that to our account as well, as we've previously seen: **For what saith the Scripture? Abraham believed God, and it was counted unto him for righteousness** (Romans 4:3). True to His loving character (God is Love), and thankfully for us, He has made a way for us that is relatively easy: believe Him and accept the righteousness of Christ and we are covered. Paul reemphasizes this in other Scriptures:

> **But to him not working, but believing on Him justifying the ungodly, his faith is counted for righteousness** (Romans 4:5).

## What is God Like?

> Here it is in a nutshell: Just as one person did it wrong and got us in all this trouble with sin and death, another person did it right and got us out of it. But more than just getting us out of trouble, he got us into life! (Romans 5:18 MSG).
>
> For He has made Him who knew no sin, *to be* sin for us, that we might become *the* righteousness of God in Him (2 Corinthians 5:21).

Holiness cannot be acted out. One cannot pretend to be holy and one cannot feel holy. (If some day you ever "feel" holy, I suggest that Satan has been tampering with your antenna!) Our Holiness is by faith in Christ as Galatians 2:20 explains: . . . *that* **life I now live in the flesh, <u>I live by faith</u> toward the Son of God, who loved me and gave Himself on my behalf.**

Angelic beings from Heaven recognized God's holiness: **In the year that King Uzziah died, I saw the Lord, high and exalted, seated on a throne; and the train of his robe filled the temple. Above him were seraphim, each with six wings: With two wings they covered their faces, with two they covered their feet, and with two they were flying. And they were calling to one another: "Holy, holy, holy is the LORD Almighty; the whole earth is full of his glory."** (Isaiah 6:1-3 NIV). Isaiah was present at this time and he was terrified knowing that he was in the presence of such Holiness and, in verse 5, uttered this cry: **"Woe to me!" I cried. "I am ruined! For I am a man of unclean lips, and I live among a people of unclean lips, and my eyes have seen the King, the LORD Almighty."**

God gave us the Law to help us recognize and learn some things about His Holiness. The book of Leviticus is particularly useful to teach us that God is Holy. By setting out a list of rules and regulations in this book, God makes us aware that He is a different kind of Being. We cannot approach Him as we do other beings. At times, when He allowed a human to approach Him, God prepared the meeting place by making the ground Holy. This is how Moses had his first encounter with God: **And He said, Do not come near here. Pull off your sandals from your feet, for the place on which you stand *is* holy ground. And He said, I *am* the God of your fathers, the God of Abraham, the God of Isaac, and the God of Jacob. And Moses hid his face, for he was afraid to look upon God** (Exodus 3:5-6). We notice from this Scripture that Moses already knew enough about God's holiness to be afraid, and recognized that he was in the presence of Holiness.

Holiness can only be put in its proper perspective when we understand that the ultimate penalty for not recognizing it is death. God made it very clear that death was a just punishment for ignoring this law. Thankfully, for all of us, He does not invoke this all the time. Here are some warnings to us, that a place, or thing that He deemed Holy, was to be treated with utmost respect.

In Numbers 19:13 (NIV), God classifies the tabernacle as a Holy place and orders excommunication for any man who refused to purify himself before entering the Holy area: **If they fail to purify themselves after touching a human corpse, they defile the LORD's tabernacle. They must be cut off from Israel. Because the water of cleansing has not been sprinkled on them, they are unclean; their uncleanness remains on them.**

In Exodus 30:33 God sets oil apart as Holy and commands that it only be used in a certain way or excommunication would be the just punishment: **Whoever compounds any like it, or whoever puts *any* of it upon a stranger, shall even be cut off from his people.**

In the Mosaic Law, God placed much emphasis on His Holiness. In Leviticus 16, He warns Moses that the sanctuary is holy, and is to be treated with the utmost respect. Prior to coming into the presence of a Holy God, Aaron was required to do the following: (plus many other regulations mentioned elsewhere).

- sacrifice a young bull (v3)

- sacrifice a ram (v3)

- take a bath (v4)

- put on sacred lined underwear (v4)

- wear a sacred linen sash (v4)

- wear a sacred linen turban (v4)

Failure to do as commanded could result in death. As we see in Leviticus 16:2, when Aaron approached God's Holiness, he was to be careful not to come into the presence of God at time of his choosing: **. . . and Jehovah said to Moses, Speak to Aaron your brother, that he does not come <u>at all times</u> into the sanctuary within the veil before the mercy-seat, which is on the Ark, <u>so that he will not die</u>. For I will appear in the cloud on the mercy-seat.**

In Leviticus 10:1-2, we find that God killed two men who refused to obey His law regarding specific rules as to how fire was to be offered because they disrespected His Holiness: **And Nadab and Abihu, the sons of Aaron, each took his censer and put fire in it, and put incense on it, and offered strange fire before Jehovah, which He had not commanded them. And there went out fire from Jehovah and devoured them, and they died before Jehovah.**

We can be sure that these individuals were not the only ones to have committed a sin against God on that particular day but they died because God had made a law. He has the power to give life or take life. Whether we like it or not, and whether we agree with His justice or not, He has the power to execute justice as He sees fit. Because of His great mercy, His choice is to give life, and He does so most of the time. However, to teach us reverence and respect for His Holiness, He took two lives that day. He really is Holy, and He will not always tolerate our disobedience.

While we cannot fully comprehend the depth of His Holiness, we learn from Scripture that He will not always disregard our ignorance. We are not likely to ever be called on the carpet for a lack of understanding, but blatant disrespect and disobedience could surely be called into account. He sees our hearts and He knows our weaknesses. A willing and submissive heart, wanting to know His ways will be matched with His patience, love and longsuffering. Hearts with no desire to respect God or learn His ways need to pay attention to this fact: some men died and will be eternally separated from Him because they refused to recognize that God is Holy. This is borne out in several Scriptures, here are a couple:

> **A man who hardens his neck when reproved shall be suddenly broken, and there will be no healing** (Proverbs 29:1).
>
> **He who believes on the Son has everlasting life, and he who does not believe the Son shall not see life, but the wrath of God abides upon him** (John 3:36).

God's name is Holy. This He made abundantly clear by issuing a warning in one of the Ten Commandments: **You shall not take the name of Jehovah your God in vain. For Jehovah will not hold him guiltless that takes His name in vain** (Exodus 20:7). It is clear from this that if we use His name in any other way except with reverence, we bring guilt down upon our heads. Guilt deserves punishment and may be administered at any time He chooses. He may choose to show mercy but it is dangerous to take Him for granted. John Gill's *Exposition of the Entire Bible* (BibleClassics.com) puts it this way: ". . . the name of God ought never to be mentioned but in a grave and serious manner, and with an awe of the greatness of his majesty upon the mind" (Bible Study

Tools). Christians need to understand this and be extremely careful not to offend Him. How could we treat Him and His Son with such disrespect when we claim to worship them?

The world has no respect for God or His name. Further, sinners are known to hate God and His Son. It was worded this strongly when Jesus said: **The world cannot hate you, but it hates Me because I testify of it, that its works are evil** (John 7:7). This hatred is clearly expressed by the world, when they use His Holy name as a curse. Whenever a sinner wants to express anger, annoyance, contempt or hatred, they use the name of God or the name of His Son, Jesus. Of all the words in the English language (about 500,000) it is strange in one sense, that the name of God and His Son are favorites when the annoyed ones want to issue a curse. Year after year men never get tired of using those same curse words. It never goes out of fashion. They claim they don't believe in Him yet His name is on their lips continuously.

An easy trap for Christians to fall into is to excuse movies and books that use the name of our Sovereign God and His Son in vain because it is 'just entertainment'. We cannot help it if people on the street and in the workplace take His name in vain, but to tolerate such in our entertainment is offensive. Is it possible that we are just as guilty as they are if we do this? If you believe this, and have done it in the past, ask God to forgive you. The next time His name is used in vain in a book, pitch it out; or on TV, shut it off; or in a theater, walk out. The choice is quite simple: offend God and be declared guilty by Him or sacrifice the pleasure.

What sinners (and sometimes Christians) fail to realize is that all cursing is being "videotaped" and recorded: **There is nothing hidden that will not be revealed. There is nothing kept secret that will not come to light** (Mark 4:22 GW). The author of Ecclesiastes confirms this in 12:14: **For God shall bring every work into judgment, with every secret thing, whether** *it be* **good, or whether** *it be* **evil.**

The Law in Leviticus clearly states how serious God views the taking of His name in vain: **And he that blasphemes the Name of Jehovah shall surely be put to death. All the congregation shall surely stone him. And the stranger as well, even as he that is born in the land; when he blasphemes the Name, he shall be put to death** (24:16). The Holiness of God and the sacredness of His name have never changed. He reassures us of this: **For I** *am* **Jehovah,** *I* **change not** (Malachi 3:6).

## What is God Like?

Our contact with God is limited. Very few have ever heard Him audibly and we are unable to touch Him or see Him. He has, however, given us one sacred part of Himself: His *name*. We may use His name in holy reverence or we may call upon His name in time of need. This is a great and awesome gift, but it comes with a grave responsibility. To help us understand His holiness, He solemnly warned us not to misuse His name. As mentioned above, this warning listed in one of the Ten Commandments and Leviticus 24:11-14 indicates just how serious He considers such abuse:

> **And the son of the woman of Israel blasphemed the name *of Jehovah*, and cursed. And they brought him to Moses (And his mother's name was Shelomith, the daughter of Dibri, of the tribe of Dan). And they put him under guard, so that the mind of Jehovah might be declared to them. And Jehovah spoke to Moses saying, Bring forth the despiser outside the camp. And let all that heard lay their hands on his head. Let all the congregation stone him.**

We know that this young man was not the only person to have misused the Holy name of God, then or now. On this occasion, however, this man paid for his sin with his life. Others, then and now, are shown mercy. This does not mean God has ignored the breaking of His laws or that He is slack concerning justice. It does mean that His law could be enacted at any moment and we should never take Him for granted.

As we become aware of our need to be Holy we also need to be reminded that mercy and grace is available to us while we live and breathe. He is a forgiving and patient Teacher who uses discipline to teach: **Furthermore we have had fathers of our flesh who corrected *us*, and we gave *them* reverence. Shall we not much rather be in subjection to the Father of spirits and live? For truly they chastened *us* for a few days according to their own pleasure, but He for our profit, that *we* might be partakers of His holiness** (Hebrews 12:9-10). Titus 3:4-7 confirms that we cannot attain this on our own, we must rely on His mercy and grace and with the help of Jesus Christ our Savior: **But when the kindness and love of God our Savior toward man appeared, not by works of righteousness which we have done, but according to His mercy He saved us, through the washing of regeneration and renewal of the Holy Spirit, whom He poured out on us abundantly through Jesus Christ our Savior, that being justified by His grace, we should become heirs according to the hope of eternal life.**

The greatest dilemma that sincere Christians may face today may well be this: How should we be treating this Holy God that we are attempting to serve?

Even Jesus, His Son, bowed Himself to the ground when He approached His Holy Father in prayer: **And He was withdrawn from them about a stone's throw. And He kneeled down and prayed, saying, Father, if You are willing, remove this cup from Me. Yet not My will, but Yours be done** (Luke 22:41-42). Thankfully for us, God does not seem to be too caught up in His holiness; He is more caught up with His love for us.

It may seem very uncomfortable and even intimidating for us, as mere humans with our shortcomings, to try and get up enough courage to approach One who has such awe inspiring holiness. We know that we would benefit from such an encounter, but what could possibly be in it for Him? The only explanation has to be His passionate love. Remember, He *is* love, and somehow that love gets past our frailties, our flaws, and even our blatant sins. It is worth noticing that it was God who pursued Adam, the first sinner, in the Garden and made things right in spite of his sin and in spite of God's great Holiness. And He is pursuing us still.

# 12  GOD IS A BUILDER

God was directly involved in the design and implementation of a building where He could meet with the Hebrews as they traveled: **Let them construct a Sanctuary for me so that I can live among them. You are to construct it following the plans I've given you, the design for The Dwelling and the design for all its furnishings** (Exodus 25:8-9 MSG). The building and its furnishings were portable and constructed with the most costly materials on earth. Every feature in the design of both the building and furnishings had a purpose. Although He could have easily done so Himself, He commanded the children to provide the materials, to teach them sacrificial giving. The Ark, a box constructed to carry the Ten Commandments, a pot of manna, and the rod of Aaron, was designed to remind the Israelites of His presence. The Golden Altar of Incense was a reminder of prayer and intercession continually going up to Him from His children: **. . . for my house will be called a house of prayer for all nations** (Isaiah 56:7 NIV). The laver, a basin where, according to various passages in Exodus, the priests would wash themselves before meeting with God, taught them to never enter His presence with sin in their lives. Leviticus 15:31 bears this out: **So you shall separate the sons of Israel from their uncleanness, so that they do not die in their uncleanness when they defile My tabernacle that *is* among them.** The whole building project displayed His skill and wisdom as a Master Builder and also that of a Teacher. The structure and its furnishings were a continuous object lesson to teach them, and us, something about Himself.

Consider His total involvement in the details of this building project: God provided the design, the plans and the skilled workmen: **GOD spoke to Moses: "See what I've done; I've personally chosen Bezalel son of Uri, son of Hur of the tribe of Judah. I've filled him with the Spirit of God, giving him skill and know-how and expertise in every kind of craft to create designs and work in gold, silver, and bronze; to cut and set gemstones; to carve wood–he's an all-around craftsman. Not only that, but I've given him Oholiab, son of Ahisamach of the tribe of Dan, to work with him. And to all who have an aptitude for crafts I've given the skills to make all the things I've commanded you"** (Exodus 31:1-6 MSG).

The writer to the Hebrews, in discussing the faith of Abraham, mentions that God is also the builder of a vast city: **For he looked for a city which has foundations, whose builder and maker** *is* **God** (Hebrews 11:10). This city is described in greater detail in Revelation chapter 21. The entire chapter describes a massive city with architectural details including the building materials, incredible lighting and out-of-this-world landscaping. If you are a Christian you should read this chapter to familiarize yourself with the city you will soon inhabit. Remember, while God is building, He has you in mind. If you think it's all too good to be true and that you are not worth it in His eyes, 1 Corinthians 2:9 says different: **But as it is written, "Eye has not seen, nor ear heard, nor has it entered into the heart of man, the things which God has prepared for those who love Him."**

Entrance into the city has one condition that is captured by Revelation 22:14 (GNB): **Happy are those who <u>wash their robes clean</u> and so have the right to eat the fruit from the tree of life and to go through the gates into the city.**

Now this is where it gets interesting for you and I. Jesus said His Father has built a residence for us with scores of rooms and square footage: **In My Father's house are many mansions; if** *it were* **not** *so,* **I would have told you. I go to prepare a place for you. And if I go and prepare a place for you, I will come again and receive you to Myself, so that where I am, you may be also** (John 14:2-3). The down payment for your share in this mansion has already been paid, and for you it's mortgage free. This house is similar to all homes in one respect: it is meant for people to live in—Father and His family. The ultimate purpose of our lives is to be with God and this house is being prepared so that we can all be together. Paul explains to the church at Corinth that the minute we leave this body we take possession of our new home: **For we know that if our earthly house of** *this* **tabernacle were dissolved, we have a building from God, a house not made with hands, eternal in the heavens** (2 Corinthians 5:1)

# 13 GOD HAS SECRETS

Nothing is more obvious than the fact that God has secrets. Millions of details about Himself and physical creation have yet to be discovered because they are still hidden. Much knowledge regarding the spiritual realm remains hidden and, according to Deuteronomy 29:29, God has and will disclose things as He sees fit: **The secret things** *belong* **to Jehovah our God, but the revealed things** *belong* **to us and to our sons forever, so that we may do all the words of this Law.** Revealing secrets, according to this Scripture, is for our benefit that we may learn to obey.

David indicates that God's secrets are for sharing with those of us who fear Him: **The secret of Jehovah** *is* **with those who fear Him; and He will show them His covenant** (Psalm 25:14).

Some secrets will be disclosed to us through men or women with the gifting of a prophet: **For the Lord Jehovah will do nothing unless He reveals His secret to His servants the prophets** (Amos 3:7).

Paul explains, in 1 Corinthians 2:9-16, how followers of Christ may obtain the secret and hidden things that God would like to reveal to His children: **But as it is written, "Eye has not seen, nor ear heard", nor has it entered into the heart of man, "the things which God has prepared for those who love Him". But <u>God has revealed</u>** *<u>them</u>* **<u>to us</u> by His Spirit; for the Spirit searches all things, yea, the deep things of God. For who among men knows the things of a man except the spirit of man within him? So also no one knows the things of God except the Spirit of God. But we have not received the spirit of the world, but the Spirit from God, so that we might know the things that are freely given to us by God. These things we also speak, not in words which man's wisdom teaches, but which** *the* **Holy Spirit teaches, comparing spiritual things with spiritual. But the natural man does not receive the things of** *the* **Spirit of God, for they are foolishness to him; neither can he know** *them***, because they are <u>spiritually discerned</u>. But he who is spiritual judges all things, yet he himself is judged by no one. For who has known the mind of the Lord, that he may instruct Him? But we have the mind of Christ.**

In this verse by Paul we understand that some of God's secrets are beyond our reach, at least for now: **O** *the* **depth of** *the* **riches both of** *the* **wisdom and knowledge of God! How unsearchable** *are* **His judgments, and His ways past finding out!** (Romans 11:33).

Deep down we all like to know secrets. Tell a child that there is something he or she cannot know until later and you will have a child who will pester you until they get to know the secret. Curiosity is built into our bones and God takes advantage of this. When there are things about Him that we don't know, we are likely to go digging. We study and seek and knock until the door is open. God likes that kind of digging. Jesus encouraged our curiosity by these words: **And I say to you, Ask and it shall be given you. Seek and you shall find. Knock and it shall be opened to you** (Luke 11:9). When He looks down and sees a child of His searching for truth, for answers and solutions, He is pleased and will not withhold from us any good thing. He's like that.

# 14 GOD DEMANDS WORSHIP

God programmed every human to worship, it's in our DNA. Worship is defined by the Oxford Dictionary as: *1. the feeling or expression of reverence and adoration for a deity; 2. great admiration or devotion.* The desire to reverence and adore some other creature, other than ourselves, is built into all of us. We get to select who we adore as an act of our free will. However, God put it there for Himself.

Once we have taken care of the basic necessities of life we go looking for someone or something to worship. Life is dreadfully empty and boring without it. We are all looking and searching. We hear a song and if we like it, we may just love the singer. We see an actor and admire his features, his physique or his skills, and he becomes an object of our affections. The fact they don't even know us or care about us is not important. We have found someone to worship and we unashamedly tell others around us how good our actor or singer really is. If we find it necessary, we will even create our own images to worship. Men are known to carve objects of animals or snakes from wood then bow down in worship to their new god. In Exodus the Hebrews took their jewelry and formed a calf from it to make their own god: And he took *them* **from their hand, and fashioned it with an engraving tool. And he made it a molten calf. And they said, These** *are* **your gods, O Israel, who brought you up out of the land of Egypt** (Exodus 32:4). It seems that anything will do when the longing to worship is not satisfied.

Of course this is not what God intended when He placed the desire to worship into the heart of man. The sole purpose for creating the human and placing a worship center inside of him was to have mutual adoration happening between God and man. Anyone who loved you enough to die for you is worthy of your worship.

God commanded Moses: **Worship no god but me. Do not make for yourselves images of anything in heaven or on earth or in the water under the earth. Do not bow down to any idol or worship it, because I am the LORD your God and <u>I tolerate no rivals</u>. I bring punishment on those who hate me and on their descendants down to the third and fourth generation** (Exodus 20:3-5 GNB).

On a human level, we may find this a bit strange. We would not usually demand or expect anyone to worship us. We hope for love from people close to us, and to a large extent we receive such from mothers, fathers and our spouses, etc. But the concept of demanding worship from one another is foreign to the average person. How can God justify His demand for our worship?

First, we need to acknowledge that while the command to worship is serious and binding, it is only to those who *choose* to do so. Man is still given a choice to obey or disobey this command. To disobey, however, means we must face the consequences (remember, we don't make the rules, He does). The consequences for disobedience are not at all pleasant. The disobedient are given the opportunity to live on His earth and enjoy all of its treasures and benefits, but at the end of our 80 or so years will be separated from Him. Forever!

For those who dislike Him and His ways, He did make provision for another abode, it's called Hell. It will be populated by Satan and hordes of demons. In fact, Hell was created for Satan and his angels, not for men (Matthew 25:41). Ask any sinner if they plan to go there or if they think they would like living with Satan and his demons and the vast majority will say no—or brush off the horror by saying it will be a big party. But, God made it clear—we can only serve one master. Refuse to worship Him and by default you automatically serve Satan. You were born in his kingdom and you stay in his kingdom. David said: **Behold, I was brought forth in iniquity, and in sin did my mother conceive me** (Psalm 51:5). And Jesus confirms this: **You are of the Devil as father, and the lusts of your father you will do. He was a murderer from *the* beginning, and did not abide in the truth because there is no truth in him. When he speaks a lie, he speaks of his own, for he is a liar and the father of it** (John 8:44).

You have probably heard people say that they cannot believe that God would send people to such a horrible place. But consider this: First, He did everything that could be done to save them from it, up to and including sacrificing the life of His Son to redeem them. Second, He allowed them to make a choice: serve and obey Him or serve and obey Satan. By choice, they picked the latter, so where else could they be sent? He only created two places for eternity: Heaven and Hell. If God brought them into Heaven out of pity, they would find themselves unsuited simply because they have no desire for the things of God and no desire to come under His government. It's not what they would choose; it's not what they want. What would they do there? There are no pubs in Heaven, no alcohol, no drugs, no porn, no gambling and no nightlife at all because there is no night (Revelation 21:25). They would be like fish out of water. In a short time they would ruin the peace in Heaven like they ruined things on earth. With their lust, greed, lies, rebellion and hatred, etc., they would eventually bring enough turmoil to Heaven that it would have to be destroyed just like earth will be destroyed. (Not that God would ever allow this to happen.)

The whole foundation of God's kingdom is love. His purpose for creating humans in His own image was so that He could love them and they would return that love. The Apostle John makes this point: **And we ourselves know and believe the love which God has for us. God is love, and those who live in love live in union with God and God lives in union with them** (1 John 4:16). Love is the essence of His being and the essence of His character. Jesus confirms this in John 3:16 (MSG)—the quintessential verse of love: **This is how much God loved the world: He gave his Son, his one and only Son. And this is why: so that no one need be destroyed; by believing in him, anyone can have a whole and lasting life.** If the Bible taught somewhere that "God is Justice," we would not last more than a day, because justice would have to be applied the minute we sinned, and there is a law that says the soul that sins shall surely die (See Genesis 2:17 and Ezekiel 18:4).

If the foundation of His kingdom were justice, our first father and mother would have been executed the minute they ate from the tree because the Lord had made this law: . . . **but you shall not eat of the tree of knowledge of good and evil. For in the day that you eat of it you shall surely die** (Genesis 2:17). Mercifully for us, the foundation of His kingdom is love tempered with mercy, and God, because He *is* love, always leans in that direction.

Regarding His command for us to love Him, we need to understand that a creator can make such a demand simply because He can. Since He is sovereign, He has a right to give His creations whatever commands He thinks proper. We are blessed since our Creator is loving and wise. Here are three other Scriptures where Jesus expresses His Father's love for us:

> **Jehovah has appeared to me from afar,** *saying,* **Yea, I have loved you with an everlasting love; therefore with loving-kindness I have drawn you** (Jeremiah 31:3).

> **Jehovah your God** *is* **mighty in your midst; He will save, He will rejoice over you with joy; He is silent in His love; He rejoices over you with joyful shout** (Zephaniah 3:17).

**But God commends His love toward us in that while we were yet sinners Christ died for us** (Romans 5:8).

God demands our worship because it is the only thing of value that we can truly contribute in the relationship between Him and us. It's our way of reciprocating. His command for humans to love Him makes sense in that it is the only way in which the human can find true fulfillment. He designed the human heart to love and be loved. He demanded our worship knowing that it would satisfy our greatest need. When He created us in His own image He placed the need for love in the very fiber of our DNA. Humans need love and we spend our lives seeking it. If, as new born babies, we are deprived of love we grow into strange, distorted creatures. As sinners we still seek love but in all the wrong places. If you turn on a radio and if they are not giving the news or running an advertisement they are likely playing a song about love, or love lost, spurned, betrayed, etc. The movie industry would collapse if they couldn't weave a love story into the script, no matter how adventurous or violent the story. It's not usually God's kind of unselfish love but it is man's feeble attempt to find it. Females long to be told they are loved and deep down macho men long to hear the same thing.

So, if loving Him is the true purpose for which we were created, then we are only going to find satisfaction in a love relationship with Him. This verse confirms that we were created solely for the pleasure of God: **Thou art worthy, O Lord, to receive glory and honour and power: for thou hast created all things, and for <u>thy pleasure</u> they are and were created** (Revelation 4:11 KJV).

He has placed many things at our disposal, for our pleasure and enjoyment: food, money, sex, travel, adventure, sports . . . The list is long, and yet none of these can compare to the pleasure found in a true love relationship between the Creator and His created beings. Some seem to have found enjoyment in drugs and alcohol and pursue such pleasures intensely. However, they will awaken one day to find they are trapped in a body that they have literally destroyed and a mind that continually craves that which is slowly killing them. We are created in such a way that we will seek pleasure. We are constantly looking to fill the void inside with something that will satisfy. What better thing could God have done to eliminate all our confusion than to issue a clear message for us to love Him and be satisfied to the full. Somehow, David was aware of the pleasure of God's presence when he penned these words: **You will make Me know the way of life; in Your presence *is* fullness of joys. At Your right hand *are* pleasures forevermore** (Psalm 16:11). "Fullness of joys" and "pleasures forevermore" certainly does not seem as if our Heavenly Father is forcing anything unpleasant on us. Could it be that this is what every one of us is longing for? Paul, teaching the Romans, says: . . . **for the kingdom of God is not eating and drinking, but righteousness and peace and joy in** *the* **Holy Spirit** (Romans 14:17). When God firmly stated that we must love and worship Him, it was simply a command that makes all things right in our world. Righteousness, peace and joy are an absolute must for a kingdom of pleasure. Further, Revelation 5:11-14 tells us this is how it will be in Heaven when we arrive:

> **And I looked, and I heard the voice of many angels around the throne, and the living creatures and the elders. And the number of them was myriads and myriads, and thousands of thousands, saying with a great voice, Worthy is the Lamb who was slain, to receive <u>power and riches and wisdom and strength and honor and glory and blessing</u>. And I heard every creature which is in the Heaven and on the earth, and under the earth, and those that are in the sea, and all who are in them, saying, <u>Blessing and honor and glory and power be to Him</u> sitting on the throne, and to the Lamb forever and ever. And the four living creatures said, Amen. And the twenty-four elders fell down and worshiped** *the* **One living forever and ever.**

What kind of creatures and elders are these in the verses above? Are they some sort of sophisticated robots? The Bible says they are around His throne and worship Him forever and ever. Do they have a free will like humans? Or are they doing all this worship because they are enjoying it? I submit that they are worshiping for the pleasure of it. I think this because other angelic beings that populate Heaven have a free will. This is proven by the fact that Satan, who used to be one of the 'top guns' in the Kingdom, made a choice one day and decided to try out for first place. This is recorded in Isaiah 14:12-14 (KJV). Listen to him make five "I will" proclamations regarding his new found ambition:

> **How art thou fallen from heaven, O Lucifer, son of the morning!** *How* **art thou cut down to the ground, which didst weaken the nations! For thou hast said in thine heart, <u>I will</u> ascend into heaven, <u>I will</u> exalt my throne above the stars of God: <u>I will</u> sit also upon the mount of the congregation, in the sides of the north: <u>I will</u> ascend above the heights of the clouds; <u>I will</u> be like the most High.**

When God created Satan in the beginning, there was no plan for redemption written into his contract. The "free will" clause simply stated that you can choose to serve God or not. Satan picked "not," and there was no turning back. He took a third of the angels with him but two thirds stayed, of their own free will. Because there was no redemption plan in place for rebellious angels they are doomed to be separated from God for eternity: **And the devil, who deceived them, was thrown into the lake of burning sulfur, where the beast and the false prophet had been thrown. They will be tormented day and night forever and ever** (Revelation 20:10 NIV).

Satan cannot be anything more than what he is at this moment. He cannot be forgiven and he cannot stop what he is doing. For the time being he is simply being used by God, as seen through the Bible, to test and train Christians and until God is finished with him he will continue to fulfill his purpose. Everything God created was for a purpose. Satan's origin and destiny is outlined by God in Ezekiel 28:13-19 (NIV):

**You were in Eden, the garden of God; every precious stone adorned you: carnelian, chrysolite and emerald, topaz, onyx and jasper, lapis lazuli, turquoise and beryl. Your settings and mountings were made of gold; on the day you were created they were prepared. You were anointed as a guardian cherub, for so I ordained you. You were on the holy mount of God; you walked among the fiery stones. You were blameless in your ways from the day you were created till wickedness was found in you. Through your widespread trade you were filled with violence, and you sinned. So I drove you in disgrace from the mount of God, and I expelled you, guardian cherub, from among the fiery stones. Your heart became proud on account of your beauty, and you corrupted your wisdom because of your splendor. So I threw you to the earth; I made a spectacle of you before kings. By your many sins and dishonest trade you have desecrated your sanctuaries. So I made a fire come out from you, and it consumed you, and I reduced you to ashes on the ground in the sight of all who were watching. All the nations who knew you are appalled at you; you have come to a horrible end and will be no more.'"**

Although the earthly person being addressed is the king of Tyre, the reference is obviously to Satan. This is known by Bible scholars as the Law of Double Reference.[1] When God designed humans He already had a redemption plan written into our contract from the foundation of the world.

---

[1] (J. Dwight Pentecost) "*Two events, widely separated as to the time of their fulfillment, may be brought together into the scope of one prophecy. This was done because the prophet had a message for his own day as well as for a future time . . . It was the purpose of God to give the near and far view so that the fulfillment of the one should be the assurance of the fulfillment of the other*" (Dwight Pages 46-47). *The phenomenon of double reference prophecy to reveal God's plan is common in and unique to the Bible.*

## What is God Like?

Our Redeemer is Jesus and these are His words: **Father, I desire that *those* whom You have given Me, that they may be with Me where I am, that they may behold My glory which You have given Me, for You have loved Me before *the* foundation of *the* world** (John 17:24). In Ephesians 1:7, Paul wrote these words: **In Him we have redemption through His blood, the forgiveness of sins, according to the riches of His grace.** The author of Psalms 111:9 was also aware of this plan of redemption: **He sent redemption to His people; He has commanded His covenant forever; holy and awesome *is* His name**. We can still choose to limit our worship to Him without being punished or losing the gift of Salvation that He gave us through Christ. However, doing so means we lose closer fellowship and the opportunity to bless Him; we miss out on the greatest pleasure this side of Heaven.

There is a deep rooted need to worship someone or even something. If you have ever observed a rock concert you would have noticed thousands of humans, male and female in the process of standing ovations, waving, screaming and really worshiping their favorite rock stars. These stars have become objects of worship. The fans will rave over the singers, pay money to be in their presence, lavish praise on them and endure hardships of long lineups, waiting for the "gods" to appear. God, their Creator, longs to receive such adoration and love. But no, they choose a mere man whose only skill is to sing songs and play the guitar. A sports worshiper picks a mere man who can shoot a puck into a net and showers adoration on him that the Creator of Heaven and Earth passionately desires. It doesn't matter that their gods pay them no attention or ever give them anything except to sing songs or score goals. Their satisfaction is in the fact that they have an object of worship. Even pets can be a god when they receive more affection and adoration than we are willing to give God.

In worshiping God, the most intense and perfect form of worship is telling Him that we love Him too. Once this relationship is in place and we are successfully worshiping Him the way we should, all the other relationships fall into place. The command to love and worship Him is no different than the one commanding us to love one another:

> **You shall not avenge, nor bear any grudge against the sons of your people; but you shall love your neighbor as yourself. I *am* Jehovah** (Leviticus 19:18).
>
> **These things I command you, that you love one another** (John 15:17).

### Ralph H. Matthews

**For all the Law is fulfilled in one word,** *even* **in this, "You shall love your neighbor as yourself"** (Galatians 5:14).

His kingdom runs on love. It's a no-brainer to conclude that the earth would run quite well if humans loved one another. The opposite is also true: it's a horrible place to live if there is no love among us. God's way of solving this problem was to command us to love Him first and all other relationships would automatically slide into place.

Some may be put off when they hear of a God who expects to be worshiped. This can be put into proper perspective when we consider another side of God—the side of Him that lavishes His love on the likes of us. Inspired by the words of Zephaniah 3:14 & 17, and Psalm 34:2 & 4, Mark Hayes writes a song entitled: *And the Father Will Dance.* Here are the first few words:

> *And the Father will dance over you in joy!*
>
> *He will take delight in whom He loves.*
>
> *Is that a choir I hear, singing the praises of God?*
>
> *No, the Lord God Himself is exulting o'er you in song!*

It may be difficult to imagine God dancing, especially dancing over you! But try this first: imagine you are in front of the Judge of the whole earth and you are about to be sentenced to death for your sins. Then, Jesus walks over and says, "Stop, I will take his place." And He did! Once you fully comprehend this, it's a lot easier to imagine God dancing over you.

The very essence of pleasure is in worshiping God. There is no greater pleasure. In my opinion, He would never have created earthly, fleshly pleasures, things or activities to be more pleasurable than Himself.

# 15 GOD CAN BE PERSUADED

It is impossible to manipulate God, but it is possible to persuade Him. There are many examples of man using words to persuade God, in spite of the fact that He is far superior to us in power and wisdom. He allows us to talk to Him and present our arguments. One verse actually indicates that we can reason with Him: **Come now, and let us reason together, says Jehovah; though your sins are as scarlet, they shall be as white as snow; though they are red like crimson, they shall be like wool** (Isaiah 1:18).

Persuading Him is more about Him giving us an opportunity to practice love, compassion and concern for others. It's about picking up on the mercy side of God. As the ultimate Lawgiver, God never uses His laws to get His way, to make idle threats or to display power. Once He made the statement to Moses that He was going to destroy the Hebrew children (Exodus 32:10), they had to be destroyed because His just laws demanded it. However, mercy is a must if any of Adam's race are to survive because none can meet the requirements of His law. This is our condition as described by the Psalmist: **Jehovah looked down from Heaven on the sons of men, to see if there were any who understood *and* sought God. All *have* gone aside, together they are filthy; *there is* none who does good, no, not one** (Psalm 14:2-3). However, through the dim gloom of the law that hangs over our heads, He has thrown us the life line of mercy and all we have to do is grab it and hold on. When confronted with a law that we are guilty of, He basically says, "You are now doomed but bear in mind, I love you. Remember My mercy, I can be persuaded." We would do well to memorize and meditate on Scriptures like these:

> **Jehovah *is* merciful and gracious, slow to anger, and rich in mercy** (Psalm 103:8).

> **Let the wicked forsake his way, and the unrighteous man his thoughts; and let him return to Jehovah, and He will have mercy on him; and to our God, for He will abundantly pardon** (Isaiah 55:7).

The Lord encourages us to remind Him of things as this verse indicates: **Cause Me to remember; let us enter into judgment; declare yourself, that you**

**may be justified** (Isaiah 43:26). It does not mean that He has forgotten; it simply means we are invited to use the promises already made to persuade Him. This is precisely what Moses did when interceding for the Hebrews who were about to be wiped out: **Remember Abraham, Isaac, and Israel, Your servants, to whom You swore by Your own self, and said to them, I will multiply your seed as the stars of the heavens, and all this land that I have spoken of will I give to your seed, and they shall inherit *it* forever** (Exodus 32:13).

When God came down to visit the people of Sodom, He needed only to verify the reports that had reached Him: **I will go down now and see whether they have done altogether according to the cry of it, which has come to Me. And if not, I will know** (Genesis 18:21). Abraham would have known the condition of this wicked place since his nephew, Lot lived there. He also knew that the law of God would warrant proper justice, which meant the destruction of the city. In Genesis 18:23-33, Abraham decides to persuade God to exercise mercy rather than justice. I imagine his motive was to salvage Lot and his family. In these verses, he persuades God to spare the city if 50 righteous people could be found. God agrees with Him. Abraham finally talks God down to 10 righteous people, imploring God to save the city for these few. The Lord agreed with him six times as Abraham persuaded the Lord to spare the city. One wonders what might have happened if Abraham had kept it up.

Moses successfully persuaded God in Exodus 32. The Israelites had sinned by making their own god by casting an idol in the form of a golden calf. This was a sin worthy of destruction and Moses knew that the entire nation was in danger of God's wrath: **And Jehovah said to Moses, I have seen this people, and behold, it *is* a stiff-necked people. And now leave Me alone, so that My wrath may become hot against them and so that I may consume them. And I will make of you a great nation** (verses 9-10). However, Moses was a man of great compassion and possibly the greatest of all human intercessors. He unselfishly put aside the opportunity to become the world's greatest patriarch and concentrated on his original calling, which was to lead the Hebrews into the Promised Land: **And Moses prayed to Jehovah his God, and said, "Jehovah, why does Your wrath become hot against Your people whom You have brought forth out of the land of Egypt with great power and with a mighty hand? Why should the Egyptians speak and say, 'He brought them out for harm, to kill them in the mountains and to consume them from the face of the earth?' Turn from Your fierce wrath, and be moved to pity as to this evil against Your people. Remember Abraham, Isaac, and Israel, Your servants, to whom You swore by Your own self, and said to them, I will multiply your seed as the stars of the heavens, and all this land that I have spoken of will I give to your seed, and they shall inherit *it* forever"** (Exodus 32:11-13).

## What is God Like?

God had not made an idle or unjustified threat. The sin that Israel committed deserved death according to the law that God had given, and it was now up to Him to administer justice or show mercy. However, I believe when God declared His intent in the presence of Moses, He did so knowing Moses had the heart of an intercessor; God allowed himself to be persuaded to mercy. In spite of his shortcomings, this is one area in which this leader excelled. When God chose Moses, He knew Moses could be trusted to intercede. When a choice had to be made between justice and mercy, God knew that Moses would lean toward mercy, which was exactly what God desired. Later, when Aaron and Miriam questioned the leadership of Moses, God rebuked them sharply and made this comment about him: . . . **this is not the way I treat my servant Moses. He is the most faithful person in my household. I speak with him face to face, plainly and not in riddles** (Numbers 12:7-8, GW).

There were many others such as David, Nehemiah, Ezekiel and Jeremiah who persuaded God to give them the desires of their heart. He has also given us the same opportunity, to persuade Him to show mercy and not justice. We may pray for friends and family who could, at any moment, meet the justice of God - but, who may be spared by our intercession.

# 16 GOD IS A LAWMAKER

He is the ultimate lawmaker. All other lawmakers will eventually answer to Him and all men will end up in His courtroom. Everything He created He will judge, according to the laws He established.

There must be law. The entire universe is governed by law. For everything that God spoke into existence, there are laws that pertain to them and laws that keep it all in order. If there were no Law of Gravity, rain would not fall to the earth. Without the laws of physics, all the planets would fly off into outer space and away from the sun, our source of heat, light and life. In the absence of law there would be total, utter chaos in nature and among men. We must have social laws to prevent anarchy, upheaval and general mayhem. No business can function without rules, and it is law that gives man a sense of security. We shun people who disregard law in business and we steer clear of men who are outside the law. We imprison or even kill the outlaws, because society cannot live without law. God built the necessity of law into the very fabric of our being.

God's first conversation with Adam in Genesis 1:28 (NIV) was not about law. It was about blessing: **God blessed them and said to them, "Be fruitful and increase in number; fill the earth and subdue it** . . .

As soon as these gifts were disbursed, God passed the first law mentioned in the Bible: **And the LORD God commanded the man, "You are free to eat from any tree in the garden; but you must not eat from the tree of the knowledge of good and evil, for when you eat from it you will certainly die."** (Genesis 2:16-17 NIV).

God certainly did not overwhelm Adam with numerous laws to give him any impression that he had entered a world of legalism. There was every indication that it would be a world of freedom. Adam had been given a paradise to live in, the weather was perfect, he had a beautiful wife to love and help him, and every physical need had been supplied. Since the nature of God is love and man was created in the image of God, it is quite possible that mankind could have been governed by a single law that we will call The

Law of Love. It is quite conceivable that this is the law that governs Heaven whether it is called by this name or not. It is the Law of God's nature because He is Love. It would stand to reason that Adam would know something of that love since God would certainly place that part of His image in Adam's DNA. Adam was created by the Great Lover Himself and in His very own image. God created Adam to lavish His love upon him. Adam was created with the capacity to love God if he so desired. There should be every expectation that he would be like his Creator and love everything the Creator had made. If Adam had accepted God's Law of Love he could have easily survived in blissful happiness without ever touching the tree of knowledge of good and evil. The first—verbal law was simply a test. If Adam truly loved God, he would obey Him. Jesus taught this principal: **"If you love me, keep my commands** (John 14:15 NIV).

The law governing Heaven is the Law of Love. All things done there must be done out of love. Anything done as an act of duty would mean someone is paying a debt with acts of service. This would also mean that the angelic beings occupying Heaven were created for the sole purpose of doing service for God. There would be no demonstration of love by the Creator if He had created them as servants or slaves. Therefore, when He created them out of love and they serve Him out of love, the term, "God is Love" has its full and true meaning.

The Law of Love as described above is not found in the Bible verbatim. However, the concept is fully defined in these words: God *is* Love. Everything about Him—His reason for creating, His reason for creating lavishly, and the reason He created man with a free will—indicates that He is motivated out of sheer, intense, holy love. The Law of Love had to be the only law functioning for Adam and his children. They had never been told they should not kill, steal, harbor jealousy or any other sin. When Adam and Eve disobeyed and Cain committed murder they broke the only law in existence, the Law of Love. But, as Paul notes in Romans 5:13 (BBE), **till the law came, sin was in existence, but sin is not put to the account of anyone when there is no law to be broken.** Adam and Eve broke the Law of Love by disobeying God as Jesus taught in John 14:15. Cain was not subject to **Thou shalt not kill** (Exodus 20:13 KJV), since it had not yet been given. The only law that he could have broken would have been The Law of Love, since Paul says that if there is no law to break, then no sin is committed. However, according to God, what Cain did was called *sin*: **If you do well, shall you not be accepted? And if you**

**do not do well, sin crouches at the door; and its desire *is* for you, and you shall rule over it** (Genesis 4:7). In fact, it's the very first time the word sin is used.

In this conversation, God is trying to head off a problem at the pass. He is making Cain aware of the fact the He knows what's going on inside his heart, and is trying to prevent him from killing Abel. He used the word 'sin' to classify those thoughts. We have to conclude that there was a law in effect that somehow alerted Cain that it was wrong to kill. The law was in the Law Giver and Cain was made in the Law Giver's image. It was unwritten but it was woven into Cain's DNA. It was written in Cain's conscience. It would be impossible for a man to be in the *image* of God and in the *presence* of God and not know that *He is love.* That bit of knowledge would prohibit you from killing your brother, because the Law of Love demands different. The Law of Love is inherent in the God of Love and was passed on to Adam and to his sons by "image transfer" (technically, that's not in the Bible either, but the Bible does talk about human characteristics being passed from one generational to the next),[2] so it is not unreasonable to assume that God wanted us to 'pass on' His characteristics, rather than the characteristics of sin. The Law of Love would demand that only good be practiced between the sons of Adam. Cain had a conscience, the spiritual computer that figures out right from wrong and his computer had calculated the right answer. But because he was feeling jealous rage and because he had a free will, he exercised this freedom and committed the sin of murder.

Further, if no law had been broken by Cain, then he should not have been punished. But God *did* punish him as Genesis 4:11-12 (NIV) records: "**Now you are under a curse and driven from the ground, which opened its mouth to receive your brother's blood from your hand. When you work the ground, it will no longer yield its crops for you. You will be a restless wanderer on the earth.**" In order for there to be punishment, there had to have been a law; and the only law in effect was the Law of Love.

The major advantage to this law is that it's the one and only law that humans actually need. The writer of Proverbs understood this when he said: **Hatred stirs up fights, but love covers all sins** (10:12). Love hides a sin by others, does not expose it, and can forgive and forget. Peter says: **love each other as if your life depended on it. Love makes up for practically anything** (1 Peter 4:8 MSG). Paul devotes 1 Corinthians 13 to exhort the church at Corinth to place love at the top of all human and spiritual characteristics. This is what the first and

---

[2]  Read: Exodus 20:5; Numbers 14:18; Deuteronomy 5:9

last verses (MSG) say: **If I speak with human eloquence and angelic ecstasy but don't love, I'm nothing but the creaking of a rusty gate . . . But for right now, until that completeness, we have three things to do to lead us toward that consummation: Trust steadily in God, hope unswervingly, love extravagantly. And the best of the three is love.**

The love characteristic was placed in all of us from the beginning and we choose whether to practice it or not. If Adam had chosen to obey God, the earth would have continued to be a perfect place to live. If Adam and his descendants had elected to love God, their wives, children and all their neighbors, there would never have been a need for the Ten Commandments. When we comply with the Law of Love, all these things are automatically taken care of.

Meanwhile, back to Adam, fresh from the dust . . . During his orientation, he was informed that his new world would have one law. It was a simple law that would not require a university degree to understand it. There had to be a law in order for Adam to exercise his will to say, "I will" or, "I will not." For a being to not have such a choice, God may as well have made a robot and programmed it to do everything right with no room for mistakes and immune to viruses, the perfect biological machine. But with the creative abilities of God, it is obvious that such a machine would not have been much of a challenge and it would certainly not have brought Him any pleasure, and we as robots would not have fulfilled the purpose for which we were made—to love God. Instead, He designed and built a creature like Himself, one with a will that could make up its own mind, even at the risk that this majestic design could turn against its Creator. A true blue human must have the option to sin or not to sin; to love or hate; to be happy or sad. Even with the Law of Love fully operational, there had to be at least one law that Adam could break in order to prove free will. And God ran that risk for us!

Regarding the command by God, "**. . . you shall not eat of the tree of knowledge of good and evil,**" Genesis 2:17, Adam Clark's Commentary of the Bible offers: *The prohibition was intended to exercise this faculty in man that it should constantly teach him this moral lesson, that there were some things fit and others unfit to be done, and that in reference to this point the tree itself should be both a constant teacher and monitor* (GodRules.net).

The first law God gave was quite simple. **And Jehovah God commanded the man, saying, You may freely eat of every tree in the garden, but you shall not eat of the tree of knowledge of good and evil. For in the day that you eat of it you shall surely die** (Genesis 2:16 - 17). Later, many more laws had to be added. One source lists a total of 2713 in the Old Testament alone and another 1050 commands in the New Testament (Dake Page 113). God only introduced the extra laws when nothing else worked. First, He gave man a shot at freedom based on love. After all he was made in the image of God who *is* Love: **The one who does not love has not known God. For God is love** (1 John 4:8). God had also given him a conscience to figure out right from wrong, and for a while no further laws were needed. Jesus even simplified the Law of Love with these words: **Here is a simple, rule-of-thumb guide for behavior: Ask yourself what you want people to do for you, then grab the initiative and do it for them. Add up God's Law and Prophets and this is what you get** (Matthew 7:12 MSG). We call it The Golden Rule. Even with my peanut of a brain I can understand it!

As Lawgiver, God bears the brunt of all sin. Any righteous law that is passed ultimately will rest with Him because all bona fide law originates with Him. This is what David meant after he had sinned by committing adultery with Bathsheba and having Uriah killed: **Against you, you only, have I sinned and done what is evil in your sight; so you are right in your verdict and justified when you judge** (Psalm 51:4 NIV).

Even though he had committed a serious crime against Bathsheba and Uriah, the law he broke was God's law as it was recorded in Exodus: **You shall not murder** (20:13) and **You shall not commit adultery** (20:14). These laws originated with God. Even before Moses wrote these down, God's original law—the Law of Love—was broken.

According to Romans 5:13, no law means one cannot be charged with sin: . . . **for until the Law sin was in *the* world, but sin is not imputed *when* there is no law.** From Adam to the Law of Moses, man obviously sinned, but the sins were not accounted to them. Only after a law is made can one break it and one cannot break a law that has not been issued either verbally or written. This still applies to us today: If our lawmakers had not passed the law that we must stop our vehicle at an intersection, then we would not be breaking the law by going through the intersection without stopping. If there were no law forbidding us from throwing trash on the highway then it is perfectly legal for us to litter. Not good, but not illegal. Nothing is said here about the inconvenience and destruction that would ensue without such laws. However, because we are a society of lawbreakers and because we do not operate by the Law of Love, we must still try and protect ourselves from chaos and destruction by making appropriate laws. If we refuse to acknowledge God's laws we have to make our own in order to survive. Read Romans 2:14-16: **The Gentiles do not have the Law; but whenever they do by instinct what the**

**Law commands, they are their own law, even though they do not have the Law. Their conduct shows that what the Law commands is written in their hearts. Their consciences also show that this is true, since their thoughts sometimes accuse them and sometimes defend them.**

We encounter a major problem when we ignore the Love Law, in that we must constantly write new laws to combat the clever ways in which humans find to break them. Then we constantly have to revise them or come up with new ones to try and plug the loop holes in the first ones. It is staggering to visit a law library - thousands of books full of written laws and thousands more commenting on and explaining them.

When the wise Lawmaker told Adam, "Don't touch that tree," He was gently teaching Adam that law is absolutely necessary for the survival of the species. Adam would eventually make his own laws and hopefully base them upon the principals of God's law. The amazing thing about His Love Law is its simplicity and power. It covers all sin, mistakes, errors and any other type of wrong committed against others as we've seen in Proverbs 10:12 and 1 Peter 4:8.

The Law of Love may not even be a law in the strict sense of the word. It certainly is not practiced due to fear of punishment. One cannot be forced to practice it. Laws are usually passed by someone who is basically saying, "This is something you *must* do or you must *not* do." This law of God is more like: This is what I *want* to do. It's my law and it is from my heart. I do this because I love you. I, for one, would not be surprised to find out that there is no law in Heaven and that the entire place operates on Love.

When God the Lawgiver invented the Law of Love, He did so knowing that man would mess up and there would have to be other laws in the interim. The Law of Love will again be put into operation after this Age of Grace has ended. Jesus mentions this "end" as recorded in Matthew 28:20: . . . **teaching them to observe all things, whatever I commanded you. And, behold, I am with you all the days until the end of the world. Amen.** The Law of Love will work in the new era because those who have been redeemed will have a new heart and their desire is to do the will of their Father. During their life on earth they were in constant training to live by this law, regardless of their many, fleshly, shortcomings. The Redeemed Ones have always had at least a <u>desire</u> to do His will and that desire is all that God required. Forgiveness, mercy and redemption take care of the rest.

Here is why this law works so well: There is no fear involved when the Law of Love is practiced as explained in 1 John 4:18: **There is no fear in love, but perfect love casts out fear, because fear has torment. He who fears has not been perfected in love.** This kind of love must be practiced out of our free will and for no other reason than we want to. Since it is Heaven's one and only law, those going there are being trained to live by it. Although hard to imagine, this is possible in view of three things that God has done for us:

1. He redeemed us by the blood of His Son, Jesus, forgave us our sins and we become sinless in His eyes.

2. According to Jeremiah 31:33/Hebrews 8:10, He is going to turn the clock back to where it was on the first day of creation and reprogram our hearts: **For this *is* the covenant that I will make with the house of Israel after those days, says the Lord: I will put My Laws into their mind and write them in their hearts, and I will be their God, and they shall be My people.**

3. He is going to remove Satan. No more temptation from that Snake. No more evil impulses; no more impetus to sin; no more doubt regarding our Creator, because the Snake's lying tongue will be silenced forever. Having left earth with all of its struggles, suffering, pain and the trials and testing brought by Satan, we will welcome this perfect rest. The Law of Love is something that every human has craved from the very beginning of our existence, and now, we will have arrived.

When God created man, He did something quite astonishing with regard to law: He allowed man to make laws of his own. God knew our laws would not be as good as His. He knew we would make improper laws, inadequate laws and downright bad laws, and yet He allowed it. He could have simply enforced His own perfect laws and made man comply or face the consequences. We know we can make our own laws from the very fact that we have thousands of them and we know they don't work well because we are ever trying to modify and update them. The Bible refers to our laws in Romans 2:14-16: **For when the nations, who do not have the Law, do by nature the things of the Law, these, not having the Law, <u>are a law unto themselves</u>; who show the work of the Law written in their hearts, their conscience also bearing witness, and the thoughts between one another accusing or even excusing one another, in a day when God shall judge the secrets of men by Jesus Christ according to my gospel.**

We know we must have law, so we modify and change the Laws which are written in our conscience. But in the same manner if we don't keep His, we can't keep our own. Generally, in our carnal nature, we love to make rules for others. Even the Mafia bosses have strict laws, but they are applied mostly to their subordinates.

Fortunately for us, for our basic survival, most of our laws do align with God's laws. Many nations have used the laws of the Bible as a basis for their legal system. Every legal system on earth has passed laws prohibiting murder (although they define it differently from culture to culture), and no legal system anywhere can function if lying were permitted. God dared to trust us with this freedom based on the fact that He placed a powerful tool inside us called the conscience. It can still compute right from wrong regardless of His influence. Christians will try to make laws based on God's Word when afforded the opportunity. Sinners and the world have no such desire and may often make deliberate efforts to separate themselves from God by making laws of their own choosing. But true to His great wisdom, God built integrity into the heart of every man by means of the conscience. They often do what is right even though they have no desire to worship their Creator. They often make just decisions because they have a conscience. They are *a law unto themselves* as indicated in the Scripture above. For the time being, God permits this because there must be a measure of justice in order for mankind to survive.

# 17 GOD MADE PECULIAR LAWS

At first glance some of Gods laws seem strange, and sometimes even unfair. But, God makes them anyway. We are required to obey them whether we understand them or not. That is not to say we cannot study and examine them to find their purpose, for He always has a purpose. For example consider this law in Exodus 21:2-6: **If you buy a Hebrew servant, he shall serve six years. And in the seventh he shall go out free for nothing. If he came in by himself, he shall go out by himself. If he was married, then his wife shall go out with him. If his master has given him a wife, and she has borne him sons or daughters, the wife and her children shall be her master's, and he shall go out by himself. And if the servant shall plainly say, I love my master, my wife, and my sons. I do not want to go out free, his master shall bring him to the judges. He shall also bring him to the door or to the door-post. And his master shall bore his ear through with an awl, and he shall serve him forever.**

This Scripture implies the buying of one person by another was permitted by God. This does not seem to fit the belief system or culture of today. However, if we place all of God's other laws alongside this situation it shouldn't pose much of a problem even for us. It's all about context: What if the master is required to love this man who works for him just as much as he loves himself? God did command that: **You shall not avenge, nor bear any grudge against the sons of your people; but you shall love your neighbor as yourself. I am Jehovah** (Leviticus 19:18). The servant's reply when he is about to be set free, **"I do not want to go free,"** certainly implies that such love could exist between a servant and his master and that God protected the slaves and servants by commanding masters to love them. In Luke 10, Jesus also made it clear as to who qualifies as a neighbor: anyone in need.

Another law from this passage that may seem peculiar at first is the one about a man having to leave his servant wife and their children behind. There are at least four interesting questions arising from this:

## What is God Like?

1. Would this law regarding marriage of slaves override the bonds of a normal, biblical marriage referred to in Genesis 2:24?[3] In this case, if the slave marries during his term of service but leaves his wife and children with the master when his term is up is the bonding of two, as one flesh, broken?

2. Would God be making a <u>widow</u> of this slave woman and creating <u>fatherless</u> children?

3. Would the slave be <u>committing abandonment</u> by taking this woman as a wife and producing offspring and later leaving her?

4. Why would God not permit the slave to take his wife and kids?

There is a sense in which we should never question God's judgments and ways. We do not possess enough wisdom. Created beings are never in a position to correct or advise their Creator as to how to run the Universe. He does, however, encourage us to study His laws and to try and understand His ways. The Psalmist, in Psalm 119:33 (GNB), said: **Teach me, LORD, the meaning of your laws, and I will obey them at all times.** With that in mind we may well place the above questions in context with other Scriptures that God said about the same subject.

So, let's look at the first question. Genesis 2:18 tells us that God created the woman to be a helpmate for the man: **And Jehovah God said, It is not good that the man should be alone. I will make a helper suitable for him.** This was her role in this situation. She was a helpmate for the slave and the master. In turn, both her new husband and her husband's master were both provider and covering.

In God's order of things it is not good for any man to be alone. That includes the poor man. God did not create anyone to be alone. God's wisdom is passed on through Solomon that covers the economic benefits of togetherness: **Two are better than one; because they have a good reward for their labor. For if they fall, the one will lift up his fellow; but woe to him who is alone when he falls, for he does not have another to help him** (Ecclesiastes 4:9-10). These Scriptures apply just as much to slaves as it does to the rest of us. So, slaves need and deserve helpmates. The male slave was given the option of

---

[3] "Therefore shall a man leave his father and his mother, and shall cleave to his wife and they shall be one flesh."

exercising his free will, to marry or not to marry. Once he made his choice to marry, he was accountable to God and His laws just like any other man. God did not treat him as someone stupid just because he was poor. Just as other men who enter into marriage contracts the slave would be required to think it all the way through and make his decision based on his circumstances. If he marries he will be required to stay with the master for life if he wishes to keep the woman and the children. God had enacted a law so that, after his six year contract was up, the welfare and safety of his wife and children were put ahead of his freedom.

With regard to the second question, would God be making a widow of this slave woman and create fatherless children? He does allow her to marry a slave and have children by him. When the husband's time is up and he must decide whether he stays with his wife and children or leave without them, this decision would hinge on two important factors. When he decided to marry her to begin with, he should have been man enough (mature enough) to know what he was getting into—a requirement for all of us. First, he would be required to know the laws of God like all other men and must take into consideration what would happen after his six year contract. Second, if he loved this woman as he ought to, as required by God, he would know that the only way he was going to keep her and his children was to remain working with his master for the rest of his life, as per the agreement. If the man did leave her behind, it would seem clear that God was protecting the woman and her children by keeping her under the covering of the master who had the means and the authority to protect her and her children.

We must now remind ourselves as to why this kind of marriage is permitted in the first place. We need to recognize the fact that the female slave and the male slave are not people of means. They are too poor to look after themselves. Obviously, a woman of wealth, who could take care of herself or had a family to care for her, would not be marrying a slave or be sold as a slave. By this arrangement God took care of the physical, social and marital needs of the poor.

Further, God set Himself up as this poor woman's ultimate protector: **He executes justice for the fatherless and widow** (Deuteronomy 10:18). Eleven times in Deuteronomy alone, God warns His people to take care of the orphans and widows and issues this last warning: **Cursed is he who perverts the judgment of the stranger, fatherless, and widow. And all the people shall say, Amen** (Deuteronomy 27:19).

We also see from the following two passages (along with numerous others) that God did not allow orphans and widows to be oppressed:

> **In His holy dwelling, God is the father of the fatherless, and the judge of the widows** (Psalm 68:5).

> **Do not rob the poor, because he is poor; nor press down the afflicted in the gate; for Jehovah will plead their cause, and strip the soul of those who plunder them** (Proverbs 22:22-23).

The third question: Would the slave be committing sin if he took this woman as a wife, producing offspring, and later abandoning her? Further, if a slave is allowed to temporarily take a wife and have sex with her and then leave her behind, would this encourage promiscuity? Again God has this covered by the command: **You shall not commit adultery** (Exodus 20:14). All are covered by the same law. We have to assume that because God is not a "respecter of persons," He would require the same sexual purity from the poor as He does the rich.[4] Both come under the same judgment.

That leaves us with the fourth question: Why would God not permit the slave to take his wife and kids? We see from the above that God planned for the slave's well-being in terms of his physical, social and marital needs. Regardless of his poverty God would require him to practice integrity and to act in a righteous manner. Poverty would not be an excuse because God requires all men to practice integrity. God gave him the choice to marry or not. This relationship would not be forced upon him. The slave would have to consider all the consequences. If he marries in his present condition, he would know that God's law says he must stay with his master to keep his wife and children because his master had purchased them both for fair payment (God did not condone forced labor from the poor). So, if his choice is to marry the woman given him by his master he must submit himself to the law of God and stay with the master who had bought him and his wife. If he decides to leave after his six year contract is up he must leave his family

---

[4] You shall not respect persons [show partiality] in judgment. You shall hear the small as well as the great. You shall not be afraid of the face of man, for the judgment is God's (Deuteronomy 1:17).

behind. A slave, who takes a wife, produces children (knowing the decision he must make in six years) and who is ready to walk out of the relationship at the end of his term, lacks integrity. God, in His wisdom, was protecting the woman and her children by leaving them under the care of the master, who had the means to support and protect them.

From this passage regarding slaves, we imagine the following scenario: The male slave and the female slave both have personal, social and material needs. The master has need of them both for their labor. God provides for all three parties. If the male slave decides to take a wife for himself during his slavery he must consider the consequences and agree to stay with his master for life in order to keep his wife and children. If he does not like this arrangement, he must simply wait six years to get married, in which time he will have learned his trade and will be able to take care of himself and his family. God protects the woman and her children regardless of what the male slave does. All three parties have the same responsibility towards God's law, and the needs of all are met.

Let's now consider those that offer themselves for indenture because they have no societal or monetary standing. Jesus taught in Matthew 26:11 that the poor will <u>always</u> be with us. This means that in any society some will be prosperous and some will be poor. The provision made here by God is for the prosperous to take care of the poor. Any man without a job could sell his services to another and immediately start taking care of his needs: instant employment at the going rate of fair wages, as we see in Deuteronomy 15. God also allowed for him to be free to eventually make his own start in life by forbidding contracts longer than six years, unless the servant desired otherwise. Presumably, after six years the man had learned many things working for his master. He would, in all likelihood, have learned a trade. He had been an apprentice for six years and now knew how to look after sheep, how to grow crops, how to handle tools and where to find water, etc. Not bad for a young man who started out with nothing.

If we compare this to today's society it is quite common for a young man to borrow money, go to a university and study for about 4 to 6 years to "learn his trade." When he returns home (with about a $50,000 debt) he will have no on-the-job training and must now start looking for someone to employ him. In view of this, God's way is obviously much better.

As for the necessity for men to buy and sell servants, there were many reasons. High unemployment, debt and crime have always been part of every society, just as it is today. If a man had difficulty in finding work he could sell himself or one of his children to an employer. The poor man had immediate relief and the employer had the help he needed. If a child had been sold in the transaction, the child, under God's command, should be properly taken care of. This arrangement was far better than poverty and starvation. Magistrates sold some people for their crimes and in some cases, creditors were allowed to sell their debtors to settle their debts. In both instances this is a far better way of treating crime than to snatch the criminal from the crime scene and put him in jail and leave it up to the taxpayer to pay for his keep. The criminal contributes nothing to society or his victim and is often left in jail as a useless, dangerous creature who becomes angry and bitter toward his entire world.

God required masters to respect and care for their servants. Remember Deuteronomy 15:12-13: **If your brother, a Hebrew man or a Hebrew woman, is sold knowing you and serves you six years, then in the seventh year you shall let him go free from you. And when you send him out free from you, you shall not let him go away empty.** Under God's law the buying and selling of humans was quite reasonable and safe. Ephesians 6:9 also demonstrates that protection was provided to servants and slaves: **And masters, do the same things to them, forbearing threatening, knowing that your Master also is in Heaven. There is no respect of persons with Him.**

What about slaves? There are obviously places in the Bible where God permitted the use of such a workforce. God allowed his own people, the Hebrews, to be slaves in Egypt for about 400 years. Pharaoh and his people abused them severely. God punished the Egyptians with plagues and with death for this sin. We can be certain that slaves were meant to be protected from the harsh brutality and unfair treatment, seen for example in the early history of North America and other countries. God, through Jesus, clearly states that we should do unto others as we would have them do unto us. He is not a respecter of persons and I believe that He included slaves and servants in this law.

Further, God did not approve of snatching people to force them to work for another. He took kidnapping very seriously as Deuteronomy 24:7 indicates: **If a man is found stealing a person of his brothers, the sons of Israel, and makes a slave of him, or sells him, then that thief shall die. And you shall put evil away from among you.** In 1Timothy 1:8-11, Paul speaks against kidnapping: **But we know that the law is good if a man uses it lawfully, knowing this, that the law is not made for a righteous one, but for the lawless and disobedient, for the ungodly and for sinners, for unholy and profane, for murderers of fathers and murderers of mothers, for manslayers, for fornicators, for**

**homosexuals, for <u>slave-traders</u>, for liars, for perjurers, and anything else that is contrary to sound doctrine, according to the glorious gospel of the blessed God, which was committed to my trust.**

Regarding slaves taken from outside the tribes of Israel. In Leviticus 25:44, God obviously allowed the buying of people as slaves: **Both your male slaves, and your female slaves whom you shall have, shall be of the nations that are all around you. You shall buy male slaves and female slaves from them.** He passed laws to prevent them from being abused and He did not permit kidnapping. It could very well be said that the people God approved as slaves were criminals, individuals in debt or individuals who were poor and were content to sell themselves to remedy their plight. Further, there were three significant benefits to being a slave to God's children, the Israelites:

1. Once a slave was connected to a Hebrew family they came under the protection and blessing of God.

2. They had opportunity to hear the Word of God.

3. They were automatically spared when the wicked nations they came from were destroyed by God.

God's great compassion towards oppressed slaves and servants is very visible in Deuteronomy 23:15 -16 (GNB): **If slaves run away from their owners and come to you for protection, do not send them back. They may live in any of your towns that they choose, and you are not to treat them harshly.** It is assumed from this verse that a servant or a slave who escapes from a master is doing so out of desperation, probably to avoid abuse. When this happened the slave was to be protected and kept free from oppression. It is obvious that a loving Father, who is compassionate toward all of His creation, rich or poor, would never tolerate the kind of slavery known to us in our history.

As Lawgiver, He has made many laws under the Mosaic Law that are sometimes hard to understand. Before we jump to conclusions we ought to take the safe approach by studying with an open mind, and place the laws in context. We do not possess the knowledge or wisdom to challenge His decisions. He did make some peculiar laws but He knows what He is doing. He's like that.

# 18 GOD CHANGES LAWS

The first law God gave was simple and verbal regarding the tree of the knowledge of good and evil. Adam and Eve were tested by it to see if they would obey their own conscience regarding right and wrong. As we know, they failed and their children failed. The age from Adam to the 600th year of Noah is called the Dispensation of Conscience, sometimes referred to as the Age of Innocence (Unger Page 310). The law of God was changed after the flood and man received a new set of laws under the Dispensation of Human Government (ibid). As far as we know the laws given in Genesis 9:1-17 were verbal, few, and very basic:

1. Be fruitful, multiply, and replenish the earth Rule over animals

2. Allowed animals as food, instead of grains, herbs, and vegetables only

3. Do not eat the blood of animals

4. Do not murder

5. Execute persons who murder

6. Keep God's covenant eternally

The third time God changed His laws is called the Dispensation of Law and often called the Mosaic Law (ibid). This set of laws was in writing and occupies a major portion of the Book of Exodus, Leviticus and Deuteronomy. The time period spans from the Exodus to John the Baptist:

> **From the days of John the Baptist until now, the kingdom of heaven has been subjected to violence, and violent people have been raiding it. For all the Prophets and the Law prophesied until John** (Matthew 11:12-13 NIV).

> **The Law and the Prophets were proclaimed until John. Since that time, the good news of the kingdom of God is being preached, and everyone is forcing his way into it** (Luke 16:16 NIV).

The fourth change in God's law is called the Dispensation of Grace or also the Age of Grace (ibid). It was instigated by Jesus. All of the past laws were inadequate: **But we know that whatever things the Law says, it says to those who are under the Law; so that every mouth may be stopped and all the world may be under judgment before God, because by the works of the Law none of all flesh will be justified in His sight; for through the Law *is* the knowledge of sin** (Romans 3:19-20).

This was the one main purpose of the Law in all three dispensations - to let us know that we had sinned. The Law still governs those who choose to remain under it. By it, every mouth will be silenced because it clearly condemns every sinner. It will be used to judge those who refused to accept the New Covenant in which the blood of Christ redeems them from the curse of the Law. Here are the two other purposes for the Law as stated in Paul's letter to the Galatians:

> **Why then the Law? It was added because of transgressions, <u>until the Seed should come</u> *to those* to whom it had been promised, being ordained through angels in the Mediator's hand** (Galatians 3:19). The Law was given <u>until Jesus arrived</u> on the scene.

> **So that the Law has become a <u>trainer of us</u> until Christ, that we might be justified by faith. But faith coming, we are no longer under a trainer** (Galatians 3:24-25). The Law was given <u>to be our teacher</u> until Jesus arrived.

The inadequacy of these laws is confirmed in Hebrews 10:1: **For the Law which has a shadow of good things to come, not the very image of the things, *appearing* year by year with the same sacrifices, which they offer continually, they are never able to perfect those drawing near.**

Here are a few other Scriptures that support the fact that we are no longer under the Law but now living under the Age of Grace:

> **For Christ *is* the end of the law for righteousness for everyone who believes** (Romans 10:4).

> For as many as are out of works of the Law, these are under a curse; for it is written, "Cursed *is* everyone who does not continue in all things which are written in the Book of the Law, to do them." But that no one is justified by the Law in the sight of God *is* clear, for, "The just shall live by faith" (Galatians 3:10-11).

> But when the fullness of the time came, God sent forth His Son, coming into being out of a woman, having come under Law, that He might redeem those under Law, so that we might receive the adoption of sons (Galatians 4:4-5).

> For He is our peace, He making us both one, and *He* has broken down the middle wall of partition *between us*, having abolished in His flesh the enmity (the Law of commandments *contained* in ordinances) so that in Himself He might make the two into one new man, making peace *between them* (Ephesians 2:14-15).

One may very well wonder how God could make one single law under the Age of Innocence, add a few new laws under the Dispensation of Human Government, add numerous laws (over 2000) under the Mosaic Law and revert back to one single law under the Age of Grace. He did it by first testing man with the first 3 sets of laws. He did this to prove to us that we cannot live by law. The fourth and final law brings us to the Age of Grace as He always intended. The Age of Grace is summed up by Galatians 5:14: **For <u>all the Law</u> is fulfilled in one word, *even* in this, "You shall <u>love</u> your neighbor as yourself."**

In Galatians 5:18, Paul explains that if we listen to the Spirit of God and practice this one law, we need no other laws: **But if you are led by *the* Spirit, you are not under law.** He goes on to explain in verses 22-23 that by relying on the Spirit of God there is no *need* for the Law: **But the fruit of the Spirit is: love, joy, peace, long-suffering, kindness, goodness, faith, meekness, self-control; <u>against such things there is no law.</u>**

James calls this new law by two names, the Royal Law and the Law of Liberty: **If you fulfill the royal Law according to the Scripture, "You shall love your neighbor as yourself," you do well. So speak and do as those who shall be judged by *the* Law of liberty** (James 2:8, 12).

So we see that God made changes to the laws He gave mankind. God said this about Himself: **For I *am* Jehovah, *I* change not** (Malachi 3:6). However, his overall plan encompassed the changes that man would bring. Mankind has been afforded every possible act of compassion, patience and love that could be given by our merciful Creator. The changes in His laws were for our benefit and He has been long-suffering in waiting for us to comply. On Earth, for this present age, there will be no further changes to His law and we will either accept His kindness and mercy or face the penalty of His law. Jesus, in Matthew 25:41, put it this way: **Then He also shall say to those on *the* left hand, Depart from Me, you cursed, into everlasting fire prepared for the Devil and his angels.**

God has never changed His laws to accommodate man's sin. A broken law has always been and will always be treated the same way. But out of His tender heart He has used His laws to do three things: let us know that we have sinned, train us to do right and to give us time until Jesus could die to cover our sins. As of now, these three things have been accomplished, but what happens next ought to make us shudder: there is no further change, no further mercy and no further hope. As Jesus warned in the verse above, if we do not avail ourselves of his covering, we are cursed and will be cast out of His sight. The good news is you are still under Grace. Embrace it!

# 19 GOD INVENTED OLD AGE

Have you ever wondered why a loving and compassionate God allows His children to get weak and sick, sometimes too frail to get out of bed? He has built an aging process into our DNA and no amount of exercise, vitamins, steroids or proper dieting will make a difference. This is puzzling, especially when we read that He loved us so much that He gave the life of His only Son to redeem us. Further, 1 Peter 2:24 tells us that His Son was beaten severely for the healing of our bodies. **He Himself bore our sins in His own body on the tree, that dying to sins, we might live to righteousness; by whose stripes you were healed.** Why then does He not heal all of His aging, aching, sagging saints? I believe there are two major reasons: to give us reason to call on Him, and to keep us from having to live eternally in a sin-plagued life—after all, what is redemption if we never leave this old planet?

Like all the other things, old age has been made to serve His purpose, and ultimately, serves us. In the beginning, the number of years He gave man was much longer than the life span we currently experience. Methuselah lived 969 years, (Genesis 5:27) and then he died. By comparison our, scant allotment of years is defined here: **Each of us lives for 70 years- or even 80 if we are in good health. But the best of them bring trouble and misery. Indeed, they are soon gone, and we fly away** (Psalm 90:9-10 GW).

The author of Ecclesiastes 12:1-7 records the progressive aging process that creeps up on every human that God created, no matter how healthy we are or how long we live. He designed the body we live in to become weaker with each passing year until the ticker finally stops ticking and the body lies down in death. Here is the detailed account of how each part of the body is slowly broken and allowed to deteriorate until it finally enters eternal rest. (The words in parenthesis are suggestions only.) **Remember now your Creator in the days of your youth, while the evil days do not come, nor the years draw near, when you shall say, I have no pleasure in them. So long as the sun, or the light, or the moon, or the stars, are darkened, or the clouds return after rain, in the day when the keepers (the arms) of the house (the human body) shall tremble, and the strong men are bowed, (the legs) and the grinders (the teeth) cease because there are few, and those who look out of the windows (the eyes)**

**are darkened, and the doors (the lips) shall be shut in the streets, when the sound of the grinding is low, (the hearing) and you shall rise up (awake up from sleep) at the voice of a bird, (light sleep) and all the daughters of music (the voice and lungs) are silenced; also they are afraid of the high place, (stairs and hills) and terrors along the way, and the almond tree shall blossom, (grey hair) and the grasshopper shall be a burden, and desire (sexual appetite) shall fail; because man goes to his long home, and the mourners go about the streets; or ever the silver cord (the spinal cord) is not loosed, or the golden bowl is broken, (the head or skull) or the pitcher (the heart) is broken at the fountain, or the wheel (the heart as a pump) broken at the cistern; then the dust (the body) shall return to the earth (it shall die) as it was, and the spirit shall return to God who gave it.**

The purpose of the entire script is summed up in the first verse: "Remember God when you are young." Old age is given by our Creator as an act of mercy. It is merciful in the sense that He has carefully measured out youth and strength to force us to take a more serious, discerning look at life toward the end. The pain, the fear and uncertainties of old age represent the final attempt by our Creator to remind us of eternity. God knew that the tendency of all flesh is to keep Him on the outside when we have health, wealth and strength. During old age, health, strength and the ability to get wealth is gradually removed. The man or woman who has any inclination toward God will quickly learn to rely on Him when the legs fail and the eyes grow dim and the five senses are no longer reliable.

God could have easily designed the body to get stronger with age as He did in our early years. But to get our attention and to teach us to rely on Him for spiritual strength He removes physical strength from the body. Old age is a time when every human starts to realize they need help. It is the last chance we have to get it right. Older people, at least Christians, know that they need God more than ever during old age. (Ask any older Christian how many times they have called upon God when they are in fear of losing their memory.) This is exactly what God intended. The day is approaching when time will run out for the physical body and all of its carnal desires will fade. Generally speaking, the lust for sex, money and material things diminishes during the golden years. God teaches the Christian during those years to trust Him to compensate for lack of decreasing strength, withering senses, and waning memory. If we are privileged to enter the senior years at all, we have to accept the aging process as inevitable.

Old age could be just as effective for the sinner if they have the slightest desire toward God. He mercifully extends to them the same option, when the body and the mind stop functioning, to start trusting their Creator. However, one should never wait for old age to make the most important decision of a lifetime. Consider these words (Meyers):

> *There is another consideration which should weigh with you: should you live to old age. It is a very disadvantageous time to begin to serve the Lord in. Infirmities press down both body and mind, and the oppressed nature has enough to do to bear its own infirmities; and as there is little time, so there is generally less inclination, to call upon the Lord. Evil habits are strengthened by long continuance; and every desire and appetite in the soul is a strong hold for Satan. There is little time for repentance, little for faith, none for obedience. The evil days are come, and the years in which you will feelingly be obliged to say, Alas! "we have no pleasure in them;" and, what is worse, the heart is hardened through the deceitfulness of sin.*

Meanwhile, understanding that it is truly an act of mercy by a loving God puts a totally different perspective on our "golden years." He knows we still have flaws, garments that are not totally white and that there are still warts that have to be removed prior to the big upcoming wedding: **Let us be glad and rejoice and we will give glory to Him. For the marriage of the Lamb has come, and His wife has prepared herself. And to her was granted that she should be arrayed in fine linen, clean and white. For the fine linen is the righteousness of the saints. And he said to me, Write, Blessed *are* those who have been called to the marriage supper of the Lamb. And he said to me, These are the true sayings of God** (Revelation 19:7-9).

In addition to being a tool of redemption, I believe old age was a consequence of Eden, and not part of His original plan. God placed two trees in the Garden of Eden, the Tree of the Knowledge of Good and Evil and the Tree of Life. Our first parents, Adam and Eve, picked the wrong tree and brought sin into the world. If they had picked the Tree of Life, they would have lived forever, in good health. Their bodies would have forever kept renewing itself as they do now during our youth. When they picked the "sin" tree it brought death, and our Heavenly Father had to ban them from Eden so they would not be condemn forever in sinful bodies.

> And Jehovah God said, Behold, the man has become as one of Us, to know good and evil. And now, <u>lest he put forth his hand and take also of the tree of life, and eat, and live forever</u>, therefore Jehovah God sent him out from the garden of Eden to till the ground from which he had been taken. And He drove out the man. And He placed cherubs at the east of the garden of Eden, and a flaming sword

**which turned every way, <u>to guard the way to the tree of life</u>** (Genesis 3:22-24).

He then enacted the plan of redemption. Symbolically, for Adam, God sacrificed an animal and used its skin to cover their nakedness. This was the first of countless innocent animal sacrifices that were needed until He sent His Son to die on a cross to be the eternal sacrifice for all who would accept everlasting life by faith.

Pain and trials of old age take on a totally different meaning if we live through them without fear. If we can accept old age as the final class in our "Holiness Degree," and understand that death is the last exam, then old age can truly be 'golden'. Trust God on this one and you graduate. Also, the elderly often find that the thing they do most efficiently is *rest*, the very thing He commanded we do right from the start.

The Psalmist, in Psalm 71:18 (NLT), recognized his limitations regarding his age but understood it did not exempt him from fulfilling his ultimate purpose: **Now that I am old and gray, do not abandon me, O God. Let me proclaim Your power to this new generation, Your mighty miracles to all who come after me.** God uses old age for a purpose. Every breath and every heartbeat is an act of tenderness and mercy.

# 20  GOD ISSUES WARNINGS

God's compassionate nature compels Him to issue warnings. He warns men of errors, impending danger, and of punishment that He is about to hand out. Some question His methods in delivering the warnings. Why not send a massive, powerful angel to deliver such important messages? Why not a *million* angels with megaphones to every city and town? Earthlings are accustomed to getting important messages from their governments via the news media or a letter in the mail. We are used to being warned and informed by email, fax or via audible, verbal instructions. However, God's method of warning us comes via an old book written hundreds of years ago by mere men, often of low status, and made them messengers of the most important information that man would ever hear. Nevertheless, this is God's method. Proper interpretation and understanding of their ancient warnings could mean life or death to contemporary man.

He has designed the course of nature so that warning signs precede storms, earthquakes and other destructive forces of nature. He gave us a measure of wisdom and intelligence that enables us to interpret these signs that enable us to keep out of harm's way. Jesus, in Matthew 16:2-3, issued this warning that we must listen closely to His teachings in order to interpret signs properly: **He answered and said to them, When it is evening, you say, Fair weather; for the sky is red. And in the morning, Foul weather today; for the sky is red and gloomy. Hypocrites! You can discern the face of the sky, but you cannot see the signs of the times!**

Although Jesus was remarking how the religious leaders ignored the portents of spiritual dangers, it is amazing how people will often see the signs of natural disaster, but still do nothing to avoid the destruction about to overtake them. For instance, we are able to conclude from signs in the earth's crust that certain cities are sitting on fault lines and devastating earthquakes will eventually destroy them, but no one is moving. Volcanoes in some mountains are showing signs of erupting but life in the valley goes on as if all is well. Landslides, mud slides and avalanches are inevitable for certain mountain slopes, but the villages and towns at the base remain. We have the signs but we ignore the danger.

Regarding warnings that God makes available to us but we often fail to heed, consider this weather forecast issued 24 hours prior to the New Orleans disaster in 2005:

> DEVASTATING DAMAGE EXPECTED!
>
> HURRICANE KATRINA . . . A MOST POWERFUL HURRICANE WITH UNPRECEDENTED STRENGTH . . . RIVALING THE INTENSITY OF HURRICANE CAMILLE OF 1969.
>
> MOST OF THE AREA WILL BE UNINHABITED FOR WEEKS . . . PERHAPS LONGER . . . POWER OUTAGES WILL LAST FOR WEEKS . . . AS MOST POWER POLES WILL BE DOWN AND TRANSFORMERS DESTROYED. WATER SHORTAGES WILL MAKE HUMAN SUFFERING INCREDIBLE BY MODERN STANDARDS.

Many people ignored these warnings and suffered greatly—but not because there was no warning. Those who heeded the warning were spared.

God gave us the tools and know-how to warn us but often the warnings are ignored. Even those who sometimes believe the warnings make the dreadful blunder of believing that it won't happen yet and it won't happen to me. History suggests that this is often man's biggest mistake. Then there are those who outright refuse to believe His warnings. Some are too lazy to investigate to see if there is any truth in the warnings. This is especially true regarding spiritual warnings.

The Bible is full of warnings given by God. He told the people in Noah's generation that He was about to destroy the earth with water, but only eight people heeded the warning. He warned the Egyptians that He was going to take His people out of Egypt but the information fell on deaf ears. Even ten national disasters did not deter Pharaoh in his stubbornness. God forewarned the Israelites, His precious people, that He would send them into exile if they disobeyed His laws, but they refused to listen and ended up in slavery many times.

God has another dire warning for a day in the near future which is woven all through the Bible. This warning is issued in many ways by many prophets. Isaiah, Jeremiah, Ezekiel, Daniel and the Apostle John in the book of Revelation, warn us that God is going to orchestrate a global war that will bring entire nations to destroy the land of Israel. The whole earth will be shaken and all the nations will tremble. This is not some notion based on quack doomsayers, but is borne out in Scriptures like Revelation 16:16 and Ezekiel 38:4: **And he gathered them together into a place called in the Hebrew tongue Armageddon . . . And I will turn you back, and put hooks into your jaws, and I will bring you out, and all your army, horses and horsemen, all of them clothed most perfectly, a great assembly with buckler and shield, all of them swordsmen.**

In Zechariah 2:8 (NIV), God describes exactly how He feels about Israel: **For this is what the LORD Almighty says: "After the Glorious One has sent me against the nations that have plundered you–for whoever touches you touches the apple of his eye–.** Joel Rosenberg writes an excellent book called "Epicenter" that describes this war and the consequences for those who tamper with Israel. The warning has been in place for hundreds of years, in writing, and yet only Christians believe and accept the fact that God means what He says and will one day stop issuing warnings and start destroying. Revelation 22:18-19 is the last warning issued in the Bible: **For I testify together to everyone who hears the Words of the prophecy of this Book: If anyone adds to these things, God will <u>add on him the plagues</u> that have been written in this Book. And if anyone takes away from the Words of the Book of this prophecy, God will <u>take away his part out of the Book of Life, and out of the holy city, and *from* the things which have been written in this Book.</u>**

According to these verses, anyone who ignores the warning they contain places themselves in eternal, mortal danger. Tampering with the words in this book could mean the difference between eternal life or eternal damnation. It would be good to study the book of Revelation. Since God took the time to author this book it stands to reason that we should take the time to read and study its meaning. The fact that it is a mysterious book only means we need the help of Holy Spirit to open our understanding. This may or may not be instantaneous. After all, **The unfolding of your words gives light; it gives understanding to the simple** (Psalm 119:130).

# 21 GOD IS AN ENFORCER

For every law that God has passed, He plans to enforce. Consider Ecclesiastes 12:13-14 and Psalm 96:13: **Let us hear the conclusion of the whole matter. Fear God, and keep His commandments. For this is the whole duty of man. For God shall <u>bring every work into judgment</u>**, with every secret thing, whether it is good, or whether evil . . . for He comes, for He comes to <u>judge the earth</u>; He shall <u>judge the world</u> with righteousness, and the people with His truth.**

In Matthew 12:36-37, Jesus said: **But I say to you that every idle word, whatever men may speak, they shall give account of it in the day of judgment. For by your words you shall be justified, and by your words you shall be condemned.** When He speaks of *every idle word*, we all know we're capable of issuing lots of them. Jesus expects us to heed this warning because it will be enforced. May God help us!

Jesus, out of concern, informs us in advance of His Father's dreadful power: **But I will warn you of whom you shall fear: Fear Him who, after He has killed, has authority to cast into hell. Yea, I say to you, fear Him** (Luke 12:5). This statement leaves no doubt that God is capable of not only taking a life but also banishing the person from His presence forever.

His means of enforcement is different from ours. God has the ability to catch every offender red-handed. But often, the offender is allowed to go free even though he could be tried and condemned on the spot. Generally, a man is allowed a full lifetime to clock up as many sins as he pleases (or practice righteousness), **as it is appointed to men once to die, but after this the judgment** (Hebrews 9:27). During this judgment every law will be enforced.

God can catch a lawbreaker when he is just thinking about sin: **If we have forgotten the name of our God, or stretched out our hands to a strange god, shall not God search this out? For He knows the secrets of the heart** (Psalm 44:20-21). As we have discussed before, God can enforce any broken law at any time. This should cause us to intensely search the secrets of our own hearts to examine what lurks there.

## What is God Like?

At the end of his life every lawbreaker will be called on the carpet to give an account: **. . . in a day when God shall judge the secrets of men by Jesus Christ according to my gospel** (Romans 2:16). Punishment will then be swift and just. Our justice system is not as efficient. First, we have to catch the lawbreaker in the act or collect sufficient proof to convince a judge or jury and then provide witnesses in order to convict them. We have to count on the honesty and integrity of each witness. We can never judge the intent of a man's heart but God created the thought process, therefore, He knows the motive and every nitty-gritty fact from start to finish.

God has a serious advantage over us humans regarding law enforcement. Humans sometimes plead 'not guilty' when charged with a crime with the excuse they did not know the law. Our legal system can never acknowledge their plea and will quickly remind them that ignorance of the law is no excuse. Many have been dragged off to jail this way, being totally innocent because he truly did not know the law. There isn't much our judges can do about this since, if they allowed one to go free on the basis of ignorance, they would have to let everyone go who so pled, and we can be sure that there would be lots who would try. God, however, has the advantage of knowing the heart. He will judge on the basis of what we do know and furthermore, on what we actually understood, about a particular law. He is able to do this based on the Scriptures above.

Paul proves here that God can forgive ignorance of His laws: **And I thank Christ Jesus our Lord, who strengthened me, because He counted me faithful, putting *me* into the ministry– the *one* who before was a blasphemer and a persecutor and insolent. But I obtained mercy, because being ignorant, I did *it* in unbelief** (1Timothy 1:12-13). We need not worry about Him enforcing a law against us that we do not know or understand. We need only to search our hearts deeply and deal with the things we do know.

For the moment, God has delegated authority to us humans to rule as we see fit. David said this referring to man: **You made him rule over the works of Your hands; You have put all things under his feet** (Psalm 8:6). However, God is still in command and does intervene from time to time when things get out of control. For example: **And Jehovah repented that He had made man on the earth, and He was angry to His heart. And Jehovah said, I will destroy man whom I have created, from the face of the earth, both man, and beast, and the creeping thing, and the fowls of the air. For I repent that I have made them** (Genesis 6:6-7). On that occasion He wiped the slate clean and started over with righteous Noah and his family. Every law in existence at the time was enforced to the nth degree. The only law required for their condemnation was this one: **The soul that sins, it shall die** (Ezekiel 18:20). They were all guilty of sin. And they died!

On another occasion He enforced the law immediately by destroying two cities because of their wickedness: **Then Jehovah rained upon Sodom and upon Gomorrah brimstone and fire, from Jehovah out of the heavens. And He overthrew those cities, and all the plain, and all the inhabitants of the cities, and that which grew upon the ground** (Genesis 19:24-25).

He destroyed a clan in Israel: **But the earth opened up its mouth and swallowed them with Korah, and fire devoured 250 of their followers. This served as a warning to the entire nation of Israel** (Numbers 26:10 NLT).

All rulers on earth come under one ultimate authority. This verse clearly states who that is: **Let every soul be subject to the higher authorities. For there is no authority but of God; the authorities that exist are ordained by God** (Romans 13:1). For a time He has allowed mere men to rule in His place. He will later call them into account as these verses indicate:

> **Yield to those leading you, and be submissive, for they watch for your souls, as those who must give account, that they may do it with joy and not with grief; for that is unprofitable for you** (Hebrews 13:17).

> **So then each one of us will give account concerning himself to God** (Romans 14:12).

> **But I say to you that every idle word, whatever men may speak, they shall give account of it in the day of judgment** (Matthew 12:36). This, of course, includes judges, politicians, prime ministers and presidents, etc.

He has left us His word, in writing that He plans to do some major destructive work on the earth again:

> **Behold, the day of Jehovah comes, cruel and with wrath and fierce anger, to lay the land waste; and He shall destroy its sinners out of it** (Isaiah 13:9).

> **For the anger of Jehovah is on all nations, and His fury on all their armies. He has completely destroyed them; He has delivered them to the slaughter** (Isaiah 34:2).

## What is God Like?

> At that time his voice shook the earth, but now he has promised, "Once more I will shake not only the earth but also the heavens." The words "once more" indicate the removing of what can be shaken that is, created things so that what cannot be shaken may remain (Hebrews 12:26-27 NIV).

> And the nations were full of wrath, and Your wrath came, and the time of the judging of the dead, and to give the reward to Your servants the prophets, and to the saints, and to the ones fearing Your name, to the small and to the great, and to destroy those destroying the earth (Revelation 11:18).

We see from Scripture that He is very patient in allowing man to go in any direction to pursue his own way. This, most often, is a walk toward death and were it not for a wise and compassionate Ruler, mankind would quickly self-destruct. None would be saved. We can rightly assume that when He elected to destroy in the past, it stands as a warning for those in the present.

It is amazing that our great and powerful Creator somehow has the ability to restrain Himself while we exercise our will to commit every despicable sin that He said we shouldn't. He looks on while we curse His name, murder unborn children, refuse to share the wealth, steal, rape and destroy our own bodies with drugs and alcohol. All the while He patiently waits.

Although this is tolerated for the moment, it does not go unnoticed. He has a timetable. He is fully aware of the gravity of the situation and His master plan is still intact. This is how our Lord views our planet at this moment in time: **that the creation itself also shall be delivered from the bondage of corruption into the glorious liberty of the children of God. And we know that the whole creation groans and travails in pain together until now** (Romans 8:21-22).

He is aware of the groaning and the travail, the clock is ticking and we know He will enforce His law as He said He would. At the moment, mercy continues.

# 22  GOD HAS SPOKEN TO EVERY MAN

God has spoken to every man as made clear in the following verses by David: **The heavens declare the glory of God; and the expanse proclaims His handiwork. Day to day pours forth speech, and night to night reveals knowledge. There is no speech nor are there words; their voice is not heard. Their line has gone out through all the earth and their words to the end of the world** (Psalm 19:1-4). If one picture is worth a thousand words, as the old proverb says, how much more then when the whole of nature speaks? This is one of the many ways in which God has tried to reach mankind. The message, "He lives!" is all around us and is being continually declared. God does exist. Creation could not exist without a Creator. Everywhere we look we see His fingerprints. When we look into space, we see His majesty. Look through a microscope and see His genius. Look into the ocean and witness His power. If we look at a newborn baby and conclude there is no Creator, our thinking process is limited indeed. No intellectual can honestly conclude that God did <u>not</u> create the baby because he lacks the knowledge and understanding to make such a conclusion. To make such a claim would mean he knows everything about babies and he knows how to make them, and of course no man can say that. The best man can do toward making a baby is to contribute a seed. Even though that seed is part of our very own body and we have been studying it for hundreds of years, we still do not fully understand it. It would be very presumptuous and ignorant to make a statement that there is no creator of babies. Yet, God makes this statement in the verse above: He says that <u>He</u> is evident, visible and present in everything that <u>He</u> made.

Meanwhile, He has spoken in numerous other ways. Consider the following Scriptures as to how and where His voice has tried to reach us: **But I say, Have they not heard? Yes indeed, their voice went out into <u>all the earth</u>, and their words to the end of the world** (Romans 10:18).

The voice referred to is that of preachers and prophets who have preached the good news. In Paul's day the gospel was spread to every nation. This is mentioned at least three times:

> First, I thank my God through Jesus Christ for you all, that your faith is spoken of <u>throughout the whole world</u> (Romans 1:8).
>
> . . . for the hope which is laid up for you in Heaven, of which you heard before in the Word of the truth of the gospel, which has come to you as it has also <u>in all the world</u> (Colossians 1:5-6).
>
> . . . if indeed you continue in the faith grounded and settled, and are not moved away from the hope of the gospel, which you have heard and which <u>was proclaimed in all the creation under Heaven</u>, of which I, Paul, became a minister (Colossians 1:23).

These verses prove that God has spoken to all of mankind through the gospel message, spread by Jesus and His disciples. Every people group has had the gospel preached to them at one time or another. Not even the dead who lived prior to the time of Jesus will have an excuse, as 1 Peter 4:6 demonstrates: **For to this *end* the gospel was preached also to *the* dead, that they might be judged according to men in *the* flesh, but live according to God in *the* Spirit.** He has seen to it that no human will have an excuse at the judgment and be able to say to God, "I did not know that you existed." He made sure that everyone heard by giving clear evidence that He exists.

On top of that He has even given each of us a measure of faith. **For I say, through the grace given to me, to everyone who is among you, not to think of himself more highly than he ought to think. But set your mind to be right-minded, even as God has dealt to every man the measure of faith** (Romans 12:3). We could not live an hour without faith. Faith is required when you step on a plane, ride in a car, eat at a restaurant or ride an elevator.

It takes massive amounts of faith to see your doctor. By faith you believe that he is sober on the day you see him, that he diligently studied what they taught him in school, that they covered your lumbago problem on the days he did make it to school, that he understood what he was being taught and that he still remembers. When he hands you a prescription your faith must double! By faith you must believe that someone will be able to read his handwriting, that they will interpret it correctly, that the druggist won't be having a bad day and that *he* is not on drugs. Then your God-given faith must extend to all the factory workers who make the pills. You get the picture; no faith means we do not trust. The measure of faith that God gave to every man should enable us, at the very least, to trust that He exists. It is a matter of choice as to whether we accept Him or reject Him but we can't fault Him for not revealing Himself.

In order to judge man at the end of his life it would be essential that a clear message be sent to every individual while they are living. God would not condemn a person who genuinely did not know. Based on this fact we must assume that all agnostics and atheists are people who do know that God does exist but refuse to acknowledge Him. This is exactly how Paul describes them: **For the wrath of God is revealed from Heaven against all ungodliness and unrighteousness of men, who <u>suppress the truth</u> in unrighteousness, because the thing which may be known of God is clearly revealed within them, for <u>God revealed</u>** *it* **<u>to them</u>. For the unseen things of Him from** *the* **creation of** *the* **world** *are* **clearly seen, being realized by the things that are made,** *even* **His eternal power and Godhead, for them to be <u>without excuse</u>** (Romans 1:18-20).

God also speaks through His followers who are called Christians. Back in the Old Testament, He had followers like Enoch, Methuselah, Noah and Abraham. Paul refers to such men as those whose lives are like an open book read by all men. God speaks to sinners through us: **You are our epistle written in our hearts, known and read by all men** (2 Corinthians 3:2). A Godly Christian life is, in some ways, better that a written Bible. Sinners may never pick up a Bible to read but they should be able to see God in a Christian. They cannot help but "read" a Christian's life.

God speaks to man by The Holy Spirit who is the third person of the Trinity. He is the One referred to in Genesis at the time of Creation: **And the earth was without form and empty. And darkness** *was* **on the face of the deep. And the Spirit of God moved on the face of the waters** (Genesis 1:2). He was the One the Lord consulted with when He made man: **And God said, Let Us make man in Our image, after Our likeness. And let them have dominion over the fish of the sea, and over the fowl of the heavens, and over the cattle, and over all the earth, and over all the creepers creeping on the earth** (Genesis 1:26). Holy Spirit has direct access to man's spirit and can communicate with him any time He wishes. We have all had thoughts pop into our mind at one time or another. There is no other explanation as to their source other than that of another spirit. Evil spirits also deliver thoughts, but they are unnaturally fearful, full of self-destruction or condemnation. The Holy Spirit brings thoughts of comfort, encouragement and conviction when we are about to do something wrong. Some will deny that any other spirit ever speaks to them, but that argument will not make the grade when we stand before God. He will assert that He did speak but He was rejected. There is no statement more eloquent than the blood of Jesus. A man or woman would have to be foolish indeed to think that they are going to argue with God during their court appearance: **For we must all appear before the judgment seat of Christ, so** that each one may receive the things *done* through the body, according to that which he has done, whether good or bad (2 Corinthians 5:10).

The Holy Spirit has always been present on earth and has always been involved in the affairs of man on God's behalf. It was the Spirit who strove with sinful man just prior to the flood: **And Jehovah said, My spirit shall not always strive with man, in his erring; he is flesh** (Genesis 6:3). In Nehemiah 9:30 (CEV), the people confessed that Holy Spirit had tried to warn them of their sins: **For years, you were patient, and your Spirit warned them with messages spoken by your prophets. Still they refused to listen, and you handed them over to their enemies.** The Psalmist made references to Holy Spirit as being sent by God: **You send forth Your Spirit, they are created; and You renew the face of the earth** (Psalm 104:30). In Psalm 139:7-8, David mentions the Holy Spirit as being omnipresent: **Where shall I go from Your Spirit? Or where shall I flee from Your presence? If I go up into Heaven, You are there; if I make my bed in Sheol, behold, You** *are there.*

We see from these and other Scriptures that the Spirit has been communicating with man all through the Old Testament. When Jesus was getting ready to return to Heaven, He informed us the Holy Spirit would still be in touch: **But I tell you the truth, it is expedient for you that I go away; for if I do not go away, the Comforter will not come to you. But if I depart, I will send Him to you** (John 16:7). Jesus assured that not only would Holy Spirit be with us, but He would be our Teacher: **And when He comes, He will convict the world of its sin, and of God's righteousness, and of the coming judgment. The world's sin is that it refuses to believe in Me. Righteousness is available because I go to the Father, and you will see Me no more. Judgment will come because the ruler of this world has already been judged.** (John 16:9-11 KJV).

During this visitation by Holy Spirit, God made provision that sinners will be contacted also: **And when that One comes, He will convict the world concerning sin, and concerning righteousness, and concerning judgment** (John 16:8). This is much to the advantage of Christians who are praying for sinners and family members who have not yet become Christians. We learn from this verse that the Spirit will speak to sinners about sin, righteousness and judgment. This is the essence of the Gospel. When we have done our part in sharing the gospel with them, we are entitled to ask the Holy Spirit to take the Word and help the sinner understand. We can only reach their ears, but He can reach their hearts. He is never too lazy or tired or indifferent; He will always go when asked.

The teaching referred to in John 16:9 above is not audible teaching, but is directly from God's Spirit to our spirit. There are three sources for thought that takes place inside our minds. One is obviously our own thoughts that we are capable of producing. Another would be thoughts that come when Holy Spirit is speaking to us. All these thoughts will align with God's Word as recorded in the Bible. A third source would be Satan via an evil spirit. These are identified by the fact that they do not align with God's Word, they are deceptive, and they bring fear and condemnation; the Holy Spirit will never condemn us but He will make us aware by convicting us of our sin.

Our Heavenly Father may, at times, seem silent to the natural man, but He has sent Holy Spirit to earth to communicate with us. He made a promise that the Comforter would never leave us or forsake us. And then, when it seems as if He has done all He could to communicate with us, He makes it all so very personal by dwelling inside us: **But if the Spirit of the *One* who raised up Jesus from *the* dead dwells in you, the *One* who raised up Christ from *the* dead shall also make your mortal bodies alive by His Spirit who dwells in you** (Romans 8:11). This is an amazing and marvelous thing God has done for those who choose to love Him. It is hard for our natural minds to comprehend that an all-mighty, all-powerful, Holy God would dwell inside the likes of us, but He does. And it gets better: not only does He communicate with us as mentioned above He makes the following promises:

Jesus said Holy Spirit would help our memory: **But the Comforter, the Holy Spirit whom the Father will send in My name, He shall teach you all things and bring all things to your remembrance, whatever I have said to you** (John 14:26).

He promised to give us awesome gifts: **For through the Spirit is given to one a word of wisdom; and to another a word of knowledge, according to the same Spirit; and to another faith by the same Spirit; and to another the gifts of healing by the same Spirit; and to another workings of powers, to another prophecy; and to another discerning of spirits; and to another kinds of tongues; and to another the interpretation of tongues. But the one and the same Spirit works all these things, distributing separately to each one as He desires** (1 Corinthians 12:8-11).

During critical times of persecution He promised to do the speaking for us: **But when they deliver you up, take no thought how or what you shall speak; for it shall be given you in that same hour what you shall speak. For it is not you who speak, but the Spirit of your Father who speaks in you** (Matthew 10:19-20).

He promised power in getting the Gospel out to the world: **But you shall receive power, the Holy Spirit coming upon you. And you shall be witnesses to Me both in Jerusalem and in all Judea, and in Samaria, and to** *the* **end of the earth** (Acts 1:8).

He promised supernatural dreams and visions: **And it shall be in the last days, says God, I will pour out of My Spirit upon all flesh. And your sons and your daughters shall prophesy, and your young men shall see visions, and your old men shall dream dreams** (Acts 2:17).

He gives us supernatural power to live as we should: **For if you live according to your human nature, you are going to die; but if by the Spirit you put to death your sinful actions, you will live** (Romans 8:13 GNB).

He helps us in sickness and mediates for us before our Heavenly Father: **Likewise the Spirit also helps our infirmities. For we do not know what we should pray for as we ought, but the Spirit Himself makes intercession for us with groanings which cannot be uttered. And He searching the hearts knows what** *is* **the mind of the Spirit, because He makes intercession for the saints according to** *the will of* **God** (Romans 8:26-27).

This is by no means an exhaustive list, but it gives us the knowledge that He does not leave us alone. In addition, God has given man a conscience whereby He can communicate with us. This built-in device has been imprinted with the will of God, straight out of Heaven. God's own set of morals has been downloaded into our conscience. Without ever reading a Bible, the conscience knows that it is wrong to kill. It knows it is wrong to lie. It knows it is right to be kind to others. It knows all of this *until it is tampered with.* Our conscience resides in our Spirit. If our fleshly man is allowed to ride roughshod over our spirit on a regular basis, the conscience can be damaged. In 1Timothy 4:1-2, Paul describes the process this way: **But the Spirit expressly says that in the latter times some shall depart from the faith, giving heed to seducing spirits and teachings of demons, speaking lies in hypocrisy, being seared in** *their* **own conscience.**

Healthy fingertips are capable of sensing fine materials and surfaces but if a hot iron is applied to the fingertips the cauterized skin becomes rigid and hard, and is no longer sensitive. So it is with a seared conscience: it can no longer sense right from wrong. Tamper with it long enough and the calloused conscience will not be able to tell the truth from a lie. This is an extremely dangerous situation to put one's self into because here is what happens next: **And for this cause God shall send them strong delusion, that they should**

**believe a lie, so that all those who do not believe the truth, but delight in unrighteousness, might be condemned** (2 Thessalonians 2:11-12). People who don't value their conscience set themselves up for everlasting condemnation and eternal separation from God.

# 23 GOD IS A GOOD COMMUNICATOR

God devised various ways to communicate with His creation. He met with Adam in the Garden and He spoke with him personally. In all likelihood, this particular meeting took place with God showing up in some visible form and speaking verbally to Adam. (I say this because I believe that communication between God and man was perfect before the fall, and that likely included Him being visible.)

God has used a variety of ways to communicate with His creation. In Numbers 22:28, God communicated to a stubborn man through the mouth of a donkey: **And Jehovah opened the mouth of the ass, and she said to Balaam, What have I done to you, that you have beaten me these three times?** He communicated to Moses through a bush: **And Jehovah saw that he had turned aside to see. God called to him out of the midst of the thorn bush, and said, Moses! Moses! And he said, Here I** *am* (Exodus 3:4). Somehow God, or Jesus, communicated with a fish and caused it to transport a coin into the hands of Peter to pay taxes: **But we don't want to offend these people. So go to the lake and drop in a line. Pull up the first fish you hook, and in its mouth you will find a coin worth enough for my Temple tax and yours. Take it and pay them our taxes** (Matthew 17:27 GNB). This was no streak of fisherman's luck.

God has devised at least nine specific ways in which He can communicate with man:

1 NATURE

> **The heavens declare the glory of God; and the expanse proclaims His handiwork. Day to day pours forth speech, and night to night reveals knowledge.** *There is* **no speech nor** *are* **there words; their voice is not heard. Their line has gone out through all the earth and their words to the end of the world** (Psalm 19:1- 4). The entire created world speaks of its Creator. A sound, honest mind observing

creation has only to acknowledge His Presence in it. This is the way Paul put it: **By taking a long and thoughtful look at what God has created, people have always been able to see what their eyes as such can't see: eternal power, for instance, and the mystery of his divine being. So nobody has a good excuse** (Romans 1:20 MSG). Someone once said that if a heathen stumbled onto a beach and picked up a watch, he would have to conclude that there had to be a watchmaker. Therefore, if the existence of a watch implies a watchmaker, then the existence of our world would imply an intelligent Designer.

God speaks to us through His creation. No man will ever be able to stand in front of the Judgment Seat of God and say, "I did not know you were there." To do so would be to accuse Him of being a poor communicator. As brave as an atheist may sound right now, I do not think they would ever be foolish enough to make such an accusation in front of the Almighty. I could be wrong, but I see such men standing in His presence and being struck dumb out of pure, unadulterated terror. Here are my reasons: the atheist will suddenly know that the game is over; he will know that the Judge in front of him was once merciful but now He is not; he will know that God did His best to communicate with him and he ignored every attempt; he will know that there is no more hope and he will know that there is no one to blame but himself.

Randy Alcorn writes this imaginary scene about the well-known atheist Mao Zedong in his after life: "*He could see now through all his rationalizations. His arguments against belief in a Creator had never been intellectual ones, as he had claimed. By rejecting a Creator he thought he could rid himself of a Judge. But it had not worked. His atheism had been the opiate of his soul and the executioner of uncalculated millions. But now His comforting atheism could no longer exist, even for a fleeting moment, for He had been stripped of the power to deny reality*" (Page 329).

## 2   CONSCIENCE

**For when the nations, who do not have the Law, do by nature the things of the Law, these, not having the Law, are a law unto themselves; who show the work of the Law written in their hearts, their conscience also bearing witness, and the thoughts between one another accusing or even excusing one another** (Romans 2:14-15). As this verse indicates, God has built into every one of us a sense of right and wrong. Sinners and Christians alike have this sense and it is one of the ways in which He communicates with us. No man will ever be able to stand before God and say, "I did not know that it was wrong to murder" or be able to say, "I did not know it was wrong to lie." Intuitively we know.

## 3   HE WROTE TO US

The Holy Bible was written by man's hand but God told the men what to write.

**. . . but now has been made plain, and by the prophetic Scriptures, according to the commandment of the everlasting God, made known to all nations for the obedience of faith** (Romans 16:26).

**All Scripture *is* God-breathed, and is profitable for doctrine, for reproof, for correction, for instruction in righteousness, that the man of God may be perfected, thoroughly furnished to every good work** (2 Timothy 3:16-17).

**. . . knowing this first, that no prophecy of the Scripture came into being of *its* own private interpretation. For prophecy was not borne at any time by *the* will of man, but holy men of God spoke being borne along by the Holy Spirit** (2 Peter 1:20-21).

## 4   VISIONS

Abraham's promise came through a vision: **After these things the Word of Jehovah came to Abram in a vision, saying, Fear not, Abram, I *am* your shield and your exceeding great reward** (Genesis 15:1).

Ananias received his instructions to rescue Paul by way of a vision: **And there was a certain disciple in Damascus named Ananias. And the Lord said to him in a vision, Ananias! And he said, Behold me, Lord** (Acts 9:10).

Under the New Covenant it seems that the Lord changed man's menu again and He communicated this to Peter in a vision: **I was in the city of Joppa praying, and in a trance I saw a vision. I saw something like a large sheet being let down from heaven by its four corners, and it came down to where I was I looked into it and saw four-footed animals of the earth, wild beasts, reptiles, and birds of the air. Then I heard a voice telling me, "Get up, Peter. Kill and eat.'**

"I replied, 'Surely not, Lord! Nothing impure or unclean has ever entered my mouth.' "The voice spoke from heaven a second time, "Do not call anything impure <u>that God has made clean</u>' (Acts 11:5-9).

## 5   DREAMS

The Lord terrorized Abimelech in a dream: **But God came to Abimelech in a dream by night, and said to him, Behold, you are about to die, for the woman whom you have taken; for she is a man's wife** (Genesis 20:3).

Here God teaches that He uses dreams to communicate with us:

**. . . he said, Listen carefully to what I'm telling you. If there is a prophet of GOD among you, I make myself known to him in visions, I speak to him in dreams** (Numbers 12:6).

**The prophet who has a dream, let him tell a dream. And he who has My Word, let him speak My Word faithfully** (Jeremiah 23:28).

God spoke to a heathen king in a dream to warn him: **And in the second year of the reign of King Nebuchadnezzar, Nebuchadnezzar dreamed dreams, with which his spirit was troubled and his sleep left him** (Daniel 2:1).

## 6   CHRISTIANS

Christians communicate the word of God to the world. **You are our epistle written in our hearts, known and read by all men,** *it* **having been made plain that you are the epistle of Christ, ministered by us, not having been written with ink, but with the Spirit of the living God; not on tablets of stone, but in fleshly tablets of** *the* **heart** (2 Corinthians 3:2-3). Some Christians have special gifts to preach or evangelize and often dedicate their entire lives to spread the Word. All real Christians live the Word in the home or in the workplace and by a holy life and good works, communicate the Word of God to people around them.

## 7   HOLY SPIRIT

His Holy Spirit communicates directly with our spirit: **However, when He, the Spirit of Truth, has come, He will <u>guide you into all</u>**

**truth.** For He shall not speak of Himself, but whatever He hears, He shall speak. And He will **announce to you** things to come (John 16:13).

**But the Comforter, the Holy Spirit whom the Father will send in My name, He shall teach you all things and bring all things to your remembrance, whatever I have said to you** (John 14:26).

Messages from the Holy Spirit are transmitted directly to the spirit of man. They are not broadcast, since they are extremely personal. Most of the time the recipient will say it sounded like a still, small voice. If rejected long enough, however, the Holy Spirit will cease speaking.

8    AUDIBLE VOICE

Occasionally, God shows up and speaks audibly as He did to Adam and Eve in the Garden. Jehovah had a special relationship with Moses and these verses indicate an audible conversation:

**And Jehovah said to Moses, Lo, I come to you in a thick cloud, that the people may hear when I speak with you, and believe you forever. And Moses told the words of the people to Jehovah** (Exodus 19:9).

**And Jehovah would speak to Moses face to face, as a man speaks to his friend** (Exodus 33:11).

He gave His Son an audible affirmation on this occasion which was heard by others: **And He was transfigured before them. And His face shone as the sun, and His clothing was white as the light. . . . And behold a voice out of the cloud which said, This is My beloved Son in whom I am well pleased, hear Him. And when the disciples heard, they fell on their face and were greatly terrified. And Jesus came and touched them, and said, Arise and do not be terrified** (Matthew 17:2-7).

9    PRAYER

God's most unique form of communication is prayer. He has set up a two way thought system between Himself and humans whereby communication can take place via the very thoughts that goes on inside our heads. Think it and it is instantly transmitted to Him and vice versa. The system is personal, highly secure and cannot be intercepted or interrupted by any other being. When He desires to communicate to us it goes instantly from His "transmitter" to our "antenna."

God, by His Holy Spirit, is able to communicate to any man, woman or child at any time. Satan also has this ability and does so continually. The enemy's transmissions invariably have to do with false information, fear and condemnation and will ultimately be in contradiction with the Word of God. However, thoughts brought to us by the Spirit of God will convict but not condemn us, and will always be in agreement with the Word.

The writer of Hebrews confirms that God speaks to us: **You have forgotten the encouraging words that God speaks to you as his children: "My child, pay attention when the Lord disciplines you. Don't give up when he corrects you."** (Hebrews 12:5 GW). Mark also confirms this in Mark 13:11 when Jesus said: **But whenever they lead *you* away and deliver *you* up, take no thought beforehand what you should speak or think. But speak whatever shall be given to you in that hour. For it is not you who speaks, but the Holy Spirit.** Communication does not get better than that.

# 24 GOD GIVES AND HE TAKES

God gives and takes away because He can. Since He created everything from nothing, He can give and take as He pleases. No one is able to challenge any decision He makes. Our security and hope lies in the fact that God is compassionate and wise. We may not always know what He is up to when He gives something and later takes it. We need to learn to trust Him but never take Him for granted.

He entrusted the Garden of Eden to Adam's care and then later drove him out. God took land from the occupants of Canaan and gave it to Israel. Later He drove the Israelites out because of their sin. In 1948 gave it back to them—permanently. He gave Job health, wealth and children and then took it all. Job understood this, and accepted it: **Naked I came from my mother's womb, and naked I will depart. The LORD gave and the LORD has taken away; may the name of the LORD be praised** (Job 1:21 NIV).

We must remember that the children and the money were only on loan to Job anyway. The sole purpose for all children is to bring God pleasure. In the case of Job's children, they simply went home to be with God earlier than most. God would have honored Job's sacrifices and allowed the blood from those sacrifices to cover his children. This would have been similar to the head of the home putting blood on the door posts of their house and covering all who were inside in Exodus 12:7. Later, when Job's trial was over, God gave him more children: **He also had seven sons and three daughters. And he called the name of the first, Jemima; and the name of the second, Keziah; and the name of the third, Keren-happuch. And in all the land there *were* not found women as beautiful as the daughters of Job. And their father gave them inheritance among their brothers** (Job 42:13-15). He also gave Job back double his money: **After Job had prayed for his friends, the LORD restored his fortunes and gave him twice as much as he had before** (Job 42:10 NIV).

Usually, God gives rain on a regular basis and in season. In this instance God speaks through Elijah and orders the rain to stop for 3 years: **As Jehovah, the God of Israel lives, before whom I stand, there shall not be dew nor rain these**

**years, except according to my word** (1 Kings 17:1). Later, He restores rain at the prayer of Elijah, once arrogant king Ahab and his people had been taught a lesson.

The Lord would never give something and then take it back without good cause. His purpose in doing so is usually to teach a lesson. This is confirmed in Deuteronomy 4:36: **He made you hear His voice out of Heaven so that He might <u>teach</u> you.** Again, 2 Samuel 7:21 (MKJV) tells us, **For Your Word's sake, and according to Your own heart, You have done all these great things to <u>make Your servant know</u>.**

We have a tendency to take Him and His gifts for granted. This is not beneficial to us because in using His gifts without the appropriate gratitude or recognition of their source, we have learned nothing about Him. Our whole purpose of being is to get to know Him, because we were created for His pleasure: **Thou art worthy, O Lord, to receive glory and honour and power: for thou hast created all things, and for thy pleasure they are and were created** (Revelation 4:11 KJV).

# 25 GOD CREATED SATAN

God created everything in the universe, and that includes angels. Some remained loyal to their Creator and some became evil, disobedient demons:

> **For all things were created in Him, the things in the heavens, and the things on the earth, the visible and the invisible, whether thrones or dominions or principalities or powers, all things were created through Him and for Him** (Colossians 1:16).

> **Praise Him, all His angels; praise Him, all His hosts. Praise Him, sun and moon; praise Him, all stars of light. Praise Him, heavens of heavens, and waters that *are* above the heavens. Let them praise the name of Jehovah; for He commanded, and they were created** (Psalm 148:2-5).

> **I have made the earth, and created man on it; I *with* My hands have stretched out the heavens; and all their host have I commanded** (Isaiah 45:12).

He specifically speaks of Satan in this Scripture: **You have been in Eden the garden of God; every precious stone *was* your covering, the ruby, topaz, and the diamond, the beryl, the onyx, and the jasper, the sapphire, the turquoise, and the emerald, and gold. The workmanship of your tambourines and of your flutes was prepared in you in the day that you were created** (Ezekiel 28:13).

God knew that Satan would fall, would cause war in Heaven, and would bring much evil and wickedness to the earth. God also knew that this wickedness would mean that His own Son, Jesus, must sacrifice His life to undo the work of Satan. But God has never said, "Oops." He allowed Satan to roam the earth and call it his kingdom. It seems he won it fair and square from Adam when Adam fell for his lies. He set up his own government immediately to rule the earth. When Satan, speaking to Jesus, referred to the earth as his, Jesus didn't argue with him. **Again, the Devil took Him up into a very high mountain and showed Him all the kingdoms of the world and their glory. And *he* said to Him, All these things I will give You if You will fall down and worship**

**me** (Matthew 4:8-9). However, make no mistake about it, Satan's ownership is temporary and will end abruptly at the blowing of this trumpet: **And the seventh angel sounded. And there were great voices in Heaven, saying, The kingdoms of this world have become** *the kingdoms* **of our Lord, and of His Christ. And He will reign forever and ever** (Revelation 11:15).

Satan has set up a spiritual government and it is described by Paul: **For we do not wrestle against flesh and blood, but against principalities, against powers, against the world's rulers, of the darkness of this age, against spiritual wickedness in high** *places* (Ephesians 6:12). When God allowed Satan to set up shop on earth, He was fully aware of the following:

SATAN WOULD MAKE WAR ON GOD'S PEOPLE:

**And the dragon was enraged over the woman, and went to make war with the rest of her seed, who keep the commandments of God and have the testimony of Jesus Christ** (Revelation 12:17).

SATAN WOULD TRY TO DECEIVE AND KILL GOD'S SON:

Satan tried his lying skills on Jesus: **And he brought Him to Jerusalem and sat Him on a pinnacle of the temple and said to Him, If you are the Son of God, cast yourself down from here** (Luke 4:9). Jesus knew better than play this game for two reasons. One, He would have been disobeying His Father in doing so, and two, Jesus knew that to obey Satan would mean becoming his slave. It was Jesus, by the Holy Spirit, who taught Paul this truth: **Do you not know that to whom you yield yourselves** *as* **slaves for obedience, you are slaves to him whom you obey; whether it is of sin to death, or of obedience to righteousness** (Romans 6:16).

Satan made many attempts to murder Jesus. The first attempt occurred when he used the jealously and fear of King Herod to try and kill Him as an infant. Joseph had to take the child and His mother and flee for their lives into Egypt. Later, Jesus returned to His homeland to be constantly harassed by jealous, fearful Pharisees, Sadducees and Romans. At the end of His ministry, when everything He came to do was completed, Satan used these religious leaders to kill the Son of God. However, this was no victory for Satan since this was all part of God's plan to put the last nail in the Deceiver's coffin. Jesus describes the plan: **Therefore My Father loves Me, because I lay down My life so that I might take it again. <u>No one takes it from Me</u>, but I lay it down from Myself. I have authority to lay it down, and I have authority to take it again. I have received this commandment from My Father** (John 10:17-18).

## What is God Like?

### HE WOULD ROAM THE EARTH TO STEAL, KILL AND DESTROY:

Jesus warned us in this reference to Satan: **The thief does not come except to steal and to kill and to destroy. I have come so that they might have life, and that they might have *it* more abundantly** (John 10:10).

### SATAN WOULD TRY TO CONTROL HUMANS:

Satan is a great manipulator, and sometimes he succeeds. Matthew relates the following regarding the ministry of Jesus and His encounters with demons who took over the body of a child and two men:

> **"Lord, have mercy on my son," he said. "He has seizures and is suffering greatly. He often falls into the fire or into the water . . . . Jesus rebuked the demon, and it came out of the boy, and he was healed at that moment** (Matthew 17: 15 - 18 NIV).

> **And when He had come to the other side into the country of the Gergesenes, two demon-possessed ones met Him, coming out of the tombs, exceedingly fierce, so that no one might pass by that way** (Matthew 8:28).

Some would have us believe that there are no demon possessed people around today. If this were true, it would mean that Satan has given up his favorite pastime: deceiving, killing and destroying. It would also mean that individuals who kill and torture others for sport are doing it on their own with no influence from Satan. This does not align with the Word of God. Jesus said that believers would have signs following them and one of those signs would be casting out demons (Mark 16:17). Further, believers are still casting out demons. Regarding individuals who torture and kill for sport, there is no proof whatsoever that they acted alone. There is evidence that many of these individuals tampered with things belonging to Satan before they lost control and committed their evil crimes. Many dabbled in the occult, played demonic games such as Ouija boards and Dungeons and Dragons; actively sought supernatural power; experimented with mind altering drugs; and indulged in Satan worship. There is evidence from follow-up investigations that they have had trouble with demons. Many have said things like: I heard voices; I was tormented; I saw evil beings; a spirit told me; a spirit led me; I had no control; I felt like my body was controlled by someone else; or I was filled with demonic rage. The medical profession usually attributes these reports of demonic activity to some mental defect, probably because they are not equipped and have no expertise in dealing with such. This however, is what Jesus teaches Christians: **Heal the sick, cleanse the lepers, raise the dead, cast out devils: freely ye have received, freely give** (Matthew 10:8 KJV).

HE WOULD BECOME RULER OF THIS WORLD:

Even though the world belongs to God, Paul acknowledges Satan's temporary ownership in this verse: **. . . in whom the god of this world has blinded the minds of the unbelieving ones, so that the light of the glorious gospel of Christ (who is the image of God) should not dawn on them** (2 Corinthians 4:4).

SATAN WOULD LIE TO SEDUCE HUMANS:

He invented lying for this purpose. Jesus said this of him: **You belong to your father, the devil, and you want to carry out your father's desire. He was a murderer from the beginning, not holding to the truth, for there is no truth in him. When he lies, he speaks his native language, for he is a liar and the father of lies** (John 8:44 NIV).

Satan's greatest power is his ability to deceive. By lying, Satan deceived the first two humans God placed on earth. In another example, Satan deceived even King David: **And Satan stood up against Israel and provoked David to take a census of Israel** (1 Chronicles 21:1). He uses a lie or the power of suggestion to create doubt which will then lead to a lie. Twice, by suggestion, he tried to get Jesus to question that God was His Father:

1. **The tempter came to him and said, "If you are the Son of God, tell these stones to become bread"** (Matthew 4:3). Jesus had just ended a 40 day fast, waiting on His Father. Satan tried to tempt Him into making His own food from rocks. Jesus refused to do this, although He could have easily done it. Instead, He continued to wait on His Father who sent angels to minister to Him at the end of the bout with Satan.

2. **Then the devil took him to the holy city and had him stand on the highest point of the temple. "If you are the Son of God,"** he said, **"throw yourself down. For it is written: 'He will command his angels concerning you, and they will lift you up in their hands, so that you will not strike your foot against a stone'"** (Matthew 4:5-6). Jesus had no need or desire to put His Father to such a test.

Satan's final ruse was to offer the Son of God everything he had in exchange for recognition: **Again, the devil took him to a very high mountain and** showed him all the kingdoms of the world and their splendor. "All this I will give you," he said, "if you will bow down and worship me" (Matthew 4:8-9). If Jesus had obeyed this suggestion it would have meant avoiding the cross and crucifixion. To do so would also mean that you and I could never be redeemed.

Jesus endured this test for our sakes. He demonstrated for us how we are to deal with Satan. Three times He used the only weapon necessary to defeat the lying Devil and put him to flight. He used verses of Scripture that He had authored and memorized.

1. Jesus answered, "It is written: 'Man does not live on bread alone, but on every word that comes from the mouth of God'" (Matthew 4:4).

2. Jesus answered him, "It is also written: 'Do not put the Lord your God to the test'" (Matthew 4:7).

3. Jesus said to him, "Away from me, Satan! For it is written: 'Worship the Lord your God, and serve him only'" (Matthew 4:10).

James says if we resist the devil he will clear out of our way: **Submit yourselves, then, to God. Resist the devil, and he will flee from you** (James 4:7).

He does have other powers, but to use them he must have God's permission. He needed God's permission before he could touch Job's family and his health. To a large degree this hinges on what God's saints are willing to give him. If the saints are living in accordance with God's laws, Satan cannot touch them. If they wander, the Good Shepherd will guide them back using whatever means necessary. Painful trials, sometimes administered by Satan, are quite common, but they are always mitigated by our loving Father. He ensures that any evil the enemy intends serves only the purposes of the Spirit in our lives. As Joseph said: **you thought evil against me, but God meant it for good** (Genesis 50:20).

This cunning craft of lying is powerful enough to work on the majority of humans. We do not seem to possess the skill to decipher his deceptions on our own. We have hundreds of thoughts occurring in our mind by the minute. Our only hope is to place the various thoughts we have alongside the Word of God, which is why we are to **take every thought captive and make it obey Christ** (2 Corinthians 10:5b GNB). Since Satan has the ability to place thoughts in our minds any time he pleases, we are often confused as to where the thought came from. Was it God, was it me, or was it Satan? I believe these are the three sources of internal thought. First, we obviously have the ability to produce a thought in our own mind. The second source is God by the power of His Holy Spirit. The third source is Satan and his lies or lies in the making. Only by comparing it with what God has taught us can we hope to know the truth. Men have often been deceived by such a message. One man, in recent years, was known to have shot and killed his son and reported to the police that he had heard a voice from God telling him to do it. Checking God's Word, we know that God would not have given such an order. It is highly unlikely that the man would have done this of his own free will since there was absolutely no motive. Satan, however, would have since he likes to kill.

While God was well aware of what would happen to His saints once Satan was let loose, we need to be reminded that it was and is all in accordance with the overall plan. This plan is best depicted in the life of Job. We see at the beginning of his story that Job was totally protected and Satan could not touch him. **Have You not made a hedge around him, and around his house, and around all that he has on every side? You have blessed the work of his hands, and his livestock have increased in the land** (Job 1:10). When God brought Job to Satan's attention, there is no doubt that Satan had already been surveying Job and his property and that his "intel" was up to date. He knew full well that the man was untouchable because of the hedge. He also knew that neither he nor his demons could penetrate that hedge.

Meanwhile, God was very pleased with this man. Verse 8 says: **And Jehovah said to Satan, Have you set your heart against My servant Job, because *there is* none like him in the earth, a perfect and upright man, one who fears God and turns away from evil?** However, as we see from the remaining chapters in Job, there were some rough spots that needed to be taken care of in Job's life, and God removed the hedge for a while and used Satan in the process. With God's permission Satan used his other powers (other than lying) to influence the Sabeans to take Job's property. He sent fire from the sky to burn his sheep and servants. He used the Chaldeans to take his camels and kill his servants. He sent wind to demolish his house and kill Job's children. And finally he had power to smite Job with boils. Satan did all this with God's knowledge and permission. Follow the story to its end and we see that God had a plan, the plan was good, and Job ultimately agreed. At one point along the way, Job, in all of his misery said this: **God may kill me, but still I will trust him and offer my defense** (Job 13:15 CEV).

When Satan speaks to a human mind, he does so in a clever way and we need to be aware of his methods. Paul calls it scheming: **I don't want Satan to**

**outwit us. After all, we are not ignorant about Satan's scheming** (2 Corinthians 2:11 GW). He speaks inside our head, uses our own thought processes and he does not speak with an accent. He can even imitate our own voice. Most sinners—and even saints—often don't recognize where the thoughts come from. Most times we mistake the evil thoughts as our own. (Consider the incident in 1Kings 22:22 where a lying spirit approaches God and suggest it could enter the minds all Ahab's prophets and cause them to lie to Ahab.) As Christians, we are taught to handle the thoughts this way: **For the weapons of our warfare *are* not fleshly, but mighty through God to the pulling down of strongholds, pulling down imaginations and every high thing that exalts itself against the knowledge of God** (2 Corinthians 10:4-5a). When the Christian discovers the voice of Satan speaking, Paul instructs us to grab hold of that thought, refuse it the ability to develop into a sin, and demolish it immediately (e.g., when an evil thought appears in your mind, pretend you are grabbing the speaking demon by the throat and you are wringing its neck). Romans 12:2 teaches that when we first come back to God through Jesus, our minds need cleansing: **And do not be conformed to this world, but be transformed by the renewing of your mind, in order to prove by you what *is* that good and pleasing and perfect will of God.** Once we stop allowing our mind to be conformed, this will take care of the past. 2 Corinthians 10:4-5 takes care of the present and the future.

God had a plan in mind from the beginning that Satan would serve Him one way or another. While in obedience, Satan served God as lead worshiper in Heaven: **You have been in Eden the garden of God; every precious stone *was* your covering, the ruby, topaz, and the diamond, the beryl, the onyx, and the jasper, the sapphire, the turquoise, and the emerald, and gold. The workmanship of your tambourines and of your flutes was prepared in you in the day that you were created** (Ezekiel 28:13). However, God was not thwarted when Satan rebelled.

When God created angels they were given the same power of choice He gave man. The only difference is that for angels there was no plan of redemption. There was no place for sin in their contract. Mess up once and there was no way back. All angels would know this was how it worked. Two thirds of the angels remembered this and stuck with their contract. Satan, because of his pride, decided to rebel against God, put Him off the throne and rule Heaven himself: **You *were* perfect in your ways from the day that you were created, until iniquity was found in you** (Ezekiel 28:15). He organized a rebellion in Heaven, taking one third of the angels with him and God empowered Michael to throw him out: **And there was war in Heaven. Michael and his angels warring against the dragon. And the dragon and his angels warred, but did not prevail. Nor was place found for them in Heaven any more. And the great dragon was cast out, the old serpent called Devil, and Satan, who deceives the whole world. He was cast out into the earth, and his angels were cast out with him** (Revelation 12:7-9).

After he got himself kicked out of Heaven, God used him to test men. In the following verse, Paul commands that a scandalous sinner in the church at Corinth be expelled to learn things he refused to learn any other way: **. . . hand this man over to Satan for his body to be destroyed, so that his spirit may be saved in the Day of the Lord** (1 Corinthians 5:5 GNB).

It would seem from Paul's second letter to the Corinthians that the process worked: **This punishment by the majority *is* enough for such a one; so that, on the contrary, you should rather forgive and comfort *him*, lest perhaps such a one should be swallowed up with overwhelming sorrow. So I beseech you to confirm *your* love toward him** (2 Corinthians 2:6-8). There was another occasion Paul found Satan's service useful: **Among these are Hymeneus and Alexander, whom I have delivered to Satan so that they may learn not to blaspheme** (1Timothy 1:20). One version (RV) actually says: **whom I delivered unto Satan, that they might be taught not to blaspheme.** Look at *who* is being used to do the teaching!

When he is of no more use, God will dispose of Satan: **And the Devil who deceived them was cast into the Lake of Fire and Brimstone, where the beast and the false prophet *were*. And he will be tormented day and night forever and ever** (Revelation 20:10).

In his book, *Destined for the Throne*, Paul Billheimer speaks of Satan's usefulness: "God permits him to carry on a guerrilla warfare. God could put Satan completely away, but He has chosen to use him to give the Church "on the job" training in overcoming" (Page 17).

HE WOULD BRING ACCUSATIONS AGAINST HUMANS:

This is made clear in Revelation: **And I heard a great voice saying in Heaven, Now has come the salvation and power and the kingdom of our God, and the authority of His Christ. For the accuser of our brothers is cast down, who accused them before our God day and night** (Revelation 12:10). This verse points toward a future date when Satan, the accuser, will be removed permanently. Meanwhile, you and I must face this menace, but not alone. The Righteous Judge has assigned you a lawyer for your defense: **My little children, I write these things to you so that you may not sin. And if anyone sins, we have an Advocate with the Father, Jesus Christ the righteous** (1 John 2:1).

To acknowledge that God created Satan and left him in our midst to test us eliminates any confusion as to why this dragon is always parked outside our door. Once we know why he is there and that God has everything under control, we should have no fear in doing battle with him. Using the weapons the Lord gave us, with the help of the Holy Spirit, we can whip him every time. God set it up that way.

# 26 GOD CREATED SATAN CUNNING AND POWERFUL

Upon completion, everything on earth was GOOD. Try to imagine a perfect earth: perfect weather; perfect temperature; perfect animals; perfect crops; no mosquitoes; no taxes; and above all, two perfect humans. Adam had a perfect wife and she lived in a perfect house. Then along comes this imperfect, sinful creature, Satan. God did not stop him. Satan basically walked into Eden and took over. What had rightfully been given to Adam became Satan's in a matter of minutes. Within hours, sin and disobedience changed everything. Eden was no longer paradise and Adam had to toil for a living and Eve, during Cain's birth, would know what pain was for the first time. They were driven from their home and would never be permitted to return. However, God has never said, "Oops." If we study His plan we find He knows the beginning and the end and His plans are always good.

The crowning glory of creation was man. The whole of creation was all about man. God wanted the best that He had ever created to be like Himself and He wanted fellowship with this creature and his descendants. He could have left it just like that. Yet, He had already created Satan and He made him smart. Among the angels, Satan was no slouch: he convinced one third of Heaven's population to vote for him in his bid to oust God. Arriving on earth, he was still at peak performance: **Now the serpent was more cunning than any beast of the field which Jehovah God had made** (Genesis 3:1). You will notice that it did not say that Satan was more cunning than humans, but he did out smart Adam. In a very real sense, one of God's best creations in Heaven is now being used to test the best He has on earth. We see from the description of Satan given in Ezekiel 28:12 that he lacked nothing in wisdom and beauty: **Son of man, lift up a lament over the king of Tyre, and say to him, So says the Lord Jehovah: You seal the measure, full of wisdom and perfect in beauty.**[5] Upon ruining His perfect creation, God only cursed

---

[5] Although the earthly king of Tyre is specifically mentioned in this passage, many scholars will agree that Satan is the subject and this earthly king is likened to him....

*(continued to next page)*

Satan. He did not destroy him or immediately banish him to Hell: **And Jehovah God said to the serpent, Because you have done this you *are* cursed more than all cattle, and more than every animal of the field. You shall go upon your belly, and you shall eat dust all the days of your life** (Genesis 3:14).

Then God laid the ground rules as to how humans and demons would exist together on earth from that day on: **And I will put enmity between you and the woman, and between your seed and her Seed; He will bruise your head, and you shall bruise His heel** (Genesis 3:15). Enmity means hostility, battle or war. This is what Paul is describing in this verse in the New Testament: **For we do not wrestle against flesh and blood, but against principalities, against powers, against the world's rulers, of the darkness of this age, against spiritual wickedness in high *places*** (Ephesians 6:12).

As we know, this will not last forever. God has a place and a plan for Satan: **And the Devil who deceived them was cast into the Lake of Fire and Brimstone, where the beast and the false prophet *were*. And he will be tormented day and night forever and ever** (Revelation 20:10). Once he fell as a rebel, Satan had no opportunity for repentance because salvation was not extended to angels as it was to humans. Satan will continue doing what he has been doing until God is finished with him. Everything God created was for a purpose and every part of His creation, from atoms to ants to planets and angels, will all, ultimately fulfill that purpose.

Satan's cunning was multiplied by use of an army of demons. These creatures are evil and come under their master's kingdom which Paul describes in Ephesians 6:12, mentioning principalities, powers, and world rulers. Satan and his evil horde have been known to exercise amazing powers once they possess a human body. In one incident in Matthew 8:31-32, demonic spirits driven out of a man by Jesus were permitted to enter pigs, which drowned themselves rather than live with the demons.

---

Basically in this passage an earthly person is addressed, but certain statements also refer to an invisible person using the earthly person as a reference. Therefore, two persons are involved in the same passage. The principle of interpretation of such passages is to associate only such statements with each individual as could refer to him. For example this passage mentions the person has been present in the garden of Eden (Ezekiel 28:13) and we know that this specific detail refers to Satan but could not refer to the king of Tyre, (See Dake's Annotated Reference Bible 1963, page 42, Column 1 regarding the Law of Double Reference.)

Demons entered two men, in the area near Gadara and by their supernatural power, terrorized the inhabitants: **And when He had come to the other side into the country of the Gergesenes, two demon-possessed ones met Him, coming out of the tombs, exceedingly fierce, so that no one might pass by that way** (Matthew 8:28).

Satan's power is extensive when we consider other references to his activities. In the book of Job he influenced the Sabeans to attack Job's servants and kill them, brought fire from the sky and killed his sheep and more servants, influenced the Chaldeans who stole his camels and killed more servants, caused a wind storm that demolished the house containing his children, killing all of them. Quite a day's work! Further, by some devilish means he covered Job with boils. In Exodus 7 and 8, the Egyptian magicians turned a stick into a snake, turned water into blood, and produced frogs by their satanic arts. Jesus warns us that in the last days Satan will go all out to display his power to deceive men: **For false Christs and false prophets will arise and show great signs and wonders; so much so that, if it were possible, they would deceive even the elect** (Matthew 24:24).

Consider the power that Satan will display and consider the fact that he will be successful in deceiving men even though the Bible has been warning men for about 2000 years: **He exercised all the authority of the first beast. And he required all the earth and its people to worship the first beast, whose fatal wound had been healed. He did astounding miracles, even making fire flash down to earth from the sky while everyone was watching. And with all the miracles he was allowed to perform on behalf of the first beast, he deceived all the people who belong to this world. He ordered the people to make a great statue of the first beast, who was fatally wounded and then came back to life. He was then permitted to give life to this statue so that it could speak. Then the statue of the beast commanded that anyone refusing to worship it must die** (Revelation 13:12-15 NLT).

Some nations are ruled by Satan and his hierarchy. In fact, the whole unbelieving population comes under his authority according to this verse by Paul: **But also if our gospel is hidden, it is hidden to those being lost, in whom <u>the god of this world</u> has blinded the minds of the unbelieving ones, so that the light of the glorious gospel of Christ (who is the image of God) should not dawn on them** (2 Corinthians 4:3-4).

Demons can possess some people and take away their ability to speak (Matthew 9:32-33), see (Matthew 12:22), and hear (Mark 9:25). He can bring on sicknesses and diseases and has the power to torment (Matthew 15:22-28).

Satan is crafty and has learned to manipulate humans in one way or another but always with the same result. His motive is to steal, kill or destroy humans—the pride and joy of God's creation.

In Mark 9:17-28, we see Jesus commanding a demon who had entered a boy to leave the boy's body. The demon had taken the child's ability to speak, gave him seizures, caused him to foam at the mouth, gnash his teeth, and have convulsions. It had often thrown him into fire or water to kill him. This cowardly, evil creature knew no pity and would have eventually succeeded in tormenting this child to death, were it not for Jesus. You will see in verse 18 that Jesus spoke a word to that demon and it left the boy immediately. Satan has the power to influence all and totally possess some. Possession most often takes place when a human unwittingly or knowingly gives their will over to Satan. Satan and his demons are an awesome force and we need help to face such an enemy and that is exactly what Jesus provided.

In His personal encounter with Satan described in Matthew 4, Jesus had just fasted for 40 days. He was weak and hungry, but "He was dieted for combat" (Henry). Satan appeared to Him and tried to cause Him to doubt that He was the Son of God. He suggested that Jesus should turn rocks into bread to satisfy His hunger; that He should jump off the roof of the temple so that His Father could protect Him and then offered Jesus the entire world if He would just bow down and worship him. With each attempt Satan made, Jesus quoted Scripture, and with the last temptation, commanded Satan to scram. And Satan did. This entire event was for our benefit. Jesus could have told him to leave the minute he showed up the first time. Instead, He demonstrated for us that no matter how weak we may feel when attacked by Satan, all we have to do is to quote the word of God. It is essential that we understand that we must learn to live by every word that comes from the mouth of God: . . . **to teach you that man does not live on bread alone but on every word that comes from the mouth of the LORD** (Deuteronomy 8:3 NIV).

The Word is your defense against Satan, and you have the authority to tell him to bolt: **Submit yourselves, then, to God. Resist the devil, and he will flee from you** (James 4:7).

Why did God create Satan so smart? Why not give him a bad case of stupidity, at least after he ruined things in Eden? It's not like his eventual evil bent ever took God by surprise, because God knew from the beginning that he would fall. God knew that it would all fit into a perfect plan of salvation—to salvage the fallen human race. Overcomers who emerge from a war with this creature, by learning to fight evil and by placing their trust in Jesus Christ, will be fit for the New Heaven and the New Earth: **They triumphed over him by the blood of the Lamb and by the word of their testimony; they did not love their lives so much as to shrink from death** (Revelations 12:11 NIV).

# 27 GOD PUT HATRED BETWEEN MAN AND SATAN

What would you think if, when you were small, your Dad intentionally set up a fight between you and the bully from next door? Further, you discover that this was not going to be an even match. The bully was bigger and smarter than you and he was brutal. That is basically what our Heavenly Daddy did when He put enmity between Satan and us. But don't panic: the fight's outcome works to your good at the end of the day. In one sense the match is uneven in Satan's favor. In another sense, because Father is present, there is simply no contest. We are the undisputed winner and the bully will bite the dust every time because Father set the rules.

This is how and when that "match" was set up: After convincing Eve to sin, God said this to Satan: **And I will put enmity between you and the woman, and between your seed and her Seed; He will bruise your head, and you shall bruise His heel** (Genesis 3:15). Enmity is defined as a deep-rooted hatred.

God would see to it that this hostility would serve His purpose. In order to test the free will of Adam, the Lord allowed the bully to wander into Eden. The bully picked a fight with Adam and Eve and won. Adam lost everything that the Father had given him, including his dignity, and fig leaves could not restore it. Jehovah gave them temporary covering for their nakedness and then placed the deep-rooted hatred between Adam (and his offspring) and Satan. There are several good things that would result from this kind of hatred, which pertains to us:

1. The bully is going to be noticed the next time he wanders into our yard.

2. When the bully does show up again there's enough hatred on both sides to ensure a vigorous fight.

3. For Adam and his family, the Referee has fixed all the fights so that Adam could always win. That is, if he really wants to.

There is still one more, good thing that the Referee has up His sleeve. If Adam (or you, or I) don't want to put up a fight, and we seem content to let the bully knock us around, He simply allows the bully to inflict enough pain to arouse our fighting instincts, if there is any fight in us at all. Sometimes we don't fight because we are fearful or feel weak. It is even possible that we don't believe the Word of God when it tells us that we have an enemy who is out to steal from us and kill us (John 10:10). There should be enough hatred in us toward Satan to rouse us; that's why God put it there, but often it must be stirred. Regardless of how we feel toward our enemy, you can be certain of this: there is *always* enough hatred in Satan toward you to bring him into your yard. It's best to be in a fighting mood when he shows up.

Not only does Father do an excellent job of refereeing in our favor, He sent us a big Brother, Jesus. This is how He took care of the bully: **on that cross Christ freed himself from the power of the spiritual rulers and authorities; he made a public spectacle of them by leading them as captives in his victory procession** (Colossians 2:15 GNB). This is the promise that enables us to fight and win: **See what I've given you? Safe passage as you walk on snakes and scorpions, and protection from every assault of the Enemy. No one can put a hand on you** (Luke 10:19 MSG).

Before you say that all this bullying sounds too scary for words let's look at it first from the Father's viewpoint. If He hadn't organized such a match He would be basically saying, "My child is no match for this devil. I have to protect and cuddle him and keep him out of harm's way." However, the truth is we are able to beat the bully. His Word says so: **But in all these things we more than conquer through Him who loved us** (Rom 8:37). *More than* means not only can we merely conquer, there is lots left in reserve—all of His strength is your strength.

If man had been left in his sinful and rebellious state, there would have been no hope for his redemption. We would have been eternally lost. In His wisdom, God allowed Satan to wage a war of enmity or a war of hostility. His design was to create in us a desire to leave the kingdom of Satan and come back to the kingdom of God where there is redemption, safety and eternal life.

The original earthly kingdom had been given to us as we see clearly from this declaration by God: **And God said, Let Us make man in Our image, after Our likeness. And <u>let them have dominion</u> over the fish of the sea, and over the fowl of the heavens, and over the cattle, and over all the earth, and over all the creepers creeping on the earth** (Genesis 1:26). God had given man the right to rule over the earthly kingdom because it was His to give. However, there is a law that accompanies this power and it is explained this way by Paul: **Never offer any part of your body to sin's power. No part of your body should ever be used to do any ungodly thing. Instead, offer yourselves to God as people who have come back from death and are now alive. Offer all the parts of your body to God. Use them to do everything that God approves of** (Romans 6:13 GW). In other words, God gave Adam the authority to rule the earth as long as he was in subjection to Him. In verse 16, Paul explains that this law is also applicable when we yield to Satan: **Don't you know that if you offer to be someone's slave, you must obey that master? Either your master is sin, or your master is obedience. Letting sin be your master leads to death. Letting obedience be your master leads to God's approval.**

If we obey Satan, he becomes the master and we become the slave. This is what happened to Adam. He had been given the authority to rule his earthly kingdom by God; however, when Adam succumbed to the cunning lies of Satan, he yielded his authority to Satan and made himself a slave. Satan is not a good ruler. Satan's worldly kingdom is a wretched place to live. He can only offer a life of war, sickness, addictions, pain and misery. He is the source of jealously, hatred and conflict. The perfect kingdom that Adam had inherited became cursed, and Satan has been trying to destroy this kingdom ever since. The curse was in full effect when Cain burned with jealous hatred and killed his younger brother, Abel.

Remember, when Satan came to test Jesus in the same manner as he had tested Adam, he used the kingdom that Adam lost as bait (Matthew 4:8-9). Thankfully, Jesus resisted the offer, rebuked Satan and went on to win the greatest war ever fought on our behalf. If He had not, we would have been doomed. This physical, earthly kingdom is still in Satan's hands for the moment; however, Jesus has already secured the spiritual kingdom for us through the sacrifice that He made in obedience to His Father's plan. We can still walk in victory while in enemy territory. In the fullness of time, He will take back the earthly kingdom.

Meanwhile, under Satan's control, this planet is in serious trouble. In Romans 8:22, Paul says: **And we know that the whole creation groans and travails in pain together until now.** Our satanic greed, wastefulness and carelessness have put our planet in jeopardy. At the very least we are guilty of poor management and of wasting the resources God gave us. Scientists claim we have polluted our atmosphere and in effect, destroyed the earth's natural ability to protect us. We are faced with hurricanes, earthquakes, drought, floods and numerous kinds of pestilence and disease. Quite possibly, a lot of it is caused by our negligence and greed.

Satan's control over this earthly kingdom is clear and obvious. We only have to consider the distressing news that is constantly at the forefront of the news media: wars, murders, lying, cheating, adultery, fornication, abortion and every sin imaginable. One may also wonder how Satan has influenced the original design of the animal kingdom. When God finished creating them, He called them "good." Under Satan's reign, they exhibit violence and also suffer. Large portions of the animal kingdom are predators, and in their quest for survival they kill and eat their prey. It is doubtful in my mind that this was how God created them. According to His future plan, when the animal kingdom comes back under their original Ruler, **the wolf shall dwell with the lamb, and the leopard shall lie down with the kid; and the calf and the cub lion and the fatling together; and a little child shall lead them. And the cow and the bear shall feed; their young ones shall lie down together; and the lion shall eat straw like the ox. And the suckling child shall play on the hole of the asp, and the weaned child shall put his hand on the adder's den.** <u>**They shall not hurt nor destroy**</u> **in all My holy mountain; for the earth shall be full of the knowledge of Jehovah, as the waters cover the sea** (Isaiah 11:6-9).

One day the enmity that God placed between man and Satan will have served its purpose and will end. Satan will be removed from the scene and punished. **And the Devil who deceived them was cast into the Lake of Fire and Brimstone, where the beast and the false prophet were. And he will be tormented day and night forever and ever** (Revelation 20:10). That will be a good day!

# 28 GOD USES EVIL SPIRITS

All of creation is God's, and He can do as He pleases with what he created. Every living and non-living thing will fulfill its purpose—even evil spirits. It is possible that all that God does in such a case is to withdraw His divine protection and then evil spirits do what evil spirits do best: destroy, lie, steal and kill. This reference in the life of King Saul demonstrates this withdrawal of Divine protection. Saul, the king chosen by God at the Israelites insistence (1 Samuel 8:18, 22), had moved himself out from under the protection of God and was blatantly disobeying Him:

> **But the spirit of Jehovah departed from Saul, and an evil spirit from Jehovah terrified him. And Saul's servants said to him, Behold now, an <u>evil spirit</u> from God terrifies you** (1 Samuel 16:14-15).

> **And it happened when the spirit from God was on Saul, that David took a harp and played with his hand. And there was relief for Saul, and** *it was* **well with him, and the <u>evil spirit</u> departed from him** (1 Samuel 16:23).

During the rule of the judges over Israel, Abimelech became a ruler that had to be dealt with. God used an evil spirit to stop his cruelty: **And <u>God sent an evil spirit</u> between Abimelech and the men of Shechem. And the men of Shechem dealt treacherously with Abimelech, so that the cruelty to the seventy sons of Jerubbaal might come, and their blood be laid upon Abimelech their brother, who killed them, and upon the men of Shechem who helped him in the killing of his brothers** (Judges 9:23-24).

Ahab was a wicked king over Israel and needed to be brought down. God allowed a lying spirit to visit this fool of a king and even told him beforehand what was going to happen. But Ahab still didn't get it: **And there came forth a spirit, and stood before the Lord, and said, I will persuade him. And the Lord said unto him, Wherewith? And he said, I will go forth, and I will be a lying spirit in the mouth of all his prophets. And he said, Thou shalt persuade him, and prevail also: go forth, and do so. Now therefore, behold, the Lord hath put a lying spirit in the mouth of all these thy prophets, and the Lord hath**

**spoken evil concerning thee** (1 Kings 22:21-24 KJV). Ahab went to war based on the lies from the evil spirit and was killed. The evil spirit was used by God to end the reign of this evil man just as God had warned.

Whether God actually sent the spirits or only permitted them, we need to acknowledge that He can do whatever He pleases and that all things were created by Him and for His purpose. Also, if the three references above are any indication, it is fitting to say that if He sent evil spirits to Abimelech, Saul, and Ahab and brought them to their destruction, He can do so to anyone. Of course, as mentioned elsewhere, He will always give sufficient warnings prior to such drastic action.

# 29 GOD LIVES ON EARTH

God lives with His people. Being the faithful, loving Father that He is, God made this promise to Jacob in a dream: **And, behold, I *am* with you, and will keep you in every *place* where you go, and will bring you again into this land. For I will not leave you until I have done that which I have spoken of to you** (Genesis 28:15). He repeated that commitment in many ways, to many men, all through the Bible. He specifically promised that His Divine Presence would always be with Israel and because He is not a respecter of persons and He never changes, it's our promise too:

> **And I will dwell among the sons of Israel, and will be their God** (Exodus 29:45).

> **. . . then there shall be a place which Jehovah your God shall choose to cause His name to dwell there. There you shall bring all that I command you, your burnt offerings, and your sacrifices, your tithes, and the heave offering of your hand, and all your choice vows which you vow to Jehovah** (Deuteronomy 12:11).

> **Sing praises to Jehovah, who dwells in Zion; declare among the nations His deeds** (Psalm 9:11).

> **Jehovah has chosen Zion; He has desired *it* for His dwelling-place. This *is* My rest forever; here I will dwell; for I have desired it** (Psalm 132:13-14).

John 1:14 (ASV) tells us that Jesus, who is God in the flesh, actually took up residence on our planet for a time: **And the Word became flesh, and <u>dwelt among us</u> (and we beheld his glory, glory as of the only begotten from the Father), full of grace and truth.** He came to lay down His life for the likes of us, all because of love. If we could only comprehend this kind of love it would change us forever. Meanwhile, by the power of His Holy Spirit, that is exactly what our Father is up to, He is gradually changing us: . . . **Nothing between us and God, our faces shining with the brightness of his face. And so we are transfigured much like the Messiah, our lives gradually becoming brighter and**

**more beautiful as God enters our lives and we become <u>like him</u>** (2 Corinthians 3:18 MSG).

With regard to God living with us, it gets better! In Old Testament times He was ever present with man in a very real sense. He spoke with them, taught them, rebuked and chastened them, and led them. In New Testament times He made a personal visit, had an address in Bethlehem, Egypt and Nazareth. It gets better because after Jesus left the earthly plane, He sent us His Holy Spirit to dwell inside of us. (See chapter one: *God is Personal.*)

All the sacrifices that He has made for His children will culminate in this scene in Heaven when our Father sits on His throne and gathers all His children around Him: **Therefore they are before the throne of God, and they serve Him day and night in His temple. And He sitting on the throne will dwell among them** (Revelation 7:15).

# 30 GOD DOES NOT ALWAYS ANSWER PRAYER

God rarely answers prayer in the manner we expect and with timing that pleases us. He can teach us many valuable lessons from this if we truly want to learn. When the answer to a prayer does not come immediately, it does not necessarily mean that it's not going to be answered. It could mean any one of the following:

1. He has something better for us than what we have been asking for.

2. He could be delaying the answer for a good purpose.

3. He may be refusing us an answer because it would not be good for us.

4. The delay may mean He wants to teach us some important lesson.

Most of our prayers result from problems we are having and we approach God for the solution. The very thing we want removed may be what He is using to make changes in us. Here are five ways God may want to use a problem in your life:

1. He may want to DIRECT you. The Good News Bible puts it this way: **Sometimes it takes a painful experience to make us change our ways** (Proverbs 20:30 GNB).

2. He may be TESTING you: **My friends, consider yourselves fortunate when all kinds of trials come your way, for you know that when your faith succeeds in facing such trials, the result is the ability to endure** (James 1:2-3).

3. He may need to CORRECT you: **My punishment was good for me, because it made me learn your commands. The law that you gave means more to me than all the money in the world** (Psalm 119:71-72).

4. He may be PROTECTING you and/or others. This is how Joseph saw it: **You plotted evil against me, but God turned it into good, in order to preserve the lives of many people who are alive today because of what happened** (Genesis 50:20).

5. He may be PERFECTING you: **We also boast of our troubles, because we know that trouble produces endurance, endurance brings God's approval, and his approval creates hope** (Romans 5:3-4).

The writer of Proverbs teaches two other lessons we can learn from unanswered prayer. One is that we should never take God for granted and the other is that there is always a price to pay for unrepented sin. This is what Proverbs 1:24-33 implies:

> **Because I called, and you refused; I stretched out my hand, and no one paid attention; but you have despised all my advice, and would have none of my warning. I also will laugh at your trouble; I will mock when your fear comes; when your fear comes as a wasting away, and your ruin comes like a tempest when trouble and pain come upon you. Then they shall call upon me, and <u>I will not answer</u>; they shall seek me early, but they shall not find me; instead they hated knowledge and did not choose the fear of Jehovah. They would have none of my counsel; they despised all my correction, and they shall eat the fruit of their own way, and be filled with their own desires. For the turning away of the simple kills them, and the ease of fools destroys them. But whoever listens to me shall dwell safely, and shall be quiet from fear of evil.**

Consider how David had to learn that sin results in unanswered prayer when he prayed but his request went unanswered: **And David prayed to God for the child. And David fasted, and went in and lay all night upon the earth** (2 Samuel 12:16). The result is recorded in verse 18: **And it happened on the seventh day, the child died.** David had committed a grievous sin in God's eyes by having one of his faithful soldiers killed to try and cover the sin of adultery with the man's wife. God spared David's life but took the child home to be with Him.

David was submissive. He learned his lesson, repented of his sin and understood that God was still able to forgive: **And he said, While the child was still alive, I fasted and wept; for I said, Who can tell if God will be gracious to me so that the child may live? But now he is dead; why should I fast? Can**

*What is God Like?*

I bring him back again? I shall go to him, but he shall not return to me (2 Samuel 12:22 -23).

Paul prayed for the removal of a thorn in his flesh and his prayer went unanswered. **For this thing I besought the Lord three times, that it might depart from me** (2 Corinthians 12:8). The Lord had noticed that this worthy servant was having a problem with conceit and He allowed Satan to torment him to keep him humble (verse 7). We learn that this was acceptable to Paul: **And He said to me, My grace is sufficient for you, for My power is made perfect in weakness. Most gladly therefore I will rather glory in my weaknesses, that the power of Christ may overshadow me** (2 Corinthians 12:9).

Here are a few of the reasons why God will refuse to answer some prayers (Dake Page 663 Column 1)

1. REFUSING TO LISTEN TO TRUTH: **God has no use for the prayers of the people who won't listen to him** (Proverbs 28:9 MSG).

2. REFUSING TO HUMBLE YOUR SELF: **If my people, which are called by my name, shall humble themselves, and pray, and seek my face, and turn from their wicked ways; then will I hear from heaven, and will forgive their sin, and will heal their land** (2 Chronicles 7:14 KJV).

3. FORSAKING GOD: **And he went out to meet Asa, and said unto him, Hear ye me, Asa, and all Judah and Benjamin; The Lord** *is* **with you, while ye be with him; and if ye seek him, he will be found of you; but if ye forsake him, he will forsake you** (2 Chronicles 15:2 KJV).

4. PROVOKING GOD: **But because of you the LORD was angry with me and would not listen to me. "That is enough," the LORD said. "Do not speak to me anymore about this matter** (Deuteronomy 3:26 NIV).

5. HARDHEARTEDNESS: **They made their hearts as hard as flint and would not listen to the law or to the words that the LORD Almighty had sent by his Spirit through the earlier prophets. So the LORD Almighty was very angry. 'When I called, they did not listen; so when they called, I would not listen,' says the LORD Almighty** (Zechariah 7:12-13 NIV).

6. LACK OF CHARITY: **Whoever shuts their ears to the cry of the poor will also cry out and not be answered** (Proverbs 21:13 NIV).

7. REGARDING INIQUITY IN THE HEART **If I regard iniquity in my heart, the Lord will not hear** *me* (Psalm 66:18 KJV).

8. WRONG MOTIVES: **Ye ask, and receive not, because ye ask amiss, that ye may consume** *it* **upon your lusts** (James 4:3 KJV).

9. DISHONOR OF COMPANION: **Likewise, ye husbands, dwell with** *them* **according to knowledge, giving honor unto the wife, as unto the weaker vessel, and as being heirs together of the grace of life; that your prayers be not hindered** (1 Peter 3:7 KJV).

10. UNBELIEF: **And Jesus said to them, Because of your unbelief. For truly I say to you, If you have faith like a grain of mustard seed, you shall say to this mountain, Move from here to there. And it shall move. And nothing shall be impossible to you** (Matthew 17:20).

11. SIN: **But your iniquities have separated between you and your God, and your sins have hid** *his* **face from you, that he will not hear** (Isaiah 59:2 KJV).

12. PARADING PRAYER LIFE: **And when you pray, do not be like the hypocrites, for they love to pray standing in the synagogues and on the street corners to be seen by others. Truly I tell you, they have received their reward in full** (Matthew 6:5 NIV).

13. VAIN REPETITIONS: **But when ye pray, use not vain repetitions, as the heathen** *do:* **for they think that they shall be heard for their much speaking** (Matthew 6:7 KJV).

14. REFUSING TO FORGIVE: **For if ye forgive men their trespasses, your heavenly Father will also forgive you: But if ye forgive not men their trespasses, neither will your Father forgive your trespasses** (Matthew 6:14-15 KJV).

15. HYPOCRISY: **To some who were confident of their own righteousness and looked down on everyone else, Jesus told this parable: "Two men went up to the temple to pray, one a Pharisee and the other a tax collector. The Pharisee stood by himself and prayed: 'God, I thank you that I am not like other people—robbers, evildoers, adulterers—or even like this tax collector. I fast twice a week and give a tenth of all I get.' But the tax collector stood at a distance. He would not even look up to heaven, but beat his breast and said, 'God, have mercy**

on me, a sinner.' I tell you that this man, rather than the other, went home justified before God. For all those who exalt themselves will be humbled, and those who humble themselves will be exalted (Luke 18:9-14 NIV).

16. BEING DISCOURAGED: **And he spake a parable unto them *to this end*, that men ought always to pray, and <u>not to faint</u>; Saying, There was in a city a judge, which feared not God, neither regarded man: And there was a widow in that city; and she came unto him, saying, Avenge me of mine adversary. And he would not for a while: but afterward he said within himself, Though I fear not God, nor regard man; Yet because this widow troubleth me, I will avenge her, lest by her continual coming she weary me. And the Lord said, Hear what the unjust judge saith. And shall not God avenge his own elect, which cry day and night unto him, though he bear long with them? I tell you that he will avenge them speedily . . . .** (Luke 18:1-8 KJV).

17. DOUBTING—DOUBLE-MINDEDNESS: **If any of you lacks wisdom, you should ask God, who gives generously to all without finding fault, and it will be given to you. But when you ask, you must believe and not doubt, because the one who doubts is like a wave of the sea, blown and tossed by the wind. That person should not expect to receive anything from the Lord. Such a person is double-minded and unstable in all they do** (James 1:5-8 NIV).

Regarding this list of reasons for unanswered prayer, we should not be discouraged or fall into condemnation. God is not continually holding out some list, waiting for you to reach a certain degree of perfection before answering your prayer. Out of His mercy, love and compassion, He answers the prayers of His children, as any good father would. He will however, consider our need and weigh that against the greater need of our heart. He will also consider how well you are doing in the School Of Hard Knocks. If you are making no progress, guess what? He may administer some discipline. However, you may still get prayers answered even if you don't deserve it—just because He loves you. He's like that.

# 31  GOD DOES ANSWER PRAYER

God really does answer prayer, but we must do our part to avoid the kind of problems that may hinder the reply. There are conditions to getting ones prayer answered. First, it would be ridiculous to be making requests of someone whom you believe does not exist. The initial requirement for answered prayer would be to believe in God. He demands that we believe in His existence, as the writer in Hebrews puts it: **But without faith** *it is* **impossible to please** *Him,* **for he who comes to God** <u>**must believe that He is**</u> **and** *that* **He is a rewarder of those who diligently seek Him** (Hebrews 11:6). Believing in Him is a start in getting prayers answered.

Basically, when we petition God we need to be prepared to obey Him. For example, if we refuse to forgive others, then we are in no position to be asking God to answer our prayers. Mark 11:24-25 tells us that God considers this a very serious problem. His primary interest is in saving and changing us, and change is underway the minute we obey and forgive others. By faith then, we can expect answers.

None of us can get a prayer answered based on our perfection. Thankfully, perfection is not what counts. Our goodness is not, and never will be sufficient anyway. Consider the following:

> **Jehovah looked down from Heaven on the sons of men, to see if there were any who understood and sought God. All have gone aside, together they are filthy; there is none who does good, no, not one** (Psalm 14:2-3).

> **. . . for all have sinned and come short of the glory of God** (Romans 3:23).

So how does one get prayers answered? From the Scriptures above it is clear we cannot offer prayers based on good works or our good nature. But somehow God still answers the prayers of people who are not perfect and have sin in their lives. One of the most obvious examples would be Abraham. He did not fully trust God when he tried to hurry up the process to get his promised son by sleeping with Hagar. Yet, it is undeniable that Abraham still had his prayers answered.

In Exodus 4:24 (NLT), Moses had a disobedience issue regarding the circumcision of his son: **On the way to Egypt, at a place where Moses and his family had stopped for the night, the LORD confronted him and was about to kill him.** After obeying and circumcising his son, this great intercessor had many prayers answered and performed the miracles God had given him as a witness to the Egyptians.

Job had a serious trust issue with God as per his own confession: **For the thing which I greatly feared has come upon me, and that which I was afraid of has come to me** (Job 3:25). Meanwhile, it is interesting to note that before putting him in the ring with Satan, God said that Job was perfect: **And Jehovah said to Satan, Have you set your heart against My servant Job, because there is none like him in the earth, a perfect and upright man, one who fears God and turns away from evil?** (Job 1:8). When God asked Satan, **"Have you set your heart against My servant Job,"** we can be sure that God was not taken by surprise when Satan beat him badly and stripped him of his wealth, his health, and his children. At the end of the book God answered all his prayers and gave him back health, wealth and a new family. Meanwhile, the ones taken by Satan earlier were tucked away safely by God in Heaven because this righteous man had prayed and offered the right kind of sacrifices for his sons: **When these celebrations ended—sometimes after several days—Job would purify his children. He would get up early in the morning and offer a burnt offering for each of them. For Job said to himself, "Perhaps my children have sinned and have cursed God in their hearts." This was Job's regular practice** (Job 1:5 NLT). God accepted these sacrifices and took care of his children.

There were many others whose prayers were answered in spite of sin and disobedience. For example, David disobeyed by taking a census of his people (2 Samuel 24:2). He conjured up a scheme to kill Uriah to cover his adultery with the man's wife (2 Samuel 11). God still blessed him and answered his prayers. David testified: **In my trouble I cried to Jehovah, and He heard me** (Psalm 120:1). Another confirmation from David that God answers prayer is found here: **I waited patiently for Jehovah; and He bowed down to me, and heard my cry** (Psalm 40:1).

In the New Testament, a father had trouble believing in the healing power of Jesus. He admitted this: **And immediately the father of the child cried out and said with tears, Lord, I believe. Help my unbelief** (Mark 9:24). Jesus did not quote a list of Scriptures on faith to this father, or even highlight his unbelief. He simply healed his child.

How strict then is God with the *No-answer-to-prayer-if-you-sin* rule? We see from the life of the men above that they did not pass the sin test but still got results. While their works did not measure up, they still got God's attention. The conclusion lies in the fact that when God answers prayer it is always out of His great compassion and mercy. If He applied the law to our sins instead of His mercy, death would be our portion because the law was clear in this statement by the Lord: **The soul that sinneth, it shall die** (Ezekiel 18:20). In other words, forget getting prayers answered: you are condemned to death!

How is it that He passed a law that condemned us to death and then found some way to override that law to give us life and answers to our prayers? The answer is in God Himself providing a suitable sacrifice that would satisfy that law. That sacrifice was His own Son, Jesus, who came and offered Himself as a living sacrifice to pay the penalty for sin: **We need a priest who doesn't have to bring daily sacrifices as those chief priests did. First they brought sacrifices for their own sins, and then they brought sacrifices for the sins of the people. Jesus brought the sacrifice for the sins of the people once and for all when he sacrificed himself** (Hebrews 7:27 GW). Hebrews 9:14 continues: **How much more shall the blood of Christ, who through the eternal Spirit offered himself without spot to God, purge your conscience from dead works to serve the living God?**

Not only does God answer prayers, but His love covers us in this life and on into the next one. **For God so loved the world that He gave His only-begotten Son, that whoever believes in Him should not perish but have everlasting life** (John 3:16). This love rescues us from Hell and makes provision for us to live in Heaven with Him. Because of what Christ did for us, the invitation is wide open to prayer and we may do so with courage and confidence: **Let us therefore come boldly unto the throne of grace, that we may obtain mercy, and find grace to help in time of need** (Hebrews 4:16). It gets better! Anyone who prays knows that prayer is not easy but God sends us Help. Imagine God the Holy Spirit groaning over your prayer request: **In the same way, the Spirit helps us in our weakness. We do not know what we ought to pray for, but the Spirit himself intercedes for us through wordless groans.** (Romans 8:26 NIV). Abba is the equivalent of our word for Daddy: **And because ye are sons, God hath sent forth the Spirit of his Son into your hearts, crying, Abba, Father** (Galatians 4:6 KJV). So, we can approach him not just as Lord and Saviour, Brother, and Helper, but we can call him Daddy. Help is never far when a child cries out to Daddy for attention.

## What is God Like?

There may be times when you have prayed and waited and prayed and waited some more and still nothing seems to happen. This is a likely time for Satan to show up as your accuser, blaming and condemning you and reminding you of all your sinful ways. When you run into a problem like this be reminded that Jesus offers to arbitrate: **For [there is] one God, and one mediator between God and men, the man Christ Jesus** (1Timothy 2:5). He will always take your side for this simple reason: In His eyes you are perfect; you have been cleansed by His blood. The accuser can't touch that.

Regarding the attacks of Satan with his list of reasons why your prayers are not going to be answered by bringing sin to your remembrance, (even ones that God has forgiven), Satan is trying to make you believe that you are condemned and unworthy. After all, you did commit the sin! But look how God took care of that problem in Romans 8:1, as Paul explains it: **There is therefore now <u>no condemnation</u> to those *who are* in Christ Jesus, who walk not according to the flesh but according to the Spirit.** You could rightfully ask your enemy at this point, "Condemnation? What condemnation? Jesus has taken my sin and in God's sight I am sinless." Then you can get on with believing and waiting for an answer to your prayer.

John Wesley said that God does nothing but in answer to prayer (Chapter 11 Reflections). From this we can conclude that God considers your prayer very important. This verse is an indication of how valuable your prayers are: **Confess faults to one another, and pray for one another, that you may be healed.** *The* **effectual fervent prayer of a righteous one avails much** (James 5:16).

God has opened the way for answering our prayers. He invites us to pray and is prompted by our prayers to do something. The *how* and *when* is still His prerogative.

# 32 GOD FORGIVES

As a God of love, His greatest desire is to forgive and love you. Over and over He calls man to simply repent and He willingly forgives. More than forgiveness, He wants to shower you with benefits, healing, and other acts of kindness as summed up in this Psalm: **Bless Jehovah, O my soul, and forget not all His benefits; who forgives all your iniquities; who heals all your diseases; who redeems your life from ruin; who crowns you** *with* **loving-kindness and tender mercies** (Psalm 103:2-4).

We are creatures who have the ability to break the heart of a loving Father. We have done this so many times by wandering away from Him. Regardless, consider this passionate note from Him penned by the Psalmist: **Jehovah is merciful and gracious, slow to anger, and rich in mercy. He will not always chasten, nor will He keep His** *anger* **forever. He has not dealt with us according to our sins, nor rewarded us according to our iniquities. For as the heavens** *are* **high above the earth,** *so* **is His mercy toward those who fear Him. As far as the east** *is* **from the west,** *so* **far has He removed our transgressions from us. As a father pities his children, Jehovah pities those who fear Him. For He knows our form; He remembers that we** *are* **dust.** *As for* **man, his days** *are* **as grass; as a flower of the field, so he flourishes. For the wind passes over it, and it is gone; and its place shall know it no more. But the mercy of Jehovah** *is* **from everlasting to everlasting on those who fear Him, and His righteousness** *is* **to sons of sons** (Psalm 103:8-17).

He revealed His motive for forgiving our sins in this verse: **"I, even I, am he who blots out your transgressions, <u>for my own sake</u>, and remembers your sins no more** (Isaiah 43:25 NIV). Holding on to our sins would not make Him happy. His intense love motivates Him to wipe the slate clean. When our sin is removed and forgiven He is content.

# 33 GOD WILL NOT ALWAYS FORGIVE

Prior to the flood God forgave the children that He had created and loved on a daily basis. But, there came a day when forgiveness was no longer an option. Forgiveness had run its course and judgment was administered. Then He drowned all of them, except for Noah and his family. He gave His reason Genesis 6:3, when He emphatically stated that He would not always strive with them. God delights in extending mercy but when mercy is ignored forgiveness must end—otherwise man would learn nothing.

Time ran out for the nation of the Amorites as well. They were wicked, but God waited patiently for a long time before He gave up on them. Speaking with Abraham, God informs him that after his children had been slaves in Egypt for 400 years, Egypt would be punished and Abraham's descendants would be given the land belonging to the Amorites: **But in the fourth generation they shall come here again, for the iniquity of the Amorites is not yet full** (Genesis 15:16). He watched and waited for them all during this time. There was no improvement, and later He commanded the Israelites to wipe them out (see Joshua 24).

Jesus taught His disciples to take the good news of salvation to all men. He commanded them to present the gospel, and if it was not received, the disciples were to shake the dust of that city off their feet and abandon it. He likened the fate of such cities to ones He had burned earlier: **And whoever shall not receive you, nor hear your words, when you depart out of that house or city, shake off the dust of your feet. Truly I say to you, it shall be more tolerable for the land of Sodom and Gomorrah in the day of judgment than for that city** (Matthew 10:14-15). This ought to make us shudder, because were it not for grace, our cities could meet the same fate. There is no more forgiveness when His mercy has run its course. There are usually several adequate warnings but the day will come when forgiveness ends, and judgment begins.

Jesus teaches that there is another condition that God will refuse to forgive: **For if ye forgive men their trespasses, your heavenly Father will also forgive you: But if ye forgive not men their trespasses, neither will your Father forgive your trespasses** (Matthew 6:14-15). It's very simple: refuse to forgive others, He will not forgive us.

Paul also teaches that sin without repentance will cause God to withhold forgiveness. He will refuse some entrance into His kingdom: **Do not be deceived; neither fornicators, nor idolaters, nor adulterers, nor abusers, nor homosexuals, nor thieves, nor covetous, nor drunkards, nor revilers, nor extortioners, shall inherit *the* kingdom of God** (1 Corinthians 6:9-10). There are numerous sins we are capable of committing that are listed throughout the Bible, and because even as Christians we are sinners, we need to be actively seeking forgiveness. A genuine "repenter" will be forgiven, but a man who does not repent can never be forgiven.

Jesus issued this dire warning regarding everlasting damnation that results when God refuses to forgive this particular sin: **Truly I say to you, All sins shall be forgiven to the sons of men, and blasphemies with which they shall blaspheme. But he who blasphemes against the Holy Spirit never shall have forgiveness, but is liable to eternal condemnation** (Mark 3:28-29). How does one end up on God's list of *"The Unforgiven"*? This is a significant question that each of us should be considering. How does one blaspheme against the Holy Spirit? Studying the context in which Jesus issued the above warning, my personal conclusion (and those of numerous Biblical scholars) is this: this warning was issued to particular people on a particular day. They were the scribes who came down from Jerusalem. Jesus had performed miracles in front of their very eyes by the Holy Spirit's power, but they refused to acknowledge this power. Instead *they attributed the power to Satan.* They saw with their own eyes and heard with their own ears the demonstrated power of the Holy One, but deliberately and knowingly gave the credit to Beelzebub, a demon. How could this apply to us? If we hear His voice and see demonstrations of His power, we should always acknowledge it and give Him credit for what He has done. His great power and creativity is all around us. He is constantly speaking to us in some form or another. Remember the words of David in these verses: **The heavens declare the glory of God; and the expanse proclaims His handiwork. Day to day pours forth speech, and night to night reveals knowledge.** *There is* **no speech nor** *are* **there words; their voice is not heard** (Psalm 19:1-3). What the heavens declare we need to acknowledge. We all see His handiwork; we all hear His speech. It is everywhere.

## What is God Like?

The author of Hebrews adds one more category to the list of "*The Unforgiven.*" These are the backsliders who meet these conditions: they were enlightened; tasted the heavenly gift; experienced the power of the Holy Spirit; and they knew the Word of God. After experiencing all of that, they go back to a life of sin, accepting Satan as their spiritual leader: **For *it is* <u>impossible</u> for those who were once enlightened, and have tasted of the heavenly gift, and were made partakers of *the* Holy Spirit, and have tasted *the* good Word of God and *the* powers of the world to come, and who have fallen away; <u>it is impossible</u>, I say, to renew them again to repentance, since they crucify the Son of God afresh to themselves and put *Him* to an open shame** (Hebrews 6:4-6).

Some try to argue that these backsliders are somehow different from the rest of us. However, when you go through the above list, you will see that as followers of Christ, we were all given the same gifts in various measures. The point is made many times through the Bible and through this book: *we should never take God for granted.* The gifts that we were given as part of our salvation are far too valuable to us and far too costly to God to treat in such a trivial manner.

If you feel you may have backslidden, the possibility exists that you have not. You may have just grown cold and need to sit closer to the fire. If you still have a love for God it is doubtful that you have actually turned back, because lovers of God couldn't possibly abandon all four of these conditions. If you are thinking of giving up and renouncing Him, hear these stern warnings:

> **And Jesus said to him, No one, having put his hand to the plow and looking back, is fit for the kingdom of God** (Luke 9:62).

> **If they have escaped the corruption of the world by knowing our Lord and Savior Jesus Christ and are again entangled in it and overcome, they are worse off at the end than they were at the beginning** (2 Peter 2:20 NIV).

> **The people God accepts will live because of their faith. But he isn't pleased with anyone who turns back** (Hebrews 10:38 CEV).

# 34 GOD IS A FAITH HEALER

God heals in response to the prayer of faith. The first reference to healing in the Bible is in Genesis 17:19, where God speaks a prophetic word of healing over Sarah, who was barren. He healed her so that she conceived and had a son. The second reference comes in Exodus 15:26, and is a conditional promise in God's own words: **And he said, If you will carefully listen to the voice of Jehovah your God, and will do that which is right in His sight, and will give ear to His commandments, and keep all His Laws, I will put none of these diseases upon you, which I have brought upon the Egyptians; for I** *am* **Jehovah who heals you.**

The Psalmists confirms God's power to heal:

> **Bless Jehovah, O my soul, and forget not all His benefits; who forgives all your iniquities; who heals all your diseases** (Psalm 103:2-3).

> **He spoke the word that healed you, that pulled you back from the brink of death** (Psalm 107:20 MSG).

Jesus taught His disciples to pray for people and He gave them power to heal:

> **And when He had called to** *Him* **His twelve disciples, He gave them authority over unclean spirits, to cast them out, and to heal all kinds of sickness and all kinds of disease** (Matthew 10:1).

There is nowhere in Scripture where this command was ever rescinded, therefore it still applies. A disciple is any follower of Christ who has faith the size of a mustard seed and is willing to pray. But we must keep on praying until the answer comes.

There are at least two types of healing that God has instigated. Jesus and His disciples demonstrated one type by speaking a word in faith and authority and commanding a sickness or a demon, to leave. The sickness or demon then left.

There is another we seem to take for granted. From the beginning God designed healing for the human body. We often refer to this as natural healing. Some would say it's the kind we get from Mother Nature. There is really no such creature as Mother Nature and no such force in nature except that which God, very deliberately, put there. If Adam ever fell out of a tree and landed on his head, Eve would have observed that blood was leaking out of his head and the surrounding area was turning black and blue. As she watched, she would also see the bleeding stop and in a short time the wound disappear. There were no doctors, nurses, peroxide or band-aids. God had designed his body to take care of this kind of problem. The same healing takes place in the bodies of Adam's offspring. It is healing instigated by God—by design. We should always be thankful to Him for this healing power because without it we would not live very long. Imagine how your body would react if the ulcer in your mouth didn't heal. Or what would life be like if one caught a common cold or the flu and it didn't ever get better? After 6000 years of history, we still don't have the technology or medical knowledge to truly cure the simplest disease. We have some things that seem to help but without the immune system, that God designed, we would die. Doctors didn't design this system. Neither did scientists nor the government. It was God who put it in place and it is free. The next time you cut your finger, take a look at how the bleeding stops and the cut starts to heal and thank Him.

The first type of healing is needed because of our disobedience and sometimes the abuse we apply to our own bodies. When He uses the words "carefully listen," it's obvious that obedience was a requirement to good health. The opposite would also be true; disobedience would bring sickness and disease. However, our merciful, Heavenly Father did not abandon us in our sickness even when it results from disobedience, stupidity or self-abuse. This Scripture can be summarized as follows: "Listen to Me, obey Me and I will heal you." As hard as we try, we will mess up on the obedience part, and when that happens, chastisement will follow. Thus, His motive for chastisement: He allows sickness to get our attention so that we stop, turn around and come home.

He does demand that we have faith in order to receive the healing. Remember this verse from Hebrews: **But without faith *it is* impossible to please *Him*, for he who comes to God must believe that He is and *that* He is a rewarder of those who diligently seek Him** (Hebrews 11:6). Jesus also made this clear when He spoke to the woman with the issue of blood: **And He said** to her, **Daughter, your faith has made you well. Go in peace, and be whole from your plague** (Mark 5:34). The next time you approach Him for healing you may feel that your faith is less than that of the woman in this verse. You may feel that your faith is small and weak. If so, approach Him with the same words of the man in Mark 9:24 **And immediately the father of the child cried out and said with tears, Lord, I believe. Help my unbelief.** Your faith is certainly no weaker than his and yet he got his prayer answered.

Is all sickness due to disobedience? I believe it is in one sense. Consider this question: would Christians suffer sickness if they were perfect and sinless? Would God have allowed Satan to afflict Job if there had been no sin in his life? Would Paul have been given a thorn in his flesh if he had no problem with conceit? If yes, then God must have slipped up somewhere because to allow sickness, on a perfect child, would mean He was either helpless to do anything about it, or He's not concerned when they suffer. And of course, neither would be true. However, there are numerous examples in the Bible where sickness was used to chasten and teach precious children.

Although sin results in sickness we need to remind ourselves that we have a compassionate and merciful God. Out of compassion and mercy, He heals and protects us even when we are ignorant, sinful and disobedient. When He does not, we are required to go searching for answers because that is why He designed pain. (See chapter four on *God Believes in Pain*.)

Consider this, after God finished creation everything was GOOD. Everything remained good until Adam sinned and then had to face the consequences of sin which is all about the Law of Sowing and Reaping:

> **Do not be deceived, God is not mocked. For whatever a man sows, that he also will reap** (Galatians 6:7).
>
> **He who sows injustice reaps calamity, and the rod they wield in fury will be broken** (Proverbs 22:8 NIV).

From that point on Satan took control of what Adam would reap and it is clear from these Scriptures that sickness was only part of the harvest:

> **. . . how God anointed Jesus of Nazareth with the Holy Spirit and power, and how he went around doing good and healing all who were under the power of the devil, because God was with him** (Acts 10:38 NIV).

## What is God Like?

> **The thief does not come except to steal and to kill and to destroy. I have come so that they might have life, and that they might have it more abundantly** (John 10:10). The thief is the devil, and he aims to steal your health.

> **Then one who had been demon-possessed was brought to Him, blind and dumb. And He healed him, so much so that the blind and dumb one both spoke and saw** (Matthew 12:22). The sick had been unable to see or speak and a demon was the cause.

We should be thankful to God that He didn't just leave us to endure the consequences of our sins. He put a plan in place to rescue us from, not only the sickness problem but also the death problem that sin had caused:

> **But the fact is, it was our pains he carried—our disfigurements, all the things wrong with us. We thought he brought it on himself, that God was punishing him for his own failures. But it was our sins that did that to him, that ripped and tore and crushed him—our sins! He took the punishment, and that made us whole. Through his bruises we get healed** (Isaiah 53:4-5 MSG).

James 5:14-16 is prophetic and has now been fulfilled, Jesus did come and He even demonstrated, numerous times, how to get healing for sickness. He returned to Heaven but left us with these very simple instructions as to how you may receive your healing:

> **Is any sick among you? Let him call for the elders of the church, and let them pray over him, anointing him with oil in the name of the Lord. And the prayer of faith will cure the sick, and the Lord shall raise him up. And if he has committed sins, it will be forgiven him. Confess faults to one another, and pray for one another, that you may be healed. The effectual fervent prayer of a righteous one avails much.**

Regarding the statement above—that disobedience brings sickness—it is important to remember that this statement may foster guilt. Paul teaches in Romans 7 that all Christians struggle with the sin problem, but Romans 8:1 assures us that we are free from any condemnation: **Therefore, there is now no condemnation for those who are in Christ Jesus.** As a Christian suffering from some sickness, it would be far more appropriate to ask, "Father, what should I be learning from this lesson?" Then, pursue the lesson until it is learned and the sickness is healed. Jesus promises to pay attention to persistence: **Ask and it will be given to you; seek and you will find; knock and the door will be opened to you** (Matthew 7:7).

As seen through the Bible and this book, sickness serves other purposes. He uses it to bring us closer to Himself and two, it brings Him glory. Regarding the latter, consider this conversation between Jesus and His disciples: **And passing by, He saw a man who was blind from birth. And His disciples asked Him, saying, Master, who sinned, this man or his parents, that he was born blind? Jesus answered, Neither has this man nor his parents sinned, but that the works of God might be revealed in him** (John 9:1-3). From this translation it would seem as if neither the man nor his parents had ever committed any sin. We know this is not the case because Scripture makes it quite clear that we are all sinners. The Message Bible has a better translation to verses 2 and 3: **His disciples asked, "Rabbi, who sinned: this man or his parents, causing him to be born blind?" Jesus said, "You're asking the wrong question. You're looking for someone to blame. There is no such cause-effect here. Look instead for what God can do."** Jesus saw in the man's sickness an opportunity to bring glory to His Father by healing him. The man's sickness resulted from sin which came into the world because of the original sin of disobedience. At this moment in time we are all tainted, we are all susceptible to sickness but we can all receive healing.

# 35  GOD MAY ASK YOU QUESTIONS

God's first recorded question to man was in the Garden of Eden: **And Jehovah God called to Adam and said to him, Where are you?** (Genesis 3:9). And in verse 11, He asked two more: "Who told you that you were naked?" and, "Have you eaten of the tree which I commanded you that you should not eat?" When He inquired of Adam as to his whereabouts, it was not because He did not know where he was, or that he was stumped as to why Adam thought he was naked, or because he was wondering if Adam had really eaten of the forbidden tree. In this case, the questions asked by God were designed to give the man opportunity to be reconciled.

Someone said that when God asked a question you can be sure He is not looking for information. After all He does know everything. When He asked Adam where he was, it was not because He didn't know. God knew where he was and what he had done. Why then, does He ask questions?

> God, strictly speaking, has nothing to ask. But he asks anyhow. And this, I think, is why: nothing hooks us and pries us open like a question. You can talk all day at me, yet it obliges me nothing. I can listen or not, respond or not. But ask me one question, and I must answer or rupture our fellowship. God's inquisitiveness, His seeming curiosity, is a measure of His intimate nature. He desires relationship. He wants to talk with us, not just at us, or we at him (Buchanan Page 191).

If intimate fellowship is God's purpose, then consider the following attempts He made to get close to various people with His questions. He asked Eve: **"What is this you have done?"** The woman said, "The serpent deceived me, and I ate"** (Genesis 3:13 NIV). In Genesis 4:6 (NIV), He asked her son: **"Why are you angry? Why is your face downcast?"** After Cain had killed his brother Abel in Genesis 4:9 (NIV), God asked: **"Where is your brother Abel?"** "I don't know," he replied. "Am I my brother's keeper?"** After each question, God was giving the individual opportunity to mend the fellowship. All that was offered were lies and excuses.

Jesus often asked similar questions giving His audience the opportunity to catch on and come into fellowship. Mark 2:8 (KJV) provides us one example: **And immediately when Jesus perceived in his spirit that they so reasoned within themselves, he said unto them, Why reason ye these things in your hearts?** In Mark 4:40 (KJV), He asks His disciples: **Why are ye so fearful? how is it that ye have no faith?** In John 5:6 (CEV) Jesus is at the Pool of Bethesda: **When Jesus saw the man and realized that he had been crippled for a long time, he asked him, "Do you want to be healed?"** With each question, Jesus is giving them an opportunity to connect with Him.

Like a close, caring friend Jesus questions His disciples just after He had been resurrected. Days before, they had turned their backs on Him and fled, leaving Him alone with a Roman mob. But now He has come to find them, with a forgiving, compassionate spirit. He even prepares a meal for them after their long toil during the night. He opens the conversation with a question: **"Friends, have you caught anything?" "No!" they answered** (John 21:5 CEV). They did not have any fish, but out of embarrassment and condemnation, they could have lied, and said yes, or they could have spurned Him and said, "No, but we will in a few minutes"—like most fishermen. But, in this case these men allowed Him to reconnect with a question.

Once questioned by God we would also have to acknowledge that He is leaving little room for us to exercise our wit in the matter, since it is useless to answer with anything but the truth. We could make an excuse like Eve did when confronted by God, or we could respond like David who, when confronted by Nathan with his sin, he immediately confessed: **"I have sinned against the LORD."** (2 Samuel 12:13 NIV).

Oh that we would be wise enough to answer His questions eagerly, honestly and come quickly back into fellowship with Him.

# 36  GOD IS AN EDUCATOR

God is an excellent teacher. He uses visual aids, symbols, parables, illustrations, and allegories to get His point across and to help us remember what He teaches. In Genesis He used two literal trees to help Adam and Eve to be aware of the one law they had to obey. The visual aids would remind them of the consequences of breaking that law. An important lesson considering it involved life or death for them. The lesson was short and simple and the two trees were constant reminders of the command.

Later He used a rainbow in the sky to help us remember His promise regarding the flood. Jesus used the fig tree in Matthew 21:21 to demonstrate the power of faith. God used the slaughtering of an innocent lamb to demonstrate and help us avoid the horror of sin. This lesson—this requirement of death for covering given under the Law—pointed toward Jesus who would eventually be the sacrifice for all our sins. With the sacrifice of lambs, God was teaching that the blood of an animal was insufficient to remove man's sin. This could only be accomplished by the blood of His Son and He would one day take the place of animals. According to Hebrews 9, all the various items listed under the law were given to illustrate the New Covenant that would be activated once Jesus had fulfilled the law. The Law was used by God to help us remember that we are sinners: **As it is, however, the sacrifices serve year after year to remind people of their sins** (Hebrews 10:3 GNB). The Mosaic Law was full of symbols, all with the sole purpose of teaching us and helping us to remember (See chapter 65, *God Is Big On Symbols*).

When David committed adultery and had a man murdered (2 Samuel 11 & 12), God sent Nathan the prophet to David with a parable to teach him that God is all seeing and all-knowing and sin cannot be hidden. God taught him the simple act of looking at a woman with lust in his heart leads to adultery and then murder.

Teachers need to show discipline and God is a strict, but fair, disciplinarian. He gives tests to help the student to truly master the lessons. He will often refuse to advance the student to the next class until the last lesson has been completed. In His testing He is lenient and the trials are always meted out with compassion: **And have you forgotten the encouraging words God spoke to you as His children? He said, "My child, don't make light of the LORD's discipline, and don't give up when He corrects you** (Hebrews 12:5 NLT). He also has a way of weeding out those who are not serious about their grades: **I know your works, that you are neither cold nor hot. I would that you were cold or hot. So because you are lukewarm, and neither cold nor hot, I will vomit you out of My mouth** (Revelation 3:15-16).

One amazing trait related to the discipline of God is that He is consistent: no problem ever goes unnoticed, or is ever ignored. Even more amazing is the fact that His first action toward our sins and omissions is to apply His love to the problem. This love is applied first, prior to any form of punishment. **But God commends His love toward us in that while we were yet sinners Christ died for us** (Romans 5:8). The greatest pain for any sin is dying. He applied this to Himself and His Son, prior to subjecting the student to any. When love alone doesn't work, and most of the time it does not, then God makes use of discipline, accompanied by pain. His love is such that He cannot allow the student to continue a life of poor grades, **because the Lord disciplines the one he loves, and he chastens everyone he accepts as his son."** (Hebrews 12:6 NIV). You will always know where you stand with God if you are being chastened or reprimanded—it means He Loves you.

# 37 GOD IS KING

God is not just a king; He is the King of kings. Revelation 4 describes a scene in Heaven of our King sitting on His throne surrounded by 24 other thrones. In this scene He has 24 kings from Heaven under Him. He is above all other rulers. Every president, prime minister, governor and dictator will answer to Him. 1Timothy 6:15 -16 and Revelation 19:16 demonstrate this:

> **His appearing will be brought about at the right time by God, the blessed and only Ruler, the King of kings and the Lord of lords. He alone is immortal; he lives in the light that no one can approach. No one has ever seen him; no one can ever see him. To him be honor and eternal power! Amen.**

> **And He has on *His* garment, and on His thigh a name written, KING OF KINGS AND LORD OF LORDS.**

The Psalmists and Isaiah recognized His authority and kingship in these verses:

> **The LORD *[is]* King forever and ever: the heathen are perished out of his land** (Psalm 10:16).

> **For God *is* King of all the earth; sing praises with understanding** (Psalm 47:7).

> **For Jehovah *is* a great God, and a great King above all gods** (Psalm 95:3).

> **So says Jehovah, the King of Israel, and His redeemer Jehovah of Hosts; I *am* the first, and I *am* the last; and besides Me *there is* no God** (Isaiah 44:6).

One of the most unique things about this great King is the love He has for His subjects. In order for a human to be part of His kingdom they have to be redeemed. This poses a serious problem. Humans start their lives outside

His kingdom, and due to the sin factor, they cannot even be in His Holy presence. They too must be holy! The word "shall" in Leviticus 11:45 means it is not a suggestion, it's a law: **For I *am* Jehovah who brought you up out of the land of Egypt, to be your God. You shall therefore be holy, for I *am* holy.**

Paul explains that no one is justified in the sight of God, **because by the works of the Law none of all flesh will be justified in His sight; for through the Law *is* the knowledge of sin** (Romans 3:20). David also understood this to be a problem when he made this request of God: **And do not enter into judgment with Your servant, for in Your sight no one living is just** (Psalm 143:2). This King took care of our sin problem by dying for us Himself, and by doing so, God manifested the greatest act of love ever shown. No other earthly king has even come close to demonstrating such love for subjects who are so unlike themselves. **For we yet being without strength, in due time Christ died for the ungodly. For one will with difficulty die for a righteous one, yet perhaps one would even dare to die for a good one. But God commends His love toward us in that while we were yet sinners Christ died for us** (Romans 5:6-8).

Some might say that God took the easy road when He had Jesus do the dying while He stayed in Heaven. However, this is not the case for a Father with such love for His beloved Son because of the kind of love God embodies. It would have been easier for Him to have actually died Himself than to have Jesus crucified at the hands of sinful men. It was by no means easy to hold back His fury and wrath. With His kind of love (remembering that He *is* Love), it would have been easier to lay down His own life than to watch it happening to the only perfect Person in the entire universe, especially when He had the power to prevent it. Can you imagine an earthly king standing by, with a massive, powerful army behind him, while a small mob murdered his son?

Kings are the ultimate authority in kingdoms over which they reign. God is the ultimate authority over all kings and all kingdoms. While He is lenient and merciful, the Psalmist in Psalm 2:10 -12, warns us never to take this King for granted: **And now be wise, O kings; be instructed, O judges of the earth. Serve Jehovah with fear, and rejoice with trembling. Kiss the Son, lest He be angry, and you perish *from* the way, when His wrath is kindled in but a little time. Blessed *are* all who put their trust in Him.** Jeremiah also warns us that the everlasting King is to be feared: **But Jehovah *is* the true God, He *is* the living God, and the everlasting King. At His wrath the earth shall tremble, and the nations shall not be able to stand His fury** (Jeremiah 10:10).

## What is God Like?

When God's patience runs out and when mercy ends, Revelation 6:15-17 records that all men will answer for the sins they have committed. The sin of refusing to acknowledge Him as their King will meet with His wrath: **And the kings of the earth, and the great men, and the rich, and the chief captains, and the mighty men, and every bondman, and every freeman, hid themselves in the dens and in the rocks of the mountains. And they said to the mountains and rocks, Fall on us and hide us from *the* face of Him sitting on the throne, and from the wrath of the Lamb; for the great day of His wrath has come, and who will be able to stand?**

God rules His kingdom like a king. He will not tolerate any threat to His absolute authority. He does not allow democratic rule and is not swayed by majorities, mobs, armies or politics. He is not against destroying the very people He created and loved once their sin reaches a certain depth. Proof of this is in the fact that He has already destroyed the entire population of the earth once, except for eight righteous members of Noah's family.

For thousands of years God has watched the rise and fall of one kingdom after another. There have been very few ruled in a manner that was pleasing to Him. One that did please God was that of King David. During his reign, the nation of Israel flourished like no other and the people enjoyed safety, peace, and wealth like none before or after. (Solomon enjoyed all that his father had set up for him and God blessed him because of His promise to David. Solomon, however, did not follow the heart of God like David did.) This all resulted from the fact that King David recognized Jehovah as his King and from his heart, tried earnestly to worship Him. One day, the King of kings will usher in a brand new kingdom, under David, a man after His own heart (Jeremiah 30:9; Ezekiel 34:23). In this final kingdom He has plans to bless His subjects with every kind of pleasant thing imaginable and added to that will also erase all memories of their past misery on earth:

> **And the ransomed of Jehovah shall return and come to Zion with songs and everlasting joy on their heads; they shall obtain joy and gladness, and sorrow and sighing shall flee away** (Isaiah 35:10).
>
> **For the Lamb who is in the midst of the throne will feed them and will lead them to *the* fountains of living waters. And God will wipe away all tears from their eyes** (Revelation 7:17).

At the moment, the King is allowing earthly rulers, many of them under Satan's influence, to rule the earth. The day is coming however, when this will end and He will take complete authority: **And out of His mouth goes a**

**sharp sword, so that with it He should strike the nations. And He will shepherd them with a rod of iron. And He treads the winepress of the wine of the anger and of the wrath of Almighty God** (Revelation 19:15). The first time He came to earth, Scripture used a meek lamb to symbolize Him. The next time He comes, He will be symbolized by a lion. During His first visit He showed mercy, compassion, forgiveness and long-suffering. The next time He will be using a rod of iron and will be far more the Lion than the Lamb.

# 38 GOD HAS A PROBLEM WITH KNOWLEDGE

God knows that we need some knowledge to survive the next few minutes. Without some knowledge, we could be killed crossing the street and without a knowledge of how to obtain food we would starve to death. Without knowledge we would know nothing of Him, so He obviously approves of some kinds of knowledge. What then, was the problem with the Tree of the Knowledge of Good and Evil? Why such drastic punishment for taking fruit from that tree?

Genesis 2:17 clearly tells us that there was something foreboding about the fruit from the tree in the midst of Adams garden: . . . **but you shall not eat of the tree of knowledge of good and evil. For in the day that you eat of it you shall surely die.** Through them, slow physical death entered the world and affected all living things. Additionally, the moment they ate, they died a spiritual death, and only the born again experience could rescue them, or us, from such death. We know that this tree was not loaded with dictionaries, encyclopedias, or commentaries. It did bear some kind of fruit which is described as Eve saw it, after she had swallowed Satan's lie—hook, line and sinker: **When the woman saw that the fruit of the tree was good for food and pleasing to the eye, and also desirable for gaining wisdom, she took some and ate it. She also gave some to her husband, who was with her, and he ate it** (Genesis 3:6 NIV).

Here is a good translation of the verse that describes the tree: **And out of the ground made Jehovah God to grow every tree that is pleasant to the sight, and good for food; the tree of life also in the midst of the garden, and the tree <u>of the knowledge</u> of good and evil** (Genesis 2:9 ASV).

All we know about this "Knowledge" tree from the two verses above is as follows:

1. It was a tree that Eve could SEE (It was in a fixed place in the middle of the garden, not spiritual or invisible).

2. It was pleasant to the eye. Eve saw it as pleasant and God said it was.

3. It was good for FOOD. Eve saw that it was and God said that it was.

4. She could PICK the food. If she picked it, so it was tangible and real.

5. She could EAT the fruit. She ate it and lived, the actual fruit did not kill her or make her sick.

Before she ate, everything was good, evil was nonexistent as far as Adam and Eve were concerned. After they ate, they became aware of good *and* evil, and they certainly had knowledge of it. They obtained this knowledge by eating the fruit from The-Tree-Of-The-Knowledge-Of-Good-And-Evil (which is exactly how the Message Bible translates it).

The immediate results from eating the forbidden fruit were:

1. They both saw their nakedness.

2. Satan, who started it all, was cursed.

3. God placed a deep hatred between Satan and the seed of Eve.

4. The earth was cursed for Adam's sake and he was introduced to sorrow.

5. God prevented them from eating of the Tree of Life (a Redemption Plan had to be instigated before man would be allowed to eat of the Tree of Life).

6. They were driven from their home.

They now had the knowledge of good *and* evil. Prior to touching the forbidden tree, everything that God had created in their world was good. Everything changed when man took it upon himself to know evil. Put simply, knowledge of evil is when one partakes of, or indulges in it. The tree was just a symbol. If God had decided not to use a tree as a symbol He may have just told Adam "Don't *sin*." God put two trees in the garden to symbolize the freedom of a free will. He could have placed the forbidden tree on Mars, out of their reach, but He didn't, He placed it in the middle of their garden. He could have commanded Satan never to go near Eve, or better yet, He could have locked him up on Pluto. But none of these things would have enabled free will to be exercised. The tree was a test. Obey or disobey, it's our choice.

# 39 GOD IS A FIGHTER

God is referred to as a warrior in the Bible. He believes in war, participates in war, uses war for His own purpose, prepares and equips His children for war. Ultimately, His kingdom will win the final war. **Jehovah goes out as a warrior, He stirs up zeal like a man of wars; He shouts, yea, roars; He overcomes His enemies** (Isaiah 42:13). In the New Living Translation of the Bible God is referred to 260 times as the Lord of Heavens Armies. This means He has more than one army. Be it a spiritual or physical conflict, He is well equipped to wage war.

God went through a war in Heaven: **And there was war in Heaven. Michael and his angels warring against the dragon. And the dragon and his angels warred, but did not prevail. Nor was place found for them in Heaven any more** (Revelation 12:7).

His wars are based on righteousness and justice: **And I saw Heaven opened. And behold, a white horse! And He sitting on him was called Faithful and True. And in righteousness He judges and makes war** (Revelation 19:11).

When He ordered Israel to go to war, He was their Commander-In-Chief. He had real battle plans with which He rained down havoc on the enemies of Israel:

> **For My Angel shall go before you and bring you in to the Amorites, and the Hittites, and the Perizzites, and the Canaanites, and the Hivites, and the Jebusites. And I will cut them off** (Exodus 23:23).

> **Jehovah your God will go over before you. He will destroy these nations from before you, and you shall possess them** (Deuteronomy 31:3).

> **And it shall be, when you hear a sound of marching in the tops of the weeping trees, then you shall go out to battle. For God has gone forth before you to strike the army of the Philistines** (1 Chronicles 14:15).

His Holy Spirit also has a dangerous fighting side as Isaiah 63:10 indicates: **But they rebelled, and troubled His Holy Spirit; therefore He was turned** *to be* **their enemy,** *and* **He fought against them.**

In a song, Moses and Israel describes God as a warrior: **Jehovah** *is* **a Man of war; Jehovah** *is* **His name** (Exodus 15:3).

David, the war hero, was trained in God's boot camp and saw God as an all-powerful fighter: **Who** *is* **this King of glory? Jehovah strong and mighty, Jehovah mighty in battle** (Psalm 24:8). David also acknowledged God as his instructor and the source of his strength during battles: **He teaches my hands to war, so that a bow of bronze is bent by my arms. For You have girded me with strength for the battle; You have humbled under me those who rose up against me** (Psalm 18: 34, 39).

Why would God be a warrior? Why not speak the Word and simply destroy all of His enemies? He *does* have that kind of power. By the word of His mouth, all things were created, and by the same word they could all be eliminated. After all, who is capable of putting up any kind of real fight against God? What is it about war that would prompt God to put His precious children in such a dangerous environment where men are bent on killing each other? Why would He deliberately allow an enemy into the home or the same country where His saints live and let them fight it out? How could a God of love, who laid down the life of His own Son as proof, subject them to a powerful enemy like Satan; an enemy who has enough power and ambition that he even tried to take God Himself off His throne?

God is a warrior entirely for our sakes. Satan took property and peace from our forefather Adam, and it's our responsibility to take it back—by war! Satan does not intend to give up anything he stole without a fight. This is what Jesus meant in Matthew 11:12 when He said: **And from the days of John the Baptist until now the kingdom of Heaven is taken by violence, and the violent take it by force.** There is no negotiation in this war!

God takes this war very seriously, and knew His people would need training in the art of warfare. With His might and power, He could have wiped the Promised Land clean of all enemies before His people arrived. He could have used insects to clear every nation who occupied the land like He did in Exodus 23:28, where he used hornets to do the job. He could have engineered supernatural victories as He did when He flattened Jericho. However, God saw the necessity of teaching Israel how to fight and left enemies in the land for the sole purpose of giving Israel experience in battle:

**So then, the LORD left some nations in the land to test the Israelites who had not been through the wars in Canaan. He did this only in order to teach each generation of Israelites about war, especially those who had never been in battle before. Those left in the land were the five Philistine cities, all the Canaanites, the Sidonians, and the Hivites who lived in the Lebanon Mountains from Mount Baal Hermon as far as Hamath Pass** (Judges 3:1-3 GNB).

The primary skill they would learn during these wars was to rely upon their God and place their faith in His power. He always promised to go before them: **For My Angel shall go before you and bring you in to the Amorites, and the Hittites, and the Perizzites, and the Canaanites, and the Hivites, and the Jebusites. And I will cut them off** (Exodus 23:23). The commanding angel mentioned here was evidently a very capable warrior. On another occasion God sent a warrior angel, possibly the same one, into the Assyrian army camp and here is what ensued: **And it happened that night, the Angel of Jehovah went out and struck a hundred and eighty-five thousand in the camp of the Assyrians. And they arose early in the morning, and behold, they were all dead bodies** (2 Kings 19:35). I am positive the angel didn't even break a sweat.

We know from the above Scriptures and the words of Jesus that war is imminent. There is no way to avoid it. Jesus clearly states who the enemy is and what he is up to: **The thief does not come except to steal and to kill and to destroy** (John 10:10). One might not declare war when something is stolen, but killing and destroying is grounds for war. Although God is continually protecting us and has built "hedges" around us, as He did for Job, He clearly intends for us to stand up and fight.

We clearly have problems with this kind of war. It is also apparent that we have not taken back all that the enemy has stolen. But thankfully, God has not given up on us. One surefire way to instigate a full-fledged war between us and Satan is to allow problems in our path. That was His method in teaching the Israelites. He left eight 'problems' in their camp as we saw in Judges 3. These people were left to cause conflict with the sole purpose of teaching the Israelites to learn how to fight and overcome enemies: **And I also said, I will not drive them out from before you, but they shall be thorns in your sides, and their gods shall be a snare to you** (Judges 2:3).

Our problems are very similar. God left Satan in our nations, in our churches, in our homes and in our lives to cause trouble and war with the sole purpose of teaching us to be victorious over our enemy. Here is the proof:

> **For everything that has been born of God overcomes the world. And this is the victory that overcomes the world, our faith** (1 John 5:4).
>
> **But in all these things we more than conquer through Him who loved us. For I am persuaded that neither death, nor life, nor angels, nor principalities, nor powers, nor things present, nor things to come, nor height, nor depth, nor any other creature, shall be able to separate us from the love of God which is in Christ Jesus our Lord** (Romans 8:37-39).
>
> **I write to you, fathers, because you have known Him** *who is* **from** *the* **beginning. I have written to you, young men, because you are strong, and the Word of God abides in you, and you have overcome the evil one** (1 John 2:14).

All soldiers who go to war must face the possibility of death. That is what war is about—kill or be killed. Wars are not about politics, logistics, transportation, training or even weapons; it is ultimately about killing. No soldier in his right mind would sincerely believe he is immortal. However, in God's order of things even if we die, we still win because of what Christ did to purchase our lives. If we die trying in this flesh, it only means that our short journey and its wars are over, and we go on to something much better. And remember this: in the next life there will be no mortal flesh, no Satan, and no more war.

Obviously, only a few soldiers in God's war are called to be actual martyrs. Usually they are the ones at the front lines. For the remainder of us the war is unique indeed. To enter His war we have to die *first*. Jesus, the greatest warrior, put it this way: **No one has greater love than this, that a man lay down his life for his friends** (John 15:13). In His war against the kingdom of darkness He laid down His life and put an end to Satan's power. The death that we are all required to partake of is mentioned in Romans 6:11 by Paul: **Likewise count yourselves also to be truly dead to sin, but alive to God through Jesus Christ our Lord.** A warrior who is already dead fears nothing.

War is the most horrible activity on earth. Men meet with the primary purpose of killing one another. Soldiers understand, it is kill or be killed. Generals will often order their men into places where they often know that they will not live out the day, but they send them anyway. The killing must continue until there is a winner. Men will kill other men; wives will be made widows; children will become orphans. The fear, hate, pain and suffering caused by war are indescribable. However, the war that God orders us to enter into today is different—it's spiritual.

First, He took care of our enemy Himself by destroying his works and his power: **The one who does what is sinful is of the devil, because the devil has been sinning from the beginning. The reason the Son of God appeared was to destroy the devil's work** (1 John 3:8 NIV). Then, as 1 Corinthians 15:54-55 tells us, He took care of the death that Satan instigated: **But when this corruptible shall put on incorruption, and when this mortal shall put on immortality, then will take place the word that is written, "Death is swallowed up in victory. O death, where *is* your sting? O grave, where *is* your victory?"** Finally, He told us the outcome of the war: we are going to win: **Ye are of God, little children, and have overcome them: because greater is he that is in you, than he that is in the world** (1 John 4:4 KJV).

As God went before the Israelites, so Jesus goes ahead of us: **I have spoken these things to you so that you might have peace in Me. In the world you shall have tribulation, but be of good cheer. I have overcome the world** (John 16:33). War is not nearly as scary as it might be if we truly believe that God is at the front of the battle and we are fully protected somewhere behind Him. God clearly tells us who will win and who will lose:

> **For every child of God defeats this evil world, and we achieve this victory through our faith** (1John 5:4 NLT).
>
> **I saw before me what seemed to be a glass sea mixed with fire. And on it stood all the people who had been victorious over the beast and his statue and the number representing his name. They were all holding harps that God had given them** (Revelations 15:2 NLT).

In the days of Joshua, God left eight enemies inside the borders of Israel, to teach them the skills of war. During this time Israel was required to make bows and arrows, swords and every weapon of war they could invent. Then they were required to train themselves in the use of these weapons if they hope to beat the enemy in battle. We know from 1 Corinthians 10:11 that the Old Testament was given to illustrate our spiritual walk as the Israelites walked it out physically: **And all these things happened to them *as* examples; and *it* is written for our warning on whom the ends of the world have come.** So how do we learn war today? How do we obey our Warrior God and train for war? First, we have to acknowledge that there is a war. Jesus said we have an enemy that is out to steal from us and kill us in John 10:10. The New

Testament is filled with instructions for our modern day, spiritual warfare. Here is a very brief five step war plan:

1. FOLLOW THE LEADER

    Jesus has offered to lead us in this war. However, there is a catch, to follow Him you must die first on some sort of a cross: **Then Jesus said to His disciples, If anyone desires to come after Me, let him deny himself and take up his cross and follow Me** (Matthew 16:24). Cowardly soldiers will not follow the leader because of their fear, and are often punished or shot. Dead soldiers have no fear; they are past that.

2. PUT ON PROTECTIVE GEAR

    Soldiers do not supply their own equipment and this is true for the follower of Christ: **Therefore take to yourselves the whole armor of God, that you may be able to withstand in the evil day, and having done all, to stand. Therefore stand, having your loins girded about with truth, and having on the breastplate of righteousness and your feet shod with the preparation of the gospel of peace. Above all, take the shield of faith, with which you shall be able to quench all the fiery darts of the wicked. And take the helmet of salvation** (Ephesians 6:13-17). If this is the protection that He designed for His warriors, we can be sure that it is adequate and will offer all the protection we need.

3. PICKUP THE ULTIMATE WEAPON

    Soldiers depend on their weapons. How much more so should we have confidence in this one: **and take . . . the sword of the Spirit, which is the Word of God** (Ephesians 6:17). Your enemy, no matter how big, is no match for the Word of God. It is used as a sword and, when memorized, can be used to both anchor us and to cut down our enemy when needed.

4. IDENTIFY THE ENEMY

    **Be sensible *and* vigilant, because your adversary *the* Devil walks about like a roaring lion, seeking someone he may devour** (1 Peter 5:8). Satan is ineffective and somewhat harmless once his cover is blown. His most trusted weapon is a lie and the truth contained in the Word of God is a weapon he fears.

5. CALL IN THE TROOPS

We can handle most of the normal skirmishes in life by the power of the Holy Spirit, but often we need to go on the offensive and declare war on the enemy. When he snatches our health, our finances, or a family member, we must rise up and take back what he has stolen. This is why God wants us trained in warfare. In the book of Judges we see that once Israel was trained and ready, they were required to declare war and conquer their enemies. All too often they refused to do this and suffered years of misery, simply because the enemy was allowed to live among them. Nobody likes war, spiritual or physical, and we can make all kinds of excuses for not declaring one: it is the harvest season and we have to get the crops in; life is busy and there is so much to do; the enemy is of no immediate threat to us; after all, no one has actually declared war. There are millions of excuses that could distract them (and us) from being obedient. Meanwhile the Israelites (and Christians) tolerate the enemy in our midst and when that happens there is suffering. Often, it was only when God saw their misery and His heart would be touched with compassion that He would intervene for them. He would then inspire a leader to declare war and deliver them. He will do this for us too, and for the same reason: compassion. God expected them to learn how to fight and declare war when any member of the family was oppressed. This is also what He expects of us. When Israel would finally rise up and declare war on an enemy, they called the troops together and went out and won every war, with the Lord going before them.

When an enemy discovers that he can pick on you because you are all alone, he will do it. Satan is no gentleman and will take unfair advantage any time he sees the opportunity, but He is no match for Christians when they get together in unity and become militant. It's this kind of unity that God was promoting in this verse: **And five of you shall chase a hundred, and a hundred of you shall put ten thousand to flight. And your enemies shall fall by the sword in front of you** (Leviticus 26:8). When the battle is big—call in the troops.

God intends to test and prove us by our willingness to declare and participate in war. For most of us, declaring war is the last resort. It means total and absolute commitment. It is so easy to refrain from this kind of aggression when we have a choice to play it safe. It's easy to ignore a brother on the other side of town when Satan, the bully, comes into their home and wrecks it, takes a teenager, or destroys a marriage. It is easy to stay put when a member of the church has a fatal sickness. But suppose we loved enough, cared enough, and had enough unity among us, then we, the Church, would rise up and declare war on the enemy when he comes to steal, kill and destroy. There is every indication that this is what Paul is teaching in 2 Corinthians 10:4 (NIV): **The weapons we fight with are not the weapons of the world. On the contrary, they have divine power to demolish strongholds.**

If we used the five step war plan, along with the power of intense prayer and fasting, is there any way that an enemy could stop the Church? Not according to the guarantee Jesus gave Peter in assuring him that Hell would go down in defeat when faced with His Church: **And I also say to you that you are Peter, and on this rock I will build My church, and** *the* **gates of hell shall not prevail against it** (Matthew 16:18).

Prayer and fasting, at first glance, do not seem all that difficult—especially, when we picture someone else doing it. This is actually where our enemy excels in his offensive war. He has succeeded in stopping most of us dead in our tracks by preventing us from praying and fasting. With free access to your mind he has a million lies: "I'm just too tired (remember, his voice, in your mind, sounds just like your own thoughts); I will pray later; I can't fast while I am working; I get too weak physically when I fast; and—my personal favorite—"I will fast next week." The list goes on. As if that weren't enough, he has obstacles and stumbling blocks for your path. For the most part, he wages a pretty successful war. It's only when our wise Father lets enough pain into our lives that we finally wake up and declare war. Then we force Satan to pack up and leave.

# 40 GOD IS SILENT

Most of the time, it seems God keeps silent. I don't know about you, but God's silence troubles me. I like to *see* someone when I am talking to them, and more important, I like it when they *respond* to me when I'm talking. But God is silent. Humans communicate verbally and visually. When either of these two methods is absent, we frequently miss what is being communicated. Talking to someone on a telephone is strictly verbal and we miss all the facial expressions and body language. Ray Birdwhistell estimates that 65 to 70% of our communication is nonverbal (Young Page 116). So, if by not seeing God, are we are missing out on 70% of the communication, and if we don't hear His audible voice, is there any communication taking place at all? As we discussed in chapter 23, *God is a Good Communicator*, God's ways of communicating are different from ours. He explained this to us in Isaiah 55:8: **For My thoughts *are* not your thoughts, nor your ways My ways, says Jehovah.**

I am not the only one who has a problem with God's silence. David in a time of despair made this plea to God: **I will cry to You, O Jehovah; my Rock, do not be deaf to me, lest, *if* You be silent to me, I become like those who go down into the pit** (Psalm 28:1). Isaiah 64:12 records a similar complaint: **Will You restrain Yourself over these *things*, O Jehovah? Will You be silent and sorely afflict us?** We know from the Bible, that our Creator did not put us here on earth just to give us the cold shoulder. In fact, the opposite is true—we were created to have fellowship with Him. Zephaniah indicates something much deeper and emotional is taking place when He is silent: **Jehovah your God *is* mighty in your midst; He will save, He will rejoice over you with joy; <u>He is silent in His love</u>; He rejoices over you with joyful shout** (Zephaniah 3:17).

So, why the silence? It's possible that if Adam and Eve had not sinned, one-on-one, face-to-face communication would have continued. When they sinned, they broke that intimate kind of fellowship. There were few times after that when God had audible, verbal conversation with anyone. Moses was one of those exceptions. The day Adam and Eve died spiritually, perfect communication ceased, just as God had warned. To get back to that original place of perfect communication Adam and Eve would have had to be reborn as Jesus described in John 3:3 to Nicodemus: **Jesus answered and said to him, Truly, truly, I say to you, Unless a man is born again, he cannot see the kingdom of God.** In the Garden of Eden, no provision had yet been made for the forgiveness of their sins because Jesus had not been offered as a sacrifice for their sin, so God made a temporary sacrifice by killing the first animal and using its skin to cover their nakedness (or sin). From that day on, communication would be via the spirits—ours and His. Here are some Scriptures that prove this:

> **For as many as are led by *the* Spirit of God, they are the sons of God. The Spirit Himself bears witness with our spirit that we are the children of God** (Romans 8:14, 16).
>
> **And he who keeps His commandment dwells in Him, and He in him. And by this we know that He abides in us, by the Spirit which He gave to us** (1 John 3:24).
>
> **By this we know that we dwell in Him, and He in us, because He has given us of His Spirit** (1 John 4:13).

Until we learn to communicate with Him in the Spirit, we are met with this apparent silence. Audible, verbal communication represents a fleshly communication. God speaks to few people in an audible voice, but His most common means is via the Spirit. One of the best methods to learn to do this is to sit and listen and sometimes, pray.

# 41  GOD IS ROMANTIC

Russell Kelfer said that God is an incurable romantic (2002). He invented it and knows what real romance—the kind where one would die for the other—is all about. 1 John 4:7 assures us He is all about love: **Beloved, let us love one another, for love is of God, and everyone who loves has been born of God, and knows God. The one who does not love has not known God. For God is love.** Jesus is God in the flesh, and in John 15:12, speaks of His love for us like this: **This is My commandment, that you love one another as I have loved you. No one has greater love than this, that a man lay down his life for his friends.** And He did.

He created mankind out of love and His greatest desire is that man would love Him. As Creator, He sets Himself up to be their first love. He did this by issuing the first commandment: **You shall have no other gods before Me.** Jesus, quoting Exodus 20:3, put it this way: **"and you shall love the Lord your God with all your heart, and with all your soul, and with all your mind, and with all your strength"** (Mark 12:30).

Paul describes the intensity of that love in Romans 8:38. There is nothing like it on earth: **For I am persuaded that neither death, nor life, nor angels, nor principalities, nor powers, nor things present, nor things to come, nor height, nor depth, nor any other creature, shall be able to separate us from the love of God which is in Christ Jesus our Lord.** If we could fully comprehend this kind of love, what would it do to us? I believe it would send us to our knees for weeks or even months crying out our gratitude and pouring out our worship to Him and His Son.

God wants to be loved and will reward those who love Him: **Therefore, know that Jehovah your God, He *is* God, the faithful God who keeps covenant and mercy with them that love Him and keep His commandments, to a thousand generations** (Deuteronomy 7:9). The author of Hebrews 11:6 puts it this way: **But without faith it is impossible to please Him, for he who comes to God must believe that He is and that He is a rewarder of those who diligently seek Him.** We often make the mistake of seeking His "things" and not seeking the Maker of the things.

Through the prophet Jeremiah, God describes the intensity and duration of His love for us: **Jehovah has appeared to me from afar, saying, Yea, I have loved you with an everlasting love; therefore with loving-kindness I have drawn you** (Jeremiah 31:3).

Paul Billheimer in his book *Destined for the Throne*, explains God's love to be at the heart and sole purpose of all creation: "From this it is implicit that romance is at the heart of the universe and is key to all existence. From all eternity God purposed that at some time in the future His Son should have an Eternal Companion, described by John the Revelator as 'the bride, the Lambs wife' (Revelation. 21:9)" (Page 23). It is all about romance, lovers and a flashy, big wedding.

# 42 GOD EXPECTS MODERATION

God designed and gave us numerous gifts for our use:

> **And God blessed them. And God said to them, Be fruitful, and multiply and fill the earth, and subdue it. And have dominion over the fish of the sea and over the fowl of the heavens, and all animals that move upon the earth** (Genesis 1:28).

> **You made him rule over the works of Your hands; You have put all things under his feet: all sheep and oxen, yes, and the beasts of the field; the birds of the heavens, and the fish of the sea, and all that pass through the paths of the seas** (Psalm 8:6-8).

All was given freely, in abundance, and with no restrictions as to ownership. Regarding natural resources, He put no limitations on how much could be used or how we should use them. He has never exacted payment, or taxes of any kind, from anyone who taps into the wealth. God did require a tithe as specified in the Law, but this went toward financing and the upkeep for the Temple and wages for the Levites who cared for the Temple. There was no payment for any natural resource like sunshine, rain or the loaded fruit trees.

Any moderation we would choose to exercise in the use of these gifts would be left entirely up to us. Man was given plenty of food to eat but for the sake of his own health he would find it necessary to limit the amount he eats and to exercise caution as to what he eats. We would be required to moderate, not Him. When He designed physical resources, like minerals and oil, it was in limited quantities. Once they are gone there will be no more. He designed other things, like plants, animals, and trees, to multiply or replenish at a certain rate. He could have had designed crude oil to replenish itself, or plant life to multiply faster, but elected not to do so. He left the entire inventory for us to use and enjoy, but we will one day have to be accountable as to how we handled all this wealth.

He designed us to have recreation - in moderation. Recreational pleasure was involved when He said: **And God blessed them: and God said unto them, Be**

**fruitful, and multiply, and replenish the earth** (Genesis 1:28 ASV). First, any blessing would obviously have to be pleasurable. Second, to "be fruitful and multiply" referred to sexual intercourse, male with female. To replenish the entire earth this way would certainly mean lots of recreational pleasure. This special, pro-creational gift is given to each couple as a wedding present. It is still a common custom today, in every culture, to give presents to newlyweds. Used properly, in moderation and according to manufacturer's instructions, it will last a lifetime. No batteries required, no maintenance required, and it never goes out of style.

**Jehovah God took the man and put him into the Garden of Eden to work it and keep it** (Genesis 2:15). He gave Adam a job, which involved work, but this too was to be in moderation. When He gave him work, He meant for Adam to also stop work to engage in other activities. On this issue the Lord may have given a hint regarding the need to be moderate. While He did not initially command the man to take a day off after he had worked six, but He set the example by taking the seventh day to rest Himself: **And on the seventh day God ended His work which He had made. And He rested on the seventh day from all His work which He had made** (Genesis 2:2). We know God did not take the day off because He was tired or stressed out from six hard days of work, because God does not *get* tired. The suggested day of resting was for man's benefit. The day was all about fellowship, to talk, to reflect, to pray, to worship and have fun. Jesus explained the day of rest this way: **Then he said unto them, The Sabbath was made for man, and not man for the Sabbath** (Mark 2:27 NIV). We run into serious problems when we ignore moderation. When the Lord left it as a "suggestion" for Adam and his children to take the seventh day off, it didn't seem to work as a mere suggestion, because God later made it one of the Ten Commandments.

Paul teaches that we need to avoid extremes and practice restraint in all our dealings: **Let your moderation be known to all men. The Lord *is* at hand** (Philippians 4:5). When we choose to ignore moderation He has a way to help us get back on track. It's called chastisement.

# 43  GOD CREATED PERILS

Numerous resources were designed for our use and God placed them all at our disposal. He gave the entire earth with billions of things for us to discover on our own. He created numerous types of fish, plants, trees, fruits, herbs, chemicals, minerals and so on, but some are dangerous and could harm or kill us. Have you ever wondered how He expects us to avoid injury or death, should we accidently or carelessly stumble on some of them? And stumble on them we do. Apparently, this problem is left for us to solve. We are expected to use caution until we have explored to the point where we know whether they will benefit or harm us. God could have written a safety manual but instead He left it up to us to use our brains. None of earth's hazards have labels on them and He does not provide a WHMIS sheet with any of them (Workplace Hazardous Information System, instigated by governments to warn workers of hazards in the workplace).

Even though He created the entire earth for our benefit, we are required to learn the basic rules of safety on our own. Our sun is beautiful and useful, but also powerful and dangerous. Stay in its rays too long, it will burn you; don't eat certain plants, they could kill you; don't get too close to certain snakes, some are deadly; exercise caution around certain chemicals, they could blow up in your face; avoid poison ivy, quick sand, black widow spiders and scorpions. The list is long and they are not even listed in His Word as hazards. A limited few are mentioned in the Law of Moses as symbols, and even these were later removed from the "unclean list" when the Law was fulfilled under the New Covenant.

Among the many plants, trees and herbs He has placed at our disposal, some appear to be edible, but may in fact be extremely poisonous. They may not be good for eating, but they may be useful as medication. God did not tell us. He did not label them, even though He could have. God left it up to us to find out that the puffer fish and certain mushrooms are deadly poisonous. The lowly poppy seed is not mentioned in Scripture, and God does not give us any instructions as to what we should do with it. Yet it has become one of the most significant plants encountered by mankind. We have found that its seeds are an important food item and contain healthy oils that can be used in food and eaten. However, we can also make various drugs from the poppy, (opium and morphine) which can cause insomnia, visual hallucinations, nightmares, respiratory depression, miosis, sedation, itchiness, and euphoria. And, apparently this is exactly what some of us use the plant for and willingly risk the hazards to find a little artificial pleasure from this narcotic.

Cocaine, made from coca leaves, does strange things to the mind. It can cause paranoid thinking, violence, irritability, verbal and physical aggression. Additional symptoms include fatigue, lack of pleasure, anxiety, sleepiness, and sometimes agitation or extreme suspicion. Users throw caution to the wind and became oblivious to its destructive power, and once addicted can be likened to the walking dead. Drugs produced from this little plant have ruined millions of lives and have caused numerous governments to wage a war against its illegal use. Using morphine which comes from the poppy plant can also benefit us by easing pain during sickness. We just need sense enough to exercise caution.

The common grape can similarly be abused. We have learned to produce a likeable liquid from the grape that causes the brain to lose its ability to function and impairs the normal thinking process. It damages the liver and wrecks health and homes. Once addicted to alcohol, the user is trapped and finds it difficult to regain control of his life. Governments have cause to be concerned when, (in Canada) the cost for health care, law enforcement and lost productivity resulting from abuse of alcohol, illegal drugs and tobacco is now costing us $40 billion per year (Readers Digest March 2007). God put these plants on earth for our use. They can ruin our health and kill us or we could choose caution and use them for our benefit. He did give to every man a measure of wisdom, from which we would normally exercise caution.

There are also many natural laws, chemicals, and powerful forces in nature that He put at our disposal. They are ours to discover but with caution. Some are very dangerous and could kill such as the power of electricity or unleashing the power of chemicals such as nitroglycerin: very dangerous, but also very useful. We just need to practice caution in exploring its use.

Another significant item He has placed at our disposal is caffeine. We stumbled upon it centuries ago when we steeped the leaves from certain trees and made ourselves tea. We found it also in certain beans and we produced coffee. Certain soft drink manufacturers lace their drinks with caffeine. And do we ever love this stimulating drug in our drinks! In short order we find ourselves craving the stuff and soon we are so dependent on it that our central nervous system is demanding a fix every few hours. Once we've become dependent, the mind doesn't seem to function as well without it and we feel a bit miserable until we've get our fix.

In addition to dangers in our physical environment, God also permitted perils in our spiritual world. The earth is the home to the greatest peril of all: Satan and his hordes. They are permitted to harass and injure humans. They planned and executed the demise of Job's family and destroyed his property (Job 1:15-19). Job's wife saw enough misery from the hand of Satan that she advised her suffering husband to curse God and die. This unseen force will kill you, and steal from you as Jesus warned in John 10:10.

He did build into us a healthy fear of the unknown that automatically causes us to exercise caution. Even small children will make use of this early warning system to protect themselves from falling off a chair, if they have fallen off it once before. He expects us to be cautious to stay alive and remain healthy. Carefully learning by trial and error is acceptable and even expected. Wisdom, which is a God-given gift, will steer us toward caution. It is the key to our safety as David acknowledges:

> **I will bless Jehovah, who has given me wisdom; my heart also instructs me *in* the nights** (Psalm 16:7).
>
> **Behold, You desire truth in the inward parts; and in the hidden *part* You shall make me to know wisdom** (Psalm 51:6).

Amid all the dangers, and true to His nature, God provided for our protection by the use of the Scriptures, but first we have to learn how to use it. Not only did God place us in a potentially hostile environment, but He will deliberately place some obstacles in our path to teach us lessons as to the importance of His Word. How about circumstances that bring us to a place of dependency and trust? Deuteronomy 8:3 (GW) tells us He caused the Israelites to: **suffer from hunger and then fed you with manna, which neither you nor your ancestors had seen before. He did this to teach you that a person cannot live on bread alone but on every word that the LORD speaks.** On another occasion, God led them to a dangerous place where they could have died from thirst: **The whole Israelite community set out from the Desert of Sin, traveling from place to place as the LORD commanded. They camped at Rephidim, but there was no water for the people to drink** (Exodus 17:1 NIV). If you read the remainder of the chapter you will see that this was a test and another opportunity for Him to prove to His people that He could, and would, always take care of them.

Every trial and every pain encountered by a child of God has the sole purpose of teaching us to depend on His Word. For those who choose to believe and trust, there is protection and comfort in the words of Jehovah. Perils that we could encounter are too numerous to count. However, when we consider Psalm 91:2-13, we realize He has also made adequate provisions for our safety: **I will say of Jehovah, my refuge and my fortress; my God; in Him I will trust. Surely He will deliver you from the fowler's trap *and* from the destroying plague. He shall cover you with His feathers, and under His wings you shall trust. His truth *shall be your* shield, and buckler. You shall not fear the terror by night; nor because of the arrow *that* flies by day; *nor* for the plague *that* walks in darkness, of the destruction laying waste at noonday. No evil shall befall You, nor shall any plague come near Your dwelling. For He shall give His angels charge over You, to keep You in all Your ways. They shall bear You up in *their* hands, lest You dash your foot against a stone. You shall tread on the lion and adder; the young lion and the jackal You shall trample underfoot.**

The words of Jesus confirm that there is protection for believers: they will take up serpents; and if they drink any deadly thing, it will not hurt them (Mark 16:18). However, it is all based on faith. (Snakes and poisons are used to simply illustrate all dangers that are covered by having faith in Jesus.) We must believe that He said it and that He meant what He said.

Hazards are numerous, yet for the most part we continue to live in spite of them. Also, it is obvious that we live because of His grace. (I say obvious because if we were subject to law and not grace, we would be dead.) The promises above are based on faith; they work if you believe they will. Paul must have remembered the words of Jesus about picking up serpents, when He had an encounter with one: **And Paul had gathered a bundle of sticks, and laying *them* on the fire, a viper came out of the heat and fastened on his hand. And when the foreigners saw the creature hanging from his hand, they said to one another, No doubt this man is a murderer, whom, being saved from the sea, Justice has not allowed to live. Then indeed he shook off the creature into the fire, suffering no harm. But they expected him to become inflamed, or to fall down dead suddenly, But over much *time* expecting and seeing nothing amiss happening to him, they changed their minds and said that he was a god** (Acts 28:3-6).

The opposite of caution is carelessness. God does not appreciate carelessness and does not cater to those who are. With His power and wisdom there are many things He could do to resolve our lack of knowledge about the hidden dangers: He could audibly warn us every time we get close to some danger;

He could have our guardian angel intervene on our behalf; He could have signs posted near hazardous sites. Instead, we find that we must be vigilant lest we come to harm or even die for being careless.

We know He designed the earth with potential dangers and we have discovered we must exercise caution when roaming it. Why did He not make it perfectly safe? Why did He create so many hazards that can make living dangerous? Our planet is wonderfully and beautifully made. But the hidden snake in a fire is a good example of lurking dangers that are everywhere. It could also be quicksand, thin ice, a tropical hurricane, or a drunk driver on the highway. They all come as part of living on this planet. So, what lesson is our Heavenly Father trying to teach us in placing us in such a perilous environment? That is what the next chapter is about.

# 44 GOD DOES NOT LIKE INDEPENDENCE

God created man to be dependent upon Him. Dependence works well in a loving relationship, especially if one party is *all knowing and all powerful* and the other is not. If one party is full of love and mercy and the other is in great need of love and mercy, dependence becomes extremely important. I believe this is why God created an environment for us to live in that could be dangerous for us, as indicated in the preceding chapter. Dangers and hazards create dependence on the One who is able to deliver and guide us through the minefields of life.

God desires us to be under His wing so that He can protect us from all dangers. He made this promise to Jacob in a dream and it applies to all of us: **Yes. I'll stay with you, <u>I'll protect you wherever you go</u>, and I'll bring you back to this very ground. I'll stick with you until I've done everything I promised you"** (Genesis 28:15 MSG).

This world is rife with fear and anxiety, and 1 Peter 5:6-7 teaches that we have a way out of this as Christians: **Therefore be humbled under the mighty hand of God, so that He may exalt you in due time, casting all your anxiety onto Him, for <u>He cares for you</u>.** Proverbs 3:5 says that to whatever degree we think we are smart, it is not enough; we are smart when we learn to trust God: **Trust in Jehovah with all your heart, and lean not to your own understanding.**

Abraham, the father of those who practice faith, learned how to be dependent upon God: **Therefore *it is* of faith so that *it might be* according to grace; for the promise to be made sure to all the seed, not only to that which is of the Law, but to that also which is of *the* <u>faith of Abraham, who is the father of us all</u>** (Romans 4:16). Dependence is all about faith. In Genesis 22, Abraham is called upon to kill his only child and offer him as a human sacrifice to God. The image portrayed in this chapter is that of Isaac walking up to the altar his father had built. Although Isaac was bound by his father, there is no indication that he struggled or resisted his father's plan. With childlike faith and dependency, he trusted his father. Eventually his life was spared by the mercy of God. Meanwhile, Abraham was so dependent on God that he found it necessary to carry out such an order to offer his only son as a sacrifice. As far as Abraham and the angels who looked on were concerned, the boy Isaac was as good as dead, because Abraham intended to carry out the order. In his physical body, Isaac carried the seed for every Jew yet to be born. Therefore, every Hebrew yet to be born belonged to God because they were all offered to God on that day. This is why God had a right to have His way with the nation of Israel. They were His, because they had been offered to Him on an altar of sacrifice. His design was that they would be dependent upon Him and He would look after them.

Abraham was one of very few men who really understood that God, who is the giver of life, in this case Isaac's, had a right to claim that life. He also believed that if God took the boy's life, He could also raise him again from the dead: **Abraham had been promised that Isaac, his only son, would continue his family. But when Abraham was tested, he had faith and was willing to sacrifice Isaac, because he was sure that God could raise people to life. This was just like getting Isaac back from death** (Hebrews 11:18-19 CEV).

While these two humans stood beside the altar that day, totally independent of their own desires, something very significant happened in the history of mankind. One man became the spiritual father of all who would depend on God. The other became the physical father of the nation of Israel, the most remarkable and significant nation on earth in God's eyes.

Further, He intended to show the whole world how He wanted His kingdom to operate. He would demonstrate through Israel how He wanted things done. He gave His Commandments and Laws to the Jews to execute. God had a right to do this because Abraham had given Him the right by offering Isaac as a living sacrifice. This promise to the seed of Isaac is repeated numerous times in the Bible: **And I will walk among you and will be your God, and you shall be My people** (Leviticus 26:12). In teaching them, God would not always be gentle. Mercy, love and compassion were shown in abundance but when discipline was needed, it was delivered. His discipline confirmed that they were His, **for the Lord disciplines the one he loves, and he punishes every son he accepts as a child** (Hebrews 12:6 GNB). Through the pages of the Law, He made it clear that He would bless them when they obeyed and would curse them when they disobeyed. (An extensive list of blessings and curses are found in Deuteronomy 28.)

Later, Jesus climbed onto that "altar" and became a living sacrifice with the sole purpose of redeeming our selfish, independent souls. He willingly placed His Spirit into His Father's hands and died a horrible, painful death at the hands of a brutal mob: . . . **Christ loved us and gave himself up for us as a fragrant offering and sacrifice to God** (Ephesians 5:2 NIV).

We inherited an independent spirit from our ancestors, Adam and Eve. God had given them the option of being dependent upon Him, or they could partake of the Tree of Knowledge of Good and Evil and be independent of Him. When Satan approached Eve about the tree, he created a doubt in her mind as to the order that God had given. The suggestion was powerful and knowledge of good and evil seemed like a good thing to pursue. Eve decided to be independent of God and the law that He had issued. She took that bait, even though God attached a serious deterrent, "Eat that fruit and you die." Adam fell into the same trap and they both discovered that independence is a harsh road to travel. They did get knowledge, but without the Holy fellowship of God, it was not satisfying. Further, the penalty for their disobedience was spiritual death. Their loving Father came to their rescue and made a temporary atonement for their sin. The permanent solution came when, in extravagant love, He gave His only Son so that we could live with Him forever (John 3:16).

Independence nullifies grace. It should cause us to question ourselves why we would ever want to be independent from a God who offers such abundant grace as a free gift.

# 45 GOD IS AN ENVIRONMENTALIST

On the third day of creation God proclaimed the earth and its environment as *good*: **And God said, Let the waters under the heavens be gathered together to one place, and let the dry land appear; and it was so. And God called the dry land, Earth. And He called the gathering together of the waters, Seas. And God saw that *it was* good** (Genesis 1:9-10). What He called good could easily be classified as perfect to us.

God's first blessing was not pronounced over man; it was over the living creatures:

> **And God said, Let the waters swarm *with* swarmers *having* a living soul; and let birds fly over the earth on the face of the expanse of the heavens. And God created great sea-animals, and every living soul that creeps *with* which the waters swarmed after their kind; and every winged fowl after its kind. And God saw that *it was* good. And God blessed them, saying, Be fruitful and multiply, and fill the waters of the seas and let the fowl multiply in the earth** (Genesis 1:20-22).

Man received the second blessing in verse 28. The above verse comes from the Modern King James Version and speaks of the swarmers as having a soul. When He described the swarmers this way, was God saying they had feelings? Here are translations from seven other Bibles:

- and every living soul

- of living and moving thing

- the living creatures

- every living creature

- every type of creature that swims

- every living creature that moves

- every living soul that creeps and all the swarm of life in the waters

Not all use the word soul, which would indicate the presence of "feelings," but the common thread in all translations is life. All things He had created earlier such as mountains, planets and stars had no life in them, and did not receive any blessing that we know of. But things with life in them He blessed. In addition to life, it would not be surprising to find that these living creatures also have a soul similar to ours. Creatures that we bring into our homes like dogs and cats certainly have life and also seem to have feelings. Dogs, for example, are known to display feelings of excitement and fear. Even if they don't have a soul exactly like ours, they certainly have the capacity to hurt and "groan" as Paul points out in this verse: **And we know that the whole creation groans and travails in pain together until now** (Romans 8:22). Biologist Jonathan Balcombe writes a book about the emotive intelligence of elephants. He gives an illustration of how several elephants kept a comrade alive by placing food directly in her mouth after she had lost her trunk to a hunter's snare (Balcombe Page 136). What would prompt elephants to feed an injured buddy other than a caring soul? This sure deals a blow to "survival of the fittest," as touted by some.

The Lord must have loved the creatures He made with life in them. He demonstrates this by placing His blessing upon them and calling them good. One cannot imagine a God who *is* Love treating them any other way. After giving the animals to man, He later demonstrated His love for them by commanding that working animals get a day off from their toil and mentions them alongside the master, handmaid and strangers. Consider this verse that is written in Exodus 23:12: **You shall do your work six days, and on the seventh day you shall rest, so that your ox and your ass may rest, and the son of your handmaid, and the stranger, may be refreshed.**

In Jonah 4:11 (MSG), when God concluded that the city of Nineveh would be destroyed unless they repented, He reminded his stubborn prophet that He wanted to show compassion on the people *and* the animals: **So, why can't I likewise change what I feel about Nineveh from anger to pleasure, this big city of more than a hundred and twenty thousand childlike people who don't yet know right from wrong, to say nothing of all the innocent animals?** When God was about to call the Babylonians into account for their great wickedness, He prophesied through Habakkuk that the destruction of trees and animals were being recorded on their invoice: **You cut down the forest of Lebanon. Now** you will be cut down. You destroyed the wild animals, so now their terror will be yours** (Habakkuk 2:17 NLT).

He concerned Himself with the welfare of animals to the extent that He even commanded man to provide for the animals of the field: **But the seventh** *year* **you shall let it rest and let it alone, so that the poor of your people may eat. And what they leave, the animals of the field shall eat. In the same way you shall deal with your vineyard** *and* **with your olive yard** (Exodus 23:11). Animals of the field are often referred to as wild animals. This reference in Job 38:41 (NIV) indicates that God hears the cry of birds when they are hungry: **Who provides food for the raven when it's young cry out to God and wander about for lack of food?** An animal that works for us should feed at will, according to this command: **You shall not muzzle an ox when he treads out** *the grain* (Deuteronomy 25:4).

God obviously cares about the welfare of animals and commands that we treat them properly. **If a donkey is overloaded and falls down, you must do what you can to help, even if it belongs to someone who doesn't like you** (Exodus 23:5 CEV). The killing of animals was, and still is, extremely important to God. He gave explicit instructions as to how they were to be killed as sacrifices. They were to be respected and only used as food for man or as sacrifices to Him. He made both so He is in a position to dictate what should die and what should live. Leviticus 17:10-11 (MSG) warns that any person caught killing an animal and showing disrespect for its blood would be severely punished. **"If any Israelite or foreigner living among them eats blood, I will disown that person and cut him off from his people, for the life of an animal is in the blood. I have provided the blood for you to make atonement for your lives on the Altar; it is the blood, the life, that makes atonement."** Animals were given to us for sacrifices, for food and for our use, but never to be the object of abuse.

Likewise, the author of Proverbs suggests we show compassion toward animals: **A righteous man cares for the needs of his animal, but the kindest acts of the wicked are cruel** (Proverbs 12:10). Deuteronomy 20:19-20 should educate and encourage "tree huggers": **When you shall besiege a city a long time in making war against it to take it, you shall not destroy its trees by forcing an axe against them. For you may eat of them, and you shall not cut them down. For** *is* **the tree of the field a man that it should go before you to lay siege? Only the trees which you know that they** *are* **not trees for food, you shall destroy and cut them down. And you shall build bulwarks against the city that makes war with you, until it is subdued.**

We can easily conclude from these Scriptures that God placed high value on everything He blessed and that He cares deeply about the environment. It would also stand to reason that He would be concerned with the water His creatures live in, the air they breathe, the earth they live on and the food He originally provided for them. When He handed Adam the creatures to care for, we acquired the maintenance contract that goes with the creatures: . . . **subdue it; and have dominion over the fish of the sea, and over the birds of the heavens, and over every living thing that moveth upon the earth** (Genesis 1:28). God created Adam in his original state to reflect the image of God. A man in the image of God should behave like his Maker. It would be reasonable for God to expect that what He gave as a gift should be managed according to His standards. This was emphasized in Genesis 2:15: **And the LORD God took the man, and put him into the Garden of Eden to <u>dress it and to keep it</u>.** We are supposed to be custodians of the garden and everything in it. This law has never been rescinded.

After the flood, in Genesis 9:12 and 15, God made the same covenant with the earth (the environment), and all living creatures as He did with man: **And God said, This *is* the token of the covenant which I make between Me and you and every living creature with you, for everlasting generations: . . . and I will remember My covenant which is between Me and you and every living creature of all flesh; and the waters shall no more become a flood to destroy all flesh.** God ordered Noah to preserve two of every living thing from the previous creation but He drowned all the humans except Noah and his family. Only one male and female of every species of bird and animal made it through the flood with only a handful of humans. No reason is given for destroying the majority of animals and sparing only two of each species, (with the exception of Genesis 7:2 where "sevens" were spared) but a blessing is issued to the animals on the ark, along with humans.

When Adam sinned, Jehovah removed him from the garden where all of his needs would have been met without having to work by the sweat of his brow. He was driven out to work hard for his living. However, this seems not to be the case for the birds of the air and quite likely all animals. In Luke 12:24, Jesus explains that His Father personally provides for the birds, they do not have to labor and worry because God feeds them. His tender care toward wildlife is also demonstrated in these verses:

> **LORD God All-Powerful, my King and my God, sparrows find a home near your altars; swallows build nests there to raise their young. You bless everyone who lives in your house, and they sing your praises** (Psalm 84:3-4 CEV).

> Behold the birds of the air; for they sow not, nor do they reap, nor gather into barns. Yet your heavenly Father feeds them; are you not much better than they are? (Matthew 6:26).
>
> For only a penny you can buy two sparrows, yet not one sparrow falls to the ground without your Father's consent (Matthew 10:29 GNB).

Revelation 11:18 tells us the time is coming when God will call us into account as to how we treated the earth. Check this out: **And the nations were full of wrath, and Your wrath came, and the time of the judging of the dead, and to give the reward to Your servants the prophets, and to the saints, and to the ones fearing Your name, to the small and to the great, and to <u>destroy those destroying the earth</u>.**

From a practical viewpoint, nobody benefits from wastefulness and abuse. If resources are wasted, in the end we all suffer. God would require us to be good environmentalist like Himself. I agree with what many environmentalists are doing in trying to save wildlife and natural resources, because this is obviously in tune with what our Creator has always required. The only thing I cannot agree with is putting animal and plant life ahead of human life. Numerous programs, films, documentaries, talk shows and books are being produced to make us aware of the dangers of killing eagles and elephants, etc., but few of such are being produced that speak about the protection of human babies killed before birth. Surely a human life is of more value than any animal. Jesus made it clear as to the worth He placed on humans when He spoke these words: <u>**you** are worth more than many sparrows</u> (Matthew 10:31 NIV).

The Lord gave *humans* the entire earth, to use for our benefit. Once we understand this we can all get on with protecting the animals, the trees and the entire planet. We are hypocrites if we place more emphasis on wild life than we do human life; fix that bad attitude and we are likely to preserve both.

# 46 GOD IS THE ULTIMATE CREATOR

God has the unique ability and wisdom to create things by speaking them into existence. We cannot even begin to understand how this is done since God did not give man this kind of awesome power mentioned here: . . . **God who gives life to the dead and calls into being things that were not** (Romans 4:17 NIV). We can't raise the dead and we can't use *words* to call things into being. The best we can do is to assemble things that are already provided by God. Man can build a house but he cannot create a house. He does have the ability to assemble all its parts: lumber from trees and nails from ore that God created and so on. Even memory and imagination were created by God. A poet, when he writes a poem, must use a language that was authored by God. An artist must collect paint and canvas (materials for these provided by God), and then recall from his memory or copy something that God has already made. Try to imagine creating light. Where would you start? What ingredients would you require? How much of each would you add? If our finite minds did try to attempt such a task, the first impulse might be to collect some electromagnetic radiation, give it some intensity, add some frequency and polarization to produce light. But, as you can see, even then we would only be collecting the "ingredients" and copying what God already originated.

To truly *create*, you do not need to assemble anything. You simply speak the word and it all comes into being. God speaks a word and that entity represented by that word instantly appears. He spoke the word and planets were instantly formed; He spoke a word and the sun appeared; spoke a word and the elephant was instantly formed, alive and breathing. That's how He did it: **And God said, Let there be light. And there was light** (Genesis 1:3). Psalm 33:6 demonstrates the same creative power: **By the Word of Jehovah were the heavens made; and all the host of them by the breath of His mouth.** Not only did His Word bring it all into being, the writer of Hebrews 1:3 (CEV) says His Word keeps it all in place and in working order: **God's Son has all the brightness of God's own glory and is like him in every way. By his own mighty word, he holds the universe together.**

Another amazing fact about this kind of power to create is that He never duplicates anything. When we try to create we must make an effort to duplicate our designs for the sake of economy. We must always be conscious of budgets. If we manufacturer a plastic fork we make a mold and from it we hope to make thousands of forks. We cannot afford to make every fork different. If we make a car for consumers, economy dictates we reuse the design. However, when God makes a mere snowflake, no two in the entire universe are alike. Every mountain, grain of sand, donkey and rose bush are all different. He fabricated no molds and all were created different with a spoken word. Awesome!

In creating, God works to a plan and then brings the plan into being. In the beginning He started out with inanimate objects—planets and stars, etc.—then moved to plants and trees and things with life in them. On day five He created yet a more complex creature; one with life in its blood and a soul. Day six he created a man with life in his blood, a soul, and a spirit. This creature was made in the likeness of His Creator and would be classified as a spiritual being because God is Spirit: **God is Spirit: then let his worshipers give him worship in the true way of the spirit** (John 4:24 BBE). However, the plan would not be completed until God moved it up one more notch, to top it all off, so He created a woman. She would be the absolute crowning glory of all creation. In her very sophisticated body would grow earth's population. She would be beautiful to look at, desirable, equipped with a nurturing anatomy and temperament, be a helper second to none and every male would be allowed to have one. When her design rolled off the drafting table, God stopped creating; everything was complete. But as we know, she fell and man went with her. However, nothing takes the Ultimate Creator by surprise. His plans are never scrapped, He simply moves from the "Perfect Plan of God" to the "Permissive Plan of God." The Perfect Plan will kick in a bit later.

Meanwhile, God expects us all to fulfill the purpose for which we were created. Revelation 4:11(KJV) reminds us: **Thou art worthy, O Lord, to receive glory and honour and power: for thou hast created all things, and <u>for thy pleasure</u> they are and were created.**

# 47 GOD CREATED THE HUMAN WILL

The human will is a piece of work! Possibly nothing in the entire universe demonstrates His creativity and wisdom better; nothing is more amazing, complex and awe inspiring. He designed and built billions of them, all different and all of them equal in power. We all have one, but know little or nothing as to how it was made, or how it works. We just know it works.

Free will speaks volumes as to the nature and genius of God. Its existence proves that God has the ability to create anything He wants. It proves He is willing to share the power of self will with creatures other than Himself. And it proves that love, which is the dominant part of His nature, was the cause in creating such an awesome, powerful thing. Creating a human and giving it a will whereby the creature could reject its Creator was risky. But, out of a desire to love and be loved, He bestowed it anyway. God took the risk and is presently watching and waiting for billions of His loved ones to love Him in return. Here are some further details as to some of the characteristics of the free will, and how this masterpiece of creativity reflects on our great Creator.

Of all the billions and trillions of things that God created there was only one thing that He created that was risky. This thing, the will of angels and humans, had the potential to wreak havoc in His universe. We will deal only with the human will in this book. All the other things He created were stable and predictable and would do exactly as He had designed them to do. Trees would always be trees and fish would always be fish and would forever stick to their original design. Mountains, stars, planets, atoms and entire galaxies would never cause Him any grief. He knew that if He placed this thing called a "free will" in man there would be ginormous problems, but He did it anyway. Adam and Eve, the first two "free willers," made their choice very early to reject the will of God and do it their way. Judging by today's trends, it is possible that the majority of "free willers" would turn their back on Him and reject everything about Him. Certainly the majority of them turned their back on Him before He destroyed them in Noah's flood. The majority today, deny His very existence, some hate Him and some will even curse Him: **And they blasphemed the God of Heaven because of their pains and their sores. And they did not repent of their deeds** (Revelation 16:11). Regardless, He gives every "free willer" the option of rejecting or accepting Him. As far as God is concerned, this choice of options is the most important event happening on the earth at any given moment.

We are composed of a body, a soul and a spirit. We have a soul, we live in a body but we are a spirit. The body is obvious and tangible, finite in its dimensions, is easily recognizable and is measurable. The body functions through its five senses: taste; touch; sight; hearing; and smell. The soul is the seat of our emotions, with a wide range of spiritual, intangible, activity such as anger, joy, fear, and all the "feely" stuff. The human spirit contains the conscience, the imagination, the intellect, the memory and the will. The conscience is programmed by God to help us in deciding right from wrong. The imagination is the world's most creative tool. All things ever planned or designed, made or built, started in the "Imaginator." From a pair of socks to a cream pie; computers to super highways and space ships, to lowly tea cups; it all starts in the imagination. The intellect is designed to enable us to calculate, reason and understand the raw materials God put at our disposal and the memory enables us to retain or store this information.

The body and its five senses stop working with our physical death, but the soul and the spirit live on forever. (A glorified body, as in 2 Corinthians 5:1-4 & Philippians 3:21 (MSG), may well have senses but likely geared to sensing things in the Heavenly realm.) Whether the spirit lives in Heaven or Hell, it lives eternally. Redeemed spirits go to be with God and He has stated very clearly that our spirit and soul are everlasting: . . . **whosoever believes in Him should not perish, but have <u>everlasting life</u>** (John 3:15). And again, in John 6:54 we read: **Whoever partakes of My flesh and drinks My blood has <u>eternal life</u>, and I will raise him up at the last day.** It is obvious that our earthly body doesn't leave the planet, it is buried here and goes to rot. However, there is a mysterious transformation of the supernatural sort that takes place at death that Paul refers to here: **So also the resurrection of the dead. It is sown in corruption, it is raised in incorruption; it is sown in dishonor, it is raised in glory; it is sown in weakness, it is raised in power; it is sown a natural body, it is raised a spiritual body. There is a natural body, and there is a spiritual body** (1 Corinthians 15:42-44).

The Scriptures above, along with many others, refer to everlasting life—the good kind. Here are two that refer to the bad kind:

> **The Son of Man shall send out His angels, and they shall gather out of His kingdom all things that offend, and those who do iniquity, and shall cast them into a furnace of fire. There shall be wailing and gnashing of teeth . . . in flaming fire taking vengeance on those who do not know God and who do not obey the gospel of our Lord Jesus Christ, who shall be punished with <u>everlasting destruction</u> from the presence of the Lord and from the glory of His power** (Matthew 13:41-42; 2 Thessalonians 1:8-9).

Spirits never age, never get sick, are never damaged and once created, will never die. The soul does get damaged, hurt, broken and often needs to be restored. David made this statement regarding his soul in his famous 23$_{rd}$ Psalm: **He restores my soul; He leads me in paths of righteousness for His name's sake** (verse 3). It is likely that once in Heaven, where there is no sin and no Satan to tempt us, there will be no need for such maintenance of the soul.

Meanwhile, our spirit is ruled by our will. It makes every important decision for the inner man or the Spiritual Man. It can, if it decides to, order the soul and the body to do whatever it commands. It is the part of us that decides to follow God—or not. It decides to put the body through the ropes to train and strive to be first in a race. It commands the body to endure hardships and to ignore pain, if it so decides. It tells the soul to quit whining and get on with it. The soul may be down but the will can command it to get up, get revived, get over it and get moving.

The human will is designed to be the most powerful force on earth. Under the conditions laid out by God and in partnership with Him, it is more powerful than all the forces of Hell. The will contains the power to think and do. With this powerful gift, man is able to sit and plan incredible feats, from climbing the highest mountain, to visiting the moon, to conquering the earth. In the Old Testament, the people of Shinar had a united will to build a tower and assembled themselves to do so. Whatever ultimate evil they were up to, we are not sure, but God was concerned and came down and stopped them: **And Jehovah said, Behold! The people *are* one and they all have one language. And this they begin to do. And now <u>nothing</u> which they have imagined to do will be restrained from them** (Genesis 11:6).

Our will is the part of us that is most like our Father. It is the part of Him that we can identify with most. When Genesis 1:26 records, **And God said, Let Us make man in Our image, after Our likeness,** He was not referring to our height or weight or facial features; we are most like Him spiritually.

God watches and waits for the will to make the all-important decision as to whether it will love Him or reject Him. When He has the will of a man, He has the man.

Human bodies are complex, yet they can be touched, studied, measured, weighed and all the parts can be counted. There are thousands of studies and numerous books about the human body. The human will however, cannot be touched, weighed, measured, seen with the naked eye or examined by any medical or scientific instrument. Once created, they never wear out, there are no moving parts, and they last forever and ever. Regarding its longevity, it is the spirit, not the body, that is described in this verse, and the will is the dominate part of our spirit: **And I give to them <u>eternal life</u>, and they shall <u>never ever perish</u>, and not anyone shall pluck them out of My hand** (John 10:28). John 6:47 also tells us: **He who believes on Me has <u>everlasting</u> life.** This gift of everlasting life will be experienced by our spirit, but it is our will which determines whether we accept or reject this gift.

Our spirits are not electrical, chemical or magnetic and are not computerized. They operate 100% in the spiritual realm. We live in a body, we have a soul but *we are a spirit*. The human will is the ruling force of our spirit. It's the boss, the president and the governing force of each individual. The will is the seat of our power and all major decisions are made there. In our will we contain power to do or not do. As a triune being, our spirit, soul and body each have wants. The body wants food and fleshly pleasures; the soul wants peace, contentment and joy. The spirit has wants too and can select higher goals, the loftier ideas and spiritual satisfactions; or it can be complacent, let the taste buds rule and we become fat and sick.

Our will also controls the mind. The mind is like a sophisticated computer in some ways. It has memory, is teachable and susceptible to "viruses." The will makes the decisions as to what it will inject into the mind for it to learn and retain. It is also the basic decision of a lazy will to put nothing into the mind. It is very much like a computer in the sense of, "garbage in, garbage out." Paul said this regarding our mind: **For let this mind be in you which was also in Christ Jesus** (Philippians 2:5). By an act of my will I allow the mind of Christ to be mine. Further, if we allow Him, God is able to act out His will in us. This is confirmed in Philippians 2:13: **For it is God who works in you both to will and to do of His good pleasure.** All we have to do is to trust Him and give Him access.

The mind is also like a radio receiver with shared access—it's yours, but both God and Satan can tune in. The will decides which station it will tune into and who has to log out. Sometimes this can be confusing when we hear thoughts and are not sure who is speaking. Satan's voice is no different in accent, tone or volume than your own, or God's. Voices in the mind all sound alike and the stations are not labeled. Satan is a very crafty broadcaster and is far too shrewd to approach us in person because we would likely recognize him. His communication with us is drenched with deceit, condemnation and fear. Though I can't remember where, I once heard that Satan will feed you an ocean of truth to get you to swallow one lie. Jesus warns us about the Devil's forked tongue in a debate with the Pharisees: **You belong to your father, the devil, and you want to carry out your father's desire. He was a murderer from the beginning, not holding to the truth, for there is no truth in him. When he lies, he speaks his native language, for he is a liar and the father of lies** (John 8:44 NIV). The Bible teaches us that we can know who is speaking by aligning the voice with the Word of God.

It is interesting to note that in recent studies in psychiatry, patients who have been known to "hear voices" are now being coached by their therapists to confront the voice and flatly refuse to obey it. Seems scriptural to me. It reminds me of 2 Corinthians 10:5: . . . **pulling down imaginations and every high thing that exalts itself against the knowledge of God, and bringing into captivity every thought into the obedience of Christ.** Imaginations are thoughts that take place in our minds that are often placed there by Satan. When we realize they are there and know they are from Satan, we can take them captive and bring our mind into obedience to the thoughts of Christ. Paul teaches us how to fight the war inside the mind and to counteract such thoughts: **Finally, my brothers, whatever things are true, whatever things** *are* **honest, whatever** *things are* **right, whatever** *things are* **pure, whatever** *things are* **lovely, whatever** *things are* **of good report; if** *there is* **any virtue and if** *there is* **any praise, <u>think on these things</u>** (Philippians 4:8).

Our will is also the "knower" and the "I am" of our being. The will can function without the memory of things that pertain to our flesh and our environment. Many people have lost large portions of their memory having to do with their family, their occupation, their surroundings and even their name but their spirit continues to function. They know in their "knower" that they are still a living being and often, as an act of their will, take certain actions to regain their lost memories. Often the amount of will power applied will determine the ultimate outcome in regaining what was lost. Some individuals who have lost portions of memory have demonstrated that with will power they can retrieve some or all of their memory.

## What is God Like?

Several studies that I have encountered regarding the spirit, soul and body have suggested that the will is part of the soul, and that the soul is the dominate part of our being. I would like to disagree. Since we all seem to agree on the fact that the soul is the seat of our emotions, I contend that the soul is not a fitting place for the will. The human will has little or nothing to do with emotion. Often, it has to make important decisions related to the soul and its emotions. For example, after the loss of a loved one, there is a time of grief, and the soul undergoes a time of sorrow and pain. This is normal and healthy, and God gave us our soul for such a time. However, these emotions may not just disappear or fade away as time goes by. The will may have to make some quality decisions and say to your soul, "It's time to end the grieving, we must move on." The soul may feel as if it can't stop and want to continue grieving, but your will imposes the final decision. Some never discover this power of their will and their grieving goes on indefinitely and their life spirals downward into deeper depression.

An example of the soul being told what to do by the will is found in Psalms 42:5: **Why are you cast down, O my soul, and moan within me? Hope in God; for I shall praise Him *for* the salvation of His face**. In his soul he is hurting and moaning but his will makes a decision that he is going to change things, as an act of his will he is going to put his hope in God. In this verse he tells God how he is questioning himself and his will makes a decision that will uplift him: **Why, my soul, are you downcast? Why so disturbed within me? Put your hope in God, for I will yet praise him, my Savior and my God** (Psalms 43:5 NIV).

Here is one example of where our spirit must make an important choice and our will makes the final decision as to what we do. We know in our spirit that we must take care of our bodies. Our soul, the emotions department, will bear the brunt of our bad decisions if we don't. Bad decisions regarding our bodies bring depression, sadness, self-pity and a general state of poor mental health which in turn reflects on our physical bodies. Proper exercise and diet are the basic requirements for good health. If this decision were left to the body, which operates on the five senses, we most often find it eating too much and eating the wrong things. Then you can count on your body either being too tired, too weak or too lazy to exercise.

When our will takes control and makes a quality decision, it will tell the body it's not going to sleep in tomorrow morning. Kicking and screaming, if need be, it's going to get up and be at the gym by 6 am! And further, starting tomorrow, no more greasy fast foods and it will not be getting its daily dose of caffeine! (At this point you can be sure that your taste buds are in panic mode!) The good thing is that your soul will start to feel an immediate sense of relief. It starts to feel hope and the kind of depression that accompanies an unhealthy body starts to lift. Leave decisions about health to your feelings then your taste buds will be King of the Castle.

Abraham had a will that pleased God. When God gave him a command to offer his only son up as a sacrifice, Abraham's will was to obey. He had his will set to obey God no matter how hard and no matter what the consequences. Paul was also a man whose spirit and will were in control of his body, as indicated in this Scripture: **I discipline my body like an athlete, training it to do what it should. Otherwise, I fear that after preaching to others I myself might be disqualified** (1 Corinthians 9:27 NLT).

The Bible refers to the body and its five senses as the *outward man,* the *fleshly man* and the *carnal man.*

> **For this cause we do not faint; but though our outward man perishes, yet the inward *man* is being renewed day by day** (2 Corinthians 4:16).
>
> **But those belonging to Christ have crucified the flesh with *its* passions and lusts** (Galatians 5:24).
>
> **For the sinful nature is always hostile to God. It never did obey God's laws, and it never will. That's why those who are still under the control of their sinful nature can never please God** (Romans 8:7-8 NLT).
>
> **For ye are yet carnal: for whereas *there is* among you envying, and strife, and divisions, are ye not carnal, and walk as men** (1 Corinthians 3:3 KJV)?

Our spirit is the *inner man* or the s*piritual man:*

> **. . . that He would grant you, according to the riches of His glory, to be strengthened with might by His Spirit in the inner man** (Ephesians 3:16).
>
> **For I delight in the Law of God according to the inward man** (Romans 7:22).
>
> **. . . it is sown a natural body, it is raised a spiritual body. There is a natural body, and there is a spiritual body** (1 Corinthians 15:44).

The inner man is the one who responds to God; the one who comes alive at the moment of our salvation.

> **Likewise count yourselves also to be truly dead to sin, but alive to God through Jesus Christ our Lord** (Romans 6:11).
>
> **And He *has made you alive*, who were once dead in trespasses and sins** (Ephesians 2:1).
>
> **But because of his great love for us, God, who is rich in mercy, made us alive with Christ even when we were dead in transgressions it is by grace you have been saved** (Ephesians 2:4-5 NIV).

Satan comes at us via the flesh, or the carnal man:

> **For when we were in the flesh, the passions of sin worked in our members through the law to bring forth fruit to death** (Romans 7:5).
>
> **. . . because the carnal mind *is* enmity against God, for it is not subject to the Law of God, neither indeed can *it be*. So then they who are in the flesh cannot please God. But you are not in the flesh, but in *the* Spirit, if *the* Spirit of God dwells in you. But if anyone has not *the* Spirit of Christ, he is none of His** (Romans 8:7-9).

The human will is the most potent force on earth. When humans have a will to do so, they can bring down mountains, change the course of rivers, destroy kingdoms, build massive buildings, send men into outer space and build powerful computers and machinery that stagers the imagination.

The strength of our will ranges all the way from men with so little will power that they are content to live in poverty, to men with enough will power to conquer and rule nations. Its power ranges from men with so little they refuse to take a daily walk for the sake of their good health, to men who, by sheer will power, become the fastest runners on earth. Here is a good example of incredible will power: A young man, Terry Fox, age 22, who had suffered bone cancer, decided to raise money for cancer research by running. First, he trained and then set out to run across Canada. He conquered 5,373 kilometers (3,339 miles) and had to stop and be hospitalized due to lung cancer. Terry died from the cancer. Now the catch is that the 3,339 miles he ran to raise money was on one leg. Now that's will power! This power is a gift from God. It's in all of us; ours to use or relinquish in any way we choose.

When God created the human will, He designed it to function entirely on its own. Although He created it, knows all of its intricacies and would have the power and wisdom to crush it, He has determined to let the human will decide for itself what it wants. If God had reserved the right to interfere with man's will, it would no longer be man's will operating; it would be God's will. He has reserved for Himself the right to <u>influence</u> man's will but He never overpowers it. Ultimately, we have no control over our bodies, God could destroy it or allow sickness to ravage it or allow Satan to attack, but your will is all yours. In one sense, we have no control over our soul. If a loved one should die tomorrow, you have no control over that and your soul will do what souls are designed to do: it will experience a time of sorrow. We have no control over the amount of time we are given to live in our body. If God decides that your time is up tomorrow, there is nothing you can do about it. But exercising your free will is yours and yours alone. It is an amazing, awesome and perilous gift: perilous in that we can misuse it to our own destruction.

Let us suppose we exercised our wills with utmost prudence and wisdom. This would mean we never gave in to the flesh, but directed our soul and body only in accordance with things that the Designer approved of. Ultimately, this would be a kind of battle which is described in 2 Corinthians 10:3 by Paul: **For though walking about in flesh, we do not war according to flesh.** This war, fought in accordance with the Designers instructions, would have to be fought in this manner:

> **Put on the whole armor of God so that you may be able to stand against the wiles of the devil. For we do not wrestle against flesh and blood, but against principalities, against powers, against the world's rulers, of the darkness of this age, against spiritual wickedness in high *places*. Therefore take to yourselves the whole armor of God that you may be able to withstand in the evil day, and having done all, to stand. Therefore stand, having your loins girded about with truth, and having on the breastplate of righteousness and your feet shod with the preparation of the gospel of peace. Above all, take the shield of faith, with which you shall be able to quench all the fiery darts of the wicked. And take the helmet of salvation, and the sword of the Spirit, which is the Word of God, praying always with all prayer and supplication in *the* Spirit, and watching to this very thing with all perseverance and supplication for all saints** (Ephesians 6:11-18).

If we did what Paul instructs without faltering, waging a victorious war and measuring up to the purpose for which we were created, we may ask what life would be like. Would we be free of sickness, condemnation, depression and failures? What would our relationship with God be like? Would it be Utopia—heaven on earth? Who knows?! No man, except Jesus, has ever succeeded in living like that, and His will was set on doing His Father's will. The rest of us continue to struggle with this dual nature, the flesh and the spirit, and we are prone to failure.

Even Paul admits to these failures as he describes his own battle with the flesh in his letter to the Romans: **But I need something more! For if I know the law but still can't keep it, and if the power of sin within me keeps sabotaging my best intentions, I obviously need help! I realize that I don't have what it takes. I can will it, but I can't do it** (Romans 7:17-18 MSG). Thankfully, for Paul and for us, the solution to this dilemma is found in these verses 24 and 25: **I've tried everything and nothing helps. I'm at the end of my rope. Is there no one who can do anything for me? Isn't that the real question?** <u>**The answer, thank God, is that Jesus Christ can and does**</u>. **He acted to set things right in this life of contradictions where I want to serve God with all my heart and mind, but am pulled by the influence of sin to do something totally different.**

So, we see that to exercise this marvelous freedom of choice we must fight a part of our very own being. Nobody describes this battle better than Paul in Romans 7. In verse 24 he seems to scream out his frustration with the war going on inside him. God has provided the know-how from His Word, with equipment for protection and for offensive action when required, but we must *choose* to fight. Left alone, our flesh takes the lead. It seems so natural because that is the way we were born. This is what David meant in this verse: **Indeed, I was born guilty. I was a sinner when my mother conceived me** (Psalm 51:5 GW). God set it up so that we can exercise our freedom of choice by accepting the forgiveness of our sins through Jesus and, with the help of the Holy Spirit, win the war. Losing a few battles along the way is part of the teaching process.

To demonstrate the complexities of the human will, let's imagine that all the nations of the earth were in unity and decided to take on a project to construct a human. With the backing of large and small nations, they pooled their resources and offered every brilliant mind that is available from each country. Let's also pretend that money is no object. Entire nations have been given specific tasks. The US is required to construct the skeleton; Canada would produce the arms (you know—Canadarm); Japan will construct the brain; Russia will produce two eyes and United Kingdom will produce the heart, and so on. Let us also imagine that since some nations are already producing artificial intelligence and artificial limbs that in 50 years or so all of them, with combined efforts are able to complete their task and on a certain day they meet in a New York hospital to assemble all the parts.

After a few weeks, with the help of the best surgeons and doctors in the world, there on the operating table lies the body of a human being. The chief doctor is given the honor of testing this incredible being. He checks all the measurements, checks for blood flow and heartbeat, etc., and all seems to be working. A tap with a little hammer to the kneecap and other parts of the body proves the reflexes are all working as expected. Someone jabs him with a small needle in the leg and the creature jerks appropriately. Another fires a starter pistol near his head and the response is good, they know the hearing works. They feed him Buckley's cough medicine and watch him contort and shudder—taste buds working fine. The tests continue, and they conclude that the body seems to be in working order so they discuss what the next test should be. A brilliant scientist from Israel suggest that the next test should be in the form of a verbal command and he quickly explains that if the creature is working properly he ought to be able to get up off the table when told to do so. Since they are all in unity they stand back while the Israeli scientist is given the honor of issuing the command. They have given the creature the name Adam. So the man from Israel says, "Adam, please get up." But Adam doesn't move. The command is repeated but Adam lies very still.

They put Adam on ice and after a month of studying and checking and rechecking, the best minds on earth conclude that they are stumped. They decided to make another attempt to get Adam moving and they set a date to meet back in New York. The chairman for the project calls the meeting to order and gets right to the point. He wants to know if anyone came up with anything that would get Adam up off the table. A Christian had sneaked into the room uninvited and he stuck his hand up. There were no other hands so the chairman motioned for him to speak. The Christian says, "I have been reading the Bible and I think you have forgotten to give Adam a will. He cannot get up off the table because he has no will to do so." He was going to mention the fact that they had not provided Adam with a soul either, but decided not to push his luck. In a couple of quick sentences he explains that the Bible teaches that man is a Spirit, he lives in a body and he has a soul and that the will is the most important part of the human spirit. The room is silent. Someone finally speaks up and asks who had the responsibility of making the will. After much debate they realized that indeed the will is missing. Then the fun starts. They realize that there are no will making factories on the planet, no labs experimenting on them, no materials from which to make one and not even a manual as to how a will works. They decide to meet the following day and discuss the matter.

## What is God Like?

Meanwhile, during the night every brilliant man is striving to come up with an answer as to how this will is going to be manufactured. The men sleep very little that night—brilliant minds are like that. The next day they meet and the debate is on. From early morning until late that night they pondered: what does a will look like; how much does it weigh; does it have any moving parts; is it electric? It was tantalizing that every man in the room realized they had one, had been using it for years, but knew nothing as to how it worked or how to build one. They understood that they had made the "perfect" man in every way with all five senses working but a real man is more that flesh and bones and five senses. In order for Adam to function perfectly he must be able to hear the command given him and then make a conscious, willful decision to obey by actually getting off the table. They reasoned that, although his ears had worked by picking up the sound waves from the pistol and his body reacted by lurching it was an involuntary act. This is what his brain was programmed to do for such an incident—fight or flight. This could not be considered as a willful act. Adam is still on ice.

God, on the other hand has created wills by the billions, by the power of His Word, and placed one in each human that He created. The human will is very special and it is the part of man that is a reflection of God Himself. When we ask ourselves, "What is God like?" we learn a lot about Him when we look at our own will.

The writer of Proverbs makes this statement about the will of kings—or their hearts as the center of their being: **The king's heart *is* in the hand of the LORD, *as* the rivers of water: he turneth it whithersoever He will** (Proverbs 21:1 KJV). We understand the word heart in this verse is talking about the intangible parts of man, and not the pump that distributes blood through his body. It could be argued that, on earth, kings have the strongest hearts or the greatest amount of will power. There is none stronger or higher to challenge them and usually their will overpowers all others. If not, they are not king for long. They are also more arbitrary and uncontrollable than others. This verse indicates that God can direct the will of a man as river water is directed. In order to change the direction of a river, one must remove the soil at the river bank and the water will flow in the direction of the new ditch or tributary. There is a sense in which the water does not have to be touched. Just remove the soil and the water will follow. God can change the heart of a king by similar means. He can place things in the path of the king or create new paths for him. A king whose will is submissive to God will follow God. King David was like this. A king who is *not* submissive can also be made to go in certain directions, like Pharaoh for example. While God was directing these kings, He allowed both to exercise their individual wills without overpowering them or destroying their will power. Here are two other Scriptures that speak of God's influence on a man's will:

> **Mortals make elaborate plans, but GOD has the last word** (Proverbs 16:1 MSG).

> **We plan the way we want to live, but only GOD makes us able to live it** (Proverbs 16:9 MSG).

Consider Pharaoh's heart and how he exercised the power of his own will: **Yet Pharaoh was as stubborn as ever—he wouldn't listen to them, just as GOD had said** (Exodus 7:13 MSG). A little later we read in 9:12 that: **GOD hardened Pharaoh in his stubbornness. He wouldn't listen, just as GOD had said to Moses.** When we read that, 'God hardened Pharaoh's heart," we need to understand that this was a heart that was already hard. His will was already in defiance mode and he was exercising his will.

God has always made reasonable attempts to win the heart of His children, Pharaoh included. Since God is not a respecter of persons, Pharaoh would have been extended the same opportunity of submission as any other. Few men have been shown as much mercy as Pharaoh and yet he refused to acknowledge God. He willingly and knowingly resisted until God finally drowned him. God knew this man from his beginning to his end. His heart was in God's hands and He did with him as He pleased. As God uses Satan, so He used Pharaoh.

Before we leave Pharaoh, let us consider the mercy God showed him before finally discarding him. This first verse explains that God had a plan and Pharaoh would fit into that plan: **And Jehovah said to Moses, When you go to return into Egypt, see that you do all those wonders which I have put in your hand before Pharaoh; but I will harden his heart, that he shall not let the people go** (Exodus 4:21). Keep in mind that Pharaoh was already set in his ways and would have no intention of listening to Moses or God.

There are at least 14 other references to this stubbornness in the book of Exodus. Here are three:

> **And Jehovah said to Moses, Pharaoh's heart is hardened. He refuses to let the people go** (Exodus 7:14). It would have been easy for God to arrange a fatal heart attack or drowned Pharaoh in the Nile at this time.

> . . . **And Pharaoh's heart was hardened, and he did not listen to them, as Jehovah had said** (Exodus 7:22).

> **But Pharaoh saw that there was relief, and he hardened his heart, and did not listen to them, even as Jehovah had said** (Exodus 8:15).

Meanwhile, God's will for Pharaoh is the same as for any other man—that he would repent and be saved as it says here: **The Lord is not slow concerning His promise, as some count slowness, but is long-suffering toward us, not purposing that any should perish, but that all should come to repentance** (2 Peter 3:9).

There are other references where men's hearts become hard of their own accord but God used them for His own purpose:

> **But King Sihon of Heshbon refused to allow us to pass through, because the LORD your God made Sihon stubborn and defiant so He could help you defeat him, as He has now done** (Deuteronomy 2:30 NLT).

> **The Lord has blinded their eyes and hardened their hearts—so that their eyes cannot see, and their hearts cannot understand, and they cannot turn to Me and have Me heal them** (John 12:40 NLT).

> **For God hath put in their hearts to fulfill his will, and to agree, and give their kingdom unto the beast, until the words of God shall be fulfilled** (Revelation 17:17 KJV).

The human will can choose to obey God. When man refuses to obey, God can harden the heart (or will), which can cause man to experience pain that could bring about repentance if the man *wills* to. Here are some examples:

1. The story of Job reveals a man who is delivered to Satan for affliction. **GOD said, "All right. Go ahead–you can do what you like with him. But mind you, don't kill him"** (Job 2:6 MSG). Job had a heart to obey God. When we read the last chapter in his story we see that Job was abundantly blessed and everything Satan took was restored. As the Lord intended and as Job desired, the afflictions brought him closer to the God he loved.

2. Paul instructs the church at Corinth to take this action against a particular man (who had committed fornication): **So when you are**

assembled and I am with you in spirit, and the power of our Lord Jesus is present, hand this man over to Satan for the destruction of the flesh, so that his spirit may be saved on the day of the Lord** (1 Corinthians 5:4-5 NIV). We see that the process worked. In Paul's second letter to the Corinthians, the man repented and the church was instructed to forgive the man: **Now instead, you ought to forgive and comfort him, so that he will not be overwhelmed by excessive sorrow** (2 Corinthians 2:7 NIV).

3. Paul suffered torment from Satan to prevent him from being proud: **Therefore, in order to keep me from becoming conceited, I was given a thorn in my flesh, a messenger of Satan, to torment me** (2 Corinthians 12:7 NIV). Paul was content to put up with the suffering knowing it was doing him good after the Lord explained the purpose for the affliction: **And He said to me, My grace is sufficient for you, for My power is made perfect in weakness. Most gladly therefore I will rather glory in my weaknesses, that the power of Christ may overshadow me** (2 Corinthians 12:9). In his flesh, or carnal nature, Paul had pride but in his will, or spiritual man, he wanted nothing of it and willingly accepted the thorn.

4. In Acts 5, Ananias and Sapphira lied to Peter and the Holy Spirit and they died for it. They had no will to repent.

5. Elymas the sorcerer and false prophet, was struck blind for a season: **And now, behold, *the* hand of the Lord *is* on you. And you shall be blind, not seeing the sun for a while. And immediately a mist and a darkness fell on him, and he went about seeking *some* to lead him by the hand** (Acts 13:11). There is no record that he repented.

6. Hymenaeus and Alexander were delivered to Satan that they may learn not to blaspheme (1 Timothy 1:20).

It is uncertain as to the outcome for Elymas, Hymenaeus and Alexander but it is clear that instead of being struck dead they were shown mercy and given opportunity to change their will. Note too that they were handed over to Satan that they might *learn* something.

There is a sense in which your will is untouchable as far as its Creator is concerned. He ordained that you would have full control. Our daily struggle is in using it to command our body and soul to do the things that we know we should. Quit the carnal desires and pursue things that are healthy, wholesome and right. So why the struggle? We seem to be on the same page as God on this issue. The Designer of wills, through His Word, has taught that we must still ask, seek and knock before we can be rid of the carnal desires, even as Christians. A wishful thought passing through the mind of an addict that he would like to be free of his drugs, does not constitute an actual change in his will. But let the addict or the Christian, come to a place where they cry out from deep within their innermost being (the will) then God will intervene and set that man free. First, it must be proven to the man himself that: "I need to change." Second, there must be the desire, "a new way of life is really what I want." Third, the man must recognize, "I cannot do this by myself." God's immediate response might sound something like this: "Yes you need to change, I have waited for you to desire real life, and I know you cannot change yourself. I will do this for you." He specializes in setting sinners free, gracefully:

> **For it is by grace you have been saved, through faith and this not from yourselves, it is the gift of God not by works, so that no one can boast** (Ephesians 2:8-9 NIV).

> **But when God, our kind and loving Savior God, stepped in, he saved us from all that. It was all his doing; we had nothing to do with it. He gave us a good bath, and we came out of it new people, washed inside and out by the Holy Spirit** (Titus 3:4-5 MSG).

To sum it up, when God created the human will it is possibly the most daring thing ever created. He allows us to use it to choose everlasting life or everlasting damnation. We can use it to make Him happy or angry. With it, we make decisions to bring ourselves misery or joy.

# 48  GOD IS INTO REAL ESTATE

He owns land—all of it. Everything a Creator created from scratch, He would own. This verse is proof that God is the owner of all land: **. . . you shall be a peculiar treasure to Me above all the nations; for all the earth *is* Mine** (Exodus 19:5). Not only does He own the earth, He has the deed to all surrounding planets and galaxies: **Behold, the heaven and the heaven of heavens *belong* to Jehovah your God, the earth also, with all in it** (Deuteronomy 10:14). Our use of His land is limited. We can use it as tenants in the same manner He allowed Israel to use it: **The land shall not be sold forever; for the land *is* Mine. For you are strangers and pilgrims with Me** (Leviticus 25:23). God reminds us through Jeremiah the prophet that He made it, owns everything on it and gives property rights to whomsoever He chooses: **I have made the earth, man, and the animals on the face of the earth, by My great power and by My outstretched arm, and have given it to whom it seemed right to Me** (Jeremiah 27:5).

From Genesis 12:7, we learn that God does have a favorite piece of real estate. The parcel of land is located in the Middle East on the shores of the Mediterranean Sea. At this time the land was called Canaan. He granted it to one of His favorite sons, Abraham: **And Jehovah appeared to Abram and said, <u>I will give this land to your seed</u>. And he built an altar there to Jehovah who appeared to him.**

He even specified the duration of the deed: **For all the land which you see I will give to you, and to your seed <u>forever</u>** (Genesis 13:15). The land was surveyed (see Numbers 34) and God listed the existing tenants who would be driven out: **In the same day Jehovah made a covenant with Abram, saying, I have given this land to your seed, from the river of Egypt to the great river, the river Euphrates, the Kenites, and the Kenizzites, and the Kadmonites, and the Hittites, and the Perizzites, and the giants, and the Amorites, and the Canaanites, and the Girgashites, and the Jebusites** (Genesis 15:18-21). The tenants occupying these lands had become a stench in God's nostrils and He was about to evict them.

## What is God Like?

The gift of land to the descendants of Abraham was to be cleansed by an Angelic being sent by God: **For My Angel shall go before you and bring you in to the Amorites, and the Hittites, and the Perizzites, and the Canaanites, and the Hivites, and the Jebusites. And I will cut them off** (Exodus 23:23). It should be noted that these nations had originally been granted the land but had corrupted it. God tolerated their sin and extended mercy for hundreds of years but finally sent judgment. When He promised Abraham their land four generations earlier, He indicated that the Amorites, possibly the most wicked nation, were being evaluated: **But in the fourth generation they shall come here again, for the iniquity of the Amorites is not yet full** (Genesis 15:16).

God cares about every detail pertaining to His real estate in Israel: **But the land which you are entering to possess it *is* a land of hills and valleys, drinking water from the rain of the heavens. It is a land which Jehovah your <u>God cares for</u>. The eyes of Jehovah your God *are* <u>always upon it</u>, from the beginning of the year even to the end of the year** (Deuteronomy 11:11-12). It is not hard to imagine that He's concerned with the Middle East property when He Himself actually lives there: **So do not defile the land which you shall inhabit, in which I dwell. For I Jehovah dwell among the sons of Israel** (Numbers 35:34). He takes no small interest in Jerusalem, the capital, of Israel: **From the day that I brought My people out of the land of Egypt I have not chosen any city among all the tribes of Israel to build a house in, so that My name might be there. Nor have I chosen any man to be a ruler over My people Israel. But now <u>I have chosen Jerusalem</u>, so that My name might be there, and now I have chosen David to be over My people Israel** (2 Chronicles 6:5-6). There is no uncertainty as to how long He plans to be there: **And he built altars in the house of Jehovah, of which Jehovah had said, In Jerusalem shall My name be <u>forever</u>** (2 Chronicles 33:4).

The Lord has future plans for His capital city:

> At that time they will call Jerusalem The Throne of the LORD, and all nations will gather in Jerusalem to honor the name of the LORD. No longer will they follow the stubbornness of their evil hearts (Jeremiah 3:17 NIV).

> On that day the LORD will shield those who live in Jerusalem, so that the feeblest among them will be like David, and the house of David will be like God, like the Angel of the LORD going before them. On that day I will set out to destroy all the nations that attack Jerusalem (Zechariah 12:8-9 NIV).

> **The LORD will inherit Judah as his portion in the holy land and will again choose Jerusalem** (Zechariah 2:12 NIV).

It would seem that Israel's present day neighbors ought to exercise caution in trying to take land and change the borders around this favored nation. The original and present Owner will take decisive action. It's just a matter of when. Joel 3:1-2 says clearly: **For, behold, in those days and in that time, *when* I will bring again the exiles of Judah and Jerusalem, I will also gather all nations and will bring them down into the valley of Jehoshaphat. And I will fight with them there for My people and for My inheritance Israel, whom they have scattered among the nations, and divided My land.** God still calls it "My land." The war described in these verses and elsewhere in the Bible is massive, vicious and God will win it.

God had issues with the descendants of Abraham in the past, and still does, but the land agreement holds. He also has the power to enforce His intentions and His contract with Israel.

Property owners often undertake renovations on property they own. God is also planning to make changes, a major redevelopment for the entire planet and the neighboring area. Demolition first and then a major overhaul as 2 Peter 3:10 describes: **But the day of the Lord will come as a thief in *the* night, in which the heavens will pass away with a rushing noise, and *the* elements will melt with fervent heat. And the earth and the works in it will be burned up.** This is about a new home that He is preparing for those who love and obey Him. Those who have no time for Him will be resettled.

# 49 GOD USES WEAPONS OF MASS DESTRUCTION

The first weapon God used was a substance with the chemical formula $H_2O$, or water, and lots of it: **And Jehovah saw that the wickedness of man was great in the earth, and every imagination of the thoughts of his heart was only evil continually. And Jehovah repented that He had made man on the earth, and He was angry to His heart. And Jehovah said, I will destroy man whom I have created, from the face of the earth, both man, and beast, and the creeping thing, and the fowls of the air. For I repent that I have made them** (Genesis 6:5 -7). Chapter 7 records a flood that covered the whole earth and drowned every living creature except Noah and his family and the creatures he had with him in the ark.

Genesis 18 records a conversation between God and Abraham. At the conclusion ten righteous men could not be found in Sodom and Gomorrah. Two angels warned Lot and his family: **For we will destroy this place because great is the cry of them before the face of Jehovah. And Jehovah has sent us to destroy it** (Genesis 19:13). Then God unleashed a powerful weapon from the sky: **Then Jehovah rained upon Sodom and upon Gomorrah brimstone and fire, from Jehovah out of the heavens. And He overthrew those cities, and all the plain, and all the inhabitants of the cities, and that which grew upon the ground** (Genesis 19:24-25).

On another occasion He destroyed an entire army overnight: **And it happened in that night, that the Angel of Jehovah went out and struck a hundred and eighty five thousand in the camp of Assyria; and they rose up early in the morning, and behold, all of them *were* dead bodies** (2 Kings 19:35). The author does not say what weapon he actually used, but this single Angel was certainly capable of destroying a large army overnight. I'd call that mass destruction.

In Deuteronomy 28:21-22, God tries to warn his children to be obedient. It reveals a list of biological (and other) weapons that could be used to destroy millions: **Jehovah shall make the plague cling to you until He has consumed** you from off the land where you go to possess it. Jehovah shall strike you with lung disease and with a fever, and with an inflammation, and with an extreme burning, and with the sword, and with blasting, and with mildew. And they shall pursue you until you perish.** This sounds a lot like the biological weapons of mass destruction presently being contemplated by various nations today. In Numbers 11:33, He actually used one of them: **And while the flesh was yet between their teeth, before it was chewed, the wrath of Jehovah was kindled against the people, and Jehovah struck the people with a very great plague.** He used it again in Numbers 16:45-49, when Israel questioned the Lord's judgment against Korah and complained against Moses: **Get away from this congregation so that I may consume them as in a moment. And they fell upon their faces. And Moses said to Aaron, Take a fire-pan, and put fire in it from the altar, and put on incense, and go quickly to the congregation and make an atonement for them. For wrath has gone out from Jehovah. The plague has begun. And Aaron did as Moses commanded and ran into the midst of the congregation. And behold! The plague had begun among the people. And he put on incense, and made an atonement for the people And he stood between the dead and the living, and the plague was stayed. And those who died in the plague were fourteen thousand, seven hundred, besides the ones who died about the matter of Korah.** Quite a weapon!

According to the book of Revelation, God is planning one more final act of mass destruction. Chapter 16 indicates that His wrath will be poured out upon the earth, land and sea and upon people who refuse to repent of their sins. In Chapter 20, God gathers nations that defy Him into Israel, and, with fire from Heaven, will burn them alive with the devil who deceived them. Their bodies will be consumed, but their never-dying spirits and souls will live on.

# 50 GOD IS A JUDGE

God invented law and set the pattern for all legal systems. He is ultimately responsible for every law and every judgment. His original legal system is very simple and short on words. From these forty one words (Modern King James Version) of the Law, He is able to run the entire universe, to perfection:

1. **YOU SHALL LOVE THE LORD YOUR GOD WITH ALL YOUR HEART, AND WITH ALL YOUR SOUL, AND WITH ALL YOUR MIND. THIS IS THE FIRST AND GREAT COMMANDMENT.**

2. **AND THE SECOND IS LIKE IT, YOU SHALL LOVE YOUR NEIGHBOR AS YOURSELF.**

The original wording shows up in what we sometimes call the Mosaic Law in the book of Exodus. In Matthew 22:37, Jesus reaffirms these two laws and added: **On these two commandments hang <u>all the Law</u> and the Prophets**. For those who have a desire to obey this law it could be shortened to the three words, YOU SHALL LOVE—and even to one word, LOVE. With this one word He rules Heaven. This one word is who He is. He is Love. As the Ultimate Judge, His judgment will be based on that one word. In essence, all men will be called into account as to whether they loved or not. No man can say they love Him if they do not obey Him; no man will be able to say that they love their neighbor if they lie to or steal from him. This makes judging easy for One who can read minds.

When He sits to judge we can be sure that His judgment will be fair, all the facts will be known and no stone unturned in pursuit of perfect justice. This is what the Psalmist understood in Psalm 50:4, 6 (MSG).

> **He summons heaven and earth as a jury, he's taking his people to court. The whole cosmos attests to the fairness of this court, that here God is judge.**

His courtroom is never closed and He is presently and forever behind the bench. His court is never over-booked and it never makes a judgment that has to be passed to a higher court. Hebrews 10:30-31 confirms, the buck stops here: **For we know Him who has said, "Vengeance belongs to Me, I will repay, says the Lord." And again, "The Lord shall judge His people." It is a fearful thing to fall into the hands of the living God.** The law He presides over as Judge is easily understood. Jesus rephrased it in such a way that even a child could understand: **Therefore all things, whatever you desire that men should do to you, do even so to them; for this is the Law and the Prophets** (Matthew 7:12). Easily understood and easily judged.

As Judge, God constantly monitors motives and actions and we live in danger of His judgment due to wrong motives and sinful actions. A Righteous Judge cannot ignore His own laws, but He is able to place His love nature ahead of His justice when He sees fit. Therefore, He offers pardons on a regular basis for those who choose to accept a pardon. This is in no way a perversion of His justice system, because the penalty for the sins was willingly paid for by His Son: **But God demonstrates his own love for us in this: While we were still sinners, Christ died for us** (Romans 5:8 NIV).

Was the law satisfied when God, as Judge, issued the law in Genesis 2:17 that man would die if he sinned? According to Paul it was. Adam died an immediate, spiritual death and unless he repented, and accepted the atonement provided, he would remain dead: **For as in Adam all die, even so in Christ all will be made alive** (1 Corinthians 15:22). Paul also teaches that even Christians have to face a kind of death that he calls "crucifixion" which results from breaking the same laws: **For if we have been joined together in the likeness of His death, we shall also be *in the likeness* of His resurrection; knowing this, that our old man is crucified with *Him* in order that the body of sin might be destroyed, that from now on we should not serve sin** (Romans 6:5-6). For the follower of Christ, the law of God is satisfied. For non-followers it will be.

God has made it clear to us that He is the one and only Judge. He instructs the rest of us to stay out of the judging business (except for those *He appoints* as shown below). This is the stern warning that Jesus gave us regarding us tampering with the business of judging: **Judge not, that you may not be judged. For with whatever judgment you judge, you shall be judged; and with whatever measure you measure out, it shall be measured to you again** (Matthew 7:1-2). Here is why this is so dangerous: We often take a stab at judging and we often do so without taking the matter to "court." We do not get all the facts; we don't call in CSI Miami to examine the evidence; we don't examine and cross examine the witnesses, if we even bother to look for one. Then, the most common blunder, we don't even give the accused a chance to defend themselves. We judge poorly, and God hates it so much, He said the same poor justice we hand out is what we can expect when we are in need of true justice. Paul teaches we are incapable of judging because, basically, we're hypocrites: **Therefore you are without excuse, O man, everyone who judges; for in that in which you judge another, you condemn yourself, for you who judge do the same things** (Romans 2:1).

Here are two examples of authorized judging He allows.

> Duly appointed judges by governments:
>
> **Let every soul be subject to the higher authorities. For there is no authority but of God; the authorities that exist are ordained by God** (Romans 13:1). His orders to them are the same for saint and sinner alike: **Do not judge according to sight, but judge righteous judgment** (John 7:24).
>
> Judging that He authorizes in the Body of Christ, the Church:
>
> **What business is it of mine to judge those outside the church? Are you not to judge those inside? God will judge those outside. "Expel the wicked person from among you". I say this to shame you. Is it possible that there is nobody among you wise enough to judge a dispute between believers?** (1 Corinthians 5:12-13; 6:5 NIV).

May He help us to leave judging to Him or to those He appoints. Someone may ask, what about ungodly judges who are duly appointed by the appropriate authorities and yet dish out judgments according to their own whims? They too will have their day in His court.

As one who holds the key to eternal life, in Heaven or Hell, God has proven Himself to be a compassionate Judge because He allows His mercy to precede His justice. However, His grace and mercy should never be taken for granted.

# 51 GOD IS NOT SAFE

God loves us, but He is not safe. It is not safe to make assumptions about Him; not safe to disobey Him; not safe to ignore His laws; not safe to hurt His feelings; and it is not safe to test His patience.

God should never be taken for granted. It was C.S. Lewis who made the statement that God is not safe in The Chronicles of Narnia. Lucy asked Mr. Beaver if the great Lion, Aslan, (who represents Jesus) is quite safe: Mr. Beaver explodes, *"Safe? Don't you hear what Mrs. Beaver tells you? Who said anything about safe? 'Course He isn't safe. But He's good"* (Page 86).

Sinners are not safe when they ignore God and His laws. To know Him and become one of His children and take Him for granted is also a mistake. His destructive powers are awesome. Job understood it this way: **He gives greatness to the nations, and destroys them. He spreads out the nations, and leads them away** (12:23). It does not matter who we are. Here are God's own words, recorded in Deuteronomy 8:19 -20 regarding His *chosen* people: **And it shall be if you do at all forget Jehovah your God and walk after other gods and serve them and worship them, I testify against you today that you shall surely perish. As the nations whom Jehovah destroys before your face, so you shall perish because you would not listen to the voice of Jehovah your God.**

God is the giver of prosperity but He can also dish out poverty: **And you shall grope at noonday, as the blind gropes in darkness, and you shall not prosper in your ways. And you shall always be pressed down and spoiled forever, and no man shall save you** (Deuteronomy 28:29). It is not safe to assume that because we have a measure of prosperity that He won't take it from us. We should never take our prosperity for granted. We know that some wicked men prosper, but that doesn't mean they are safe!

God gave man the order, "Do not work on the Sabbath." Numbers 15:36 records that He had a man killed for gathering wood on the Sabbath: **And all the congregation brought him without the camp, and stoned him with stones, and he died; as the LORD commanded Moses.** The man decided he had no trust for God's provision and decided to do things his own way. Any one of us could be guilty of a similar sin, and only by His grace do we escape.

He met Moses once to kill him for neglecting to circumcise his son: **And it happened by the way, in the inn, that Jehovah met him and sought to kill him** (Exodus 4:24). Moses was in direct disobedience to an order that God had given for all Hebrews regarding circumcision. With his wife's help, his life was spared at the last minute.

God had given Moses and the priests strict orders never to touch the ark, so when a man touched the sacred Ark of the Covenant the consequences were severe: **And the anger of Jehovah was kindled against Uzza, and He struck him because he put his hand to the ark. And he died there before Jehovah** (1 Chronicles 13:10). Uzza had decided that he, not God, was the protector of the ark.

God killed two sons of Judah: **But Er, Judah's first-born, was wicked in the Lord's sight; so The Lord put him to death . . . But Onan knew that the child would not be his; so whenever he slept with his brother's wife, he spilled his semen on the ground to keep from providing offspring for his brother. What he did was wicked in the LORD's sight; so the LORD put him to death also** (Genesis 38:7, 9-10 NIV). On the day they died, these men very likely felt safe and secure. After all, this was not the first time they had disobeyed God and gotten away with it. But they were far from safe.

Consider the following passages from His word giving us a clear warning that it is not safe to take God for granted:

1. **And it happened about ten days afterward Jehovah struck Nabal so that he died** (1 Samuel 25:38). This man refused to show David hospitality.

2. **And Jehovah struck the king, (Azariah) so that he was a leper until the day of his death, and lived in a separate house** (2 Kings 15:5a). This king started out doing things right in the Lord's sight but failed to remove idol worship from his kingdom.

3. **And on a certain day, Herod sat on his throne, dressed in royal clothing, and made a speech to them. And the people gave a shout, saying, It is the voice of a god and not of a man! And immediately the angel of the Lord struck him, because he did not give God the glory. And he was eaten by worms and gave up the spirit** (Acts 12:21). Herod assumed he could take credit for something that belonged to God.

4. **And hearing these words, Ananias fell down and expired. And great fear came on all those who heard these things. And the younger ones arose, wound him up, and carrying him out, they buried him. And it was about the space of three hours afterward, when his wife (not knowing what was done) came in. And Peter answered her, Tell me whether you sold the land for so much? And she said, Yes, for so much. Then Peter said to her, How is it that you have <u>agreed together to tempt the Spirit of the Lord?</u> Behold, the feet of those who have buried your husband are at the door and they will carry you out. Then at once she fell down at his feet and expired. And the younger ones found her dead, and, carrying her out, buried her beside her husband** (Acts 5:5-10). This couple conspired to lie to a preacher about the price of their land which they had sold. One wonders if they considered it as just a little white lie. If so, their death proves that it is not safe to tell even white lies. What is remarkable is that this occurred after Jesus died and that judgment was meted out in the Age of Grace.

5. **Then Jehovah rained upon Sodom and upon Gomorrah brimstone and fire, from Jehovah out of the heavens** (Genesis 19:24). God saw the sin of these two cities as unacceptable, they had crossed the line: **And Jehovah said, Because the cry of Sodom and Gomorrah is great, and because their sin is very grievous. I will go down now and see whether they have done altogether according to the cry of it, which has come to Me. And if not, I will know** (Genesis 18:20-21). The sin recorded against these citizens was homosexuality:

   **They called to Lot, "Where are the men who came to you tonight? Bring them out to us so that we can have sex with them"** (Genesis 19:5 NIV).

   **In a similar way, Sodom and Gomorrah and the surrounding towns gave themselves up to sexual immorality and perversion. They serve as an example of those who suffer the punishment of eternal fire** (Jude 1:7 NIV).

It is obvious that the sin highlighted in the two verses above is homosexuality. We should note however, that this sin is no more or less a problem with God than any other sin. Ananias and his wife were "church goers." They only committed what we would classify as a small sin, they lied, yet when God removed mercy and applied justice they died. Christians should never feel smug about little white lies or "small sins" because we face the same delicate, precarious balance of mercy and justice. His love for the homosexual and the liar is exactly the same. He will judge us both. Lest we forget.

From the Scriptures above we can confidently conclude that it is not safe to test God. A student of the Bible would have an understanding that God is not safe. We never know what He is up to, we never know who might be next; therefore, He is to be feared. Our spirit man, once we are in good standing with Him, would understand that Mr. Beaver was right: He is good.

# 52  GOD IS IMPARTIAL

God does not have favorites, and all are treated equal: **And if ye call on the Father, who without respect of persons judgeth according to every man's work, pass the time of your sojourning here in fear** (1 Peter 1:17). Luke 12:48 tells us that to whom much is given, much is expected and to whom little is given, little is expected. That's the rule. It applies to all: saints and sinners alike. Both will receive impartial treatment.

Although it had nothing to do with punishment, God revealed this to Isaiah regarding His only Son, Jesus: **Yet it pleased Jehovah to crush Him; to grieve Him; that He should put forth His soul as a guilt-offering. He shall see His seed, He shall prolong His days, and the will of Jehovah shall prosper in His hand** (Isaiah 53:10). When a sacrifice was needed to atone for the sin of mankind, there was only one Man who could fit the bill—this was God's own Son. When the time came for the sacrifice to be offered, God was impartial and Jesus had to be offered. The death of an innocent was the only offering that could be accepted by a Holy and just God.

At times, it may have seemed that His chosen people, the apple of His eye, suffered inordinately as a result of His actions toward them. Their nation was born in Egypt where He subjected them to slavery for four hundred years. Later, they suffered long and hard at the hands of other nations, with His permission. Jesus used a parable in Luke 12:47- 48 to explain the principal of impartiality in a parable: **And that servant who knew his lord's will and did not prepare, nor did according to His will, shall be beaten with many *stripes*. But he not knowing, and doing *things* worthy of stripes, shall be beaten with few *stripes*. For to whomever much is given, of him much shall be required. And to whom men have committed much, of him they will ask the more.** The Jews were given much and much was expected. It would sound scary and unappealing to be given much knowing much is expected, except for a promise that He gives to accompany the trials: **No temptation has taken you but what is common to man; but God *is* faithful, who will not allow you to be tempted above what you are able, but with the temptation also will make a way to escape, so that you may be able to bear *it*** (1 Corinthians 10:13). His impartiality may seem brutal at times, but we need to remember He always looks on with compassion and tenderness to rescue when the lesson is too hard or the load too heavy.

God has reserved the exclusive right to give natural talents, wealth and power to whomsoever He pleases. Some may think that He should only lavish such blessings on His chosen people, the Jews or on Christians. While it is true that He does bless Jews and Christians, their blessings cover their needs and come with purpose and conditions. He purposely withholds blessings at times, to teach us lessons we need to learn. Sinners also receive their proportional share of blessings from His hand. One of the greatest blessings of wealth and power ever handed out was given to the Gentile, heathen king Nebuchadnezzar. The Lord gifted and elevated this man above all others according to Daniel: **Your Majesty, you are the greatest of kings, and God has highly honored you with power <u>over all humans, animals, and birds</u>. You are the head of gold** (Daniel 2:37-38 CEV).

# 53  GOD GETS ANGRY

God is always justified in His anger. We should read and heed His Word and never assume that His anger cannot be stirred against us. Consider the following Scriptures: **Then My anger shall be kindled against them in that day, and I will forsake them. And I will hide My face from them, and they shall be devoured, and many evils and troubles shall befall them, so that they will say in that day, Have not these evils come on us because our God *is* not among us? . . . And He said, I will hide My face from them; I will see what their end *shall be.* For they *are* a very perverse generation, sons in whom there *is* no faithfulness** (Deuteronomy 31:17; 32:20).

At one time David felt the anger of the Lord as recorded in Psalms: **There *is* no soundness in my flesh because of Your anger; nor rest in my bones because of my sin** (Psalm 38:3).

He has been known to totally shun those who make Him angry:

> **And when you spread out your hands, I will hide My eyes from you; yea, when you make many prayers, I will not hear; your hands are full of blood** (Isaiah 1:15).

> **They shall go with their flocks and with their herds to seek Jehovah; but they shall not find Him. He has withdrawn Himself from them** (Hosea 5:6).

> **For the iniquity of his covetousness I was angry and struck him; I hid Myself, and was angry, and he went on turning away in the way of his heart** (Isaiah 57:17).

No man should get God riled up. It is far too dangerous. It is indicated in His Word that although he is very merciful and compassionate, He has set limits and there is a point of no return. Consider that God said he limited our life span so he would not always have to fight with us (Genesis 6:3), and that after making that statement, God drowned the entire population of the earth except for the eight members of Noah's family. What happens to a man or woman who no longer receives pity from the Lord? **Likewise, I will no longer have pity on the people of the land," says the LORD. "I will let them fall into each other's hands and into the hands of their king. They will turn the land into a wilderness, and I will not rescue them"** (Zechariah 11:6 NLT).

This would be a dreadful situation to wake up to. It is one thing to get God angry but can we even imagine what it would be like to experience His "fierce" anger. Consider this situation in the Hebrew camp when they bowed to false gods and committed fornication with the daughters of Moab: **And Jehovah said to Moses, Take all the heads of the people and hang them up before Jehovah against the sun, so that the fierce anger of Jehovah may be turned away from Israel** (Numbers 25:4). His anger did not subside until 24,000 had died. Nations today commit the same sins and we could wonder how close some might be to His breaking point.

The writer of Hebrews 10:31 gives this warning: *It is* **a fearful thing to fall into the hands of the living God.**

Once all mercy has expired, and in the fullness of time, God plans to pour out wrath:

> **For the wrath of God is revealed from Heaven against all ungodliness and unrighteousness of men, who suppress the truth in unrighteousness, because the thing which may be known of God is clearly revealed within them, for God revealed** *it* **to them** (Romans 1:18).

> **And anyone who believes in God's Son has eternal life. Anyone who doesn't obey the Son will never experience eternal life but remains under God's angry judgment** (John 3:36 NLT).

There is, however, a measure of comfort in God's wrath for every person who has a shred of righteousness in their spirit. Saints and sinners alike have a built-in desire to see justice and it can only be done when sin is punished. One obvious reason for this built-in desire is that no one is safe while evil men practice their sin unhindered. God makes this promise to all: **Let no man deceive you with vain words, for because of these things the wrath of God comes upon the children of disobedience** (Ephesians 5:6). For those of us who think His wrath is unnecessary or excessive, we need to remind ourselves that the recipients of His wrath are men and women who were aware of His laws, flaunted them anyway, and nothing He tried to do to pursue them worked.

# 54 GOD HIDES

There is a sense in which God has always been hidden. No one has ever seen Him, and for good reason. He explained it to Moses saying: **"But you may not see my face. <u>No one can see me and live</u>"** (Exodus 33:20 MSG). Moses, not realizing what he was asking for, had requested to see the Glory of God. The Lord satisfied him by allowing only His goodness to be seen. He protected Moses from death by hiding him in the cleft of a rock while He passed by. John confirms that He has never been seen: **No one has ever seen God. The only Son, who is truly God and is closest to the Father, has shown us what God is like** (John 1:18 CEV).

Yet, there are times when even His Spiritual presence leaves the scene and He goes into hiding. He always keeps us in sight but we can't see Him. Consider this verse: **But from there you will search again for the LORD your God. And if you search for Him with all your heart and soul, you will find Him** (Deuteronomy 4:29 NLT). Finding Him is not always easy. He has intentionally set it up that way, and He has definitely gone into hiding since it would be unnecessary to seek for someone who is close and visible. As the verse above indicates the search must be intense. Anything less may be ignored. You may be accustomed to doing thorough searches, but this one will require your very heart and soul.

However, there will be times when He will surprise you. He will show up announced, or in the nick of time, or to blow your socks off. He met with Moses once. He didn't exactly blow his socks off but He did command him to remove his sandals before promoting him from leading sheep to become the world's greatest leader of men. He met with Paul the Apostle on the road to Damascus, knocked him to the ground, blinded him, healed him, and then transformed him from a terrorist to the world's greatest evangelist. When He does show Himself in that manner, watch out, there is always a divine purpose.

There are times when He hides for a reason. Consider the following Scriptures:

## What is God Like?

Here He hides because of His children's wickedness: **And He said, I will hide My face from them; I will see what their end** *shall be.* **For they** *are* **a very perverse generation, sons in whom there** *is* **no faithfulness** (Deuteronomy 32:20).

The 30th Psalm describes how David experienced the anger of the Lord, which verse 5 says lasted only for a moment, but during that time God was hiding: **LORD, when you favored me, you made my royal mountain stand firm; but when you hid your face, I was dismayed** (Psalm 30:7 NIV).

Job was a faithful servant that God severely tested. During the trial He hid Himself for a short period of time: **I travel East looking for him–I find no one; then West, but not a trace; I go North, but he's hidden his tracks; then South, but not even a glimpse. But he knows where I am and what I've done. He can cross-examine me all he wants, and I'll pass the test with honors** (Job 23:8-10 MSG).

Why does God hide? There could be a number of reasons: Spiritually we are empty, and have many weaknesses; we are often in need of healing and our list of wants is long. When we become aware of the great provisions in Almighty God, our carnal nature tends to treat Him as our own personal lottery. This seems especially true of North American Christians who live in abundance, and yet we spend most of our time striving for more and more of the material things of the world. From this He hides. This is what God said about our spiritual condition through the Psalmist: **Jehovah looked down from Heaven on the sons of men, to see if there were any who understood** *and* **sought God. All** *have* **gone aside, together they are filthy;** *there is* **none who does good, no, not one** (Psalm 14:2-3). If we try first to understand Him, and then try to seek Him, there would be no hiding.

He will hide from our selfishness, for a time, but even then there will be a lesson somewhere to make us aware of our sin. Listen to this kind reminder in the book of Isaiah: **In a little wrath I hid My face from you** *for* **a moment; but with everlasting kindness I will have mercy on you, says Jehovah your Redeemer** (Isaiah 54:8).

Ezekiel 39:23-24 explains why the Lord found it necessary to hide even from His chosen people: **And the nations shall know that the house of Israel was exiled for their iniquity. Because they sinned against Me, therefore I hid My face from them and gave them into the hand of their enemies. So they all fell by the sword. According to their uncleanness and according to their sins I**

**have done to them, and have hidden My face from them.** Ezekiel 39:29 also assures us He will not always remain hidden: **Nor will I hide My face from them anymore, for I have poured out My Spirit on the house of Israel, says the Lord Jehovah.**

For the Spirit filled Christian, He is always available to them when they diligently seek Him: **Ask and it shall be given to you; seek and you shall find; knock and it shall be opened to you. For each one who asks receives; and he who seeks finds; and to him who knocks, it shall be opened** (Matthew 7:7-8).

Finding Him is not without its reward: **And without faith it is not possible to be well-pleasing to him, for it is necessary for anyone who comes to God to have the belief that God is, and that he is a rewarder of all those who make a serious search for him** (Hebrews 11:6 BBE).

From the scriptures above we can see that our sin can cause Him to hide from us. Remember He cannot tolerate sin. Yet His intense desire is to have intimate fellowship with His children. This is still attainable by accepting the covering that His Son provides for us. His blood covers our sin allowing us back into fellowship with Him.

# 55 GOD WANTS YOU TO FIND HIM

We know that God is out there somewhere, but in our carnal nature we cannot find Him. God is aware of this and makes it possible for us to find Him in various ways. First, we must acknowledge His Son is the way to the Father: **Jesus said to him, I am the Way, the Truth, and the Life; no one comes to the Father but by Me** (John 14:6). Once that connection is in place we must find a means of communication. Neither God nor Jesus are into faxing, texting, email, or snail mail. The way to find Him is via the Spirit realm. He commands us to look for Him and the commands have instructions, warnings and conditions as seen in the following Scriptures:

- Deuteronomy 4:29 tells us trivial and halfhearted attempts will not work: **But if you shall seek Jehovah your God from there, you shall find *Him*, if you seek Him with all your heart and with all your soul.**

- Proverbs 8:17 tells us: **I love them that love me; and those that seek me early shall find me.** This may mean seeking Him at the beginning of our day, but for sure it means putting the search at the top of our priorities.

- Isaiah 55:6 warns us not to delay in our search and we should never assume He will always be available: **Seek ye the LORD while he may be found, call ye upon him while he is near.**

- Jeremiah 29:13 intimates the search must have intensity: **And ye shall seek me, and find *me*, when ye shall search for me with all your heart.**

- Hosea 5:15 advises us pain is often part of an intense and diligent search: **I will go *and* return to my place, till they acknowledge their offence, and seek my face: in their affliction they will seek me early.**

Our Father changes and transforms us in the process of our search. He has not been hiding just to be out of sight; He is out of sight so that we may long for His presence and seek to find Him. All the while, our earthbound mind is being renewed. In Romans 12:2, Paul teaches: **And be not conformed to this world: but be ye transformed by the <u>renewing of your mind</u>, that ye may prove what *is* that good, and acceptable, and perfect, will of God.** Essentially we are a spirit and we are never truly satisfied with the things of the flesh. One day the body will drop off and we will live totally in His realm. Even now, our spirit craves more than what the flesh offers. God knows this because that is exactly how He designed us. He created a vacuum in our spirit that only He can fill. When His Spirit connects with ours we are complete and whole.

Meanwhile, if you feel He is hiding from you today, remember: He is close enough to see you; He is waiting and longing for you to find Him.

# 56 GOD DOES NOT NEED A CAUSE

Here is a common argument among skeptics and atheists: *if it is true that all things need a cause then God must also need a cause."* Many philosophers and theologians have debated this cosmological argument searching for the "first cause:" the first event that caused our universe to exist as we know it. They concluded that the first cause could not be God because, in their mind, God would also need a cause. The problem with such debating is that no matter how brilliant the mind, no matter how wordy the hypothesis, how simple or how confusing its wording, we cannot arrive at the proper conclusion when trying to prove the existence of God. Here is why: we are not on the same page as God; we are not in the same realm. We are of the earthly realm and He is in a spiritual realm, and things are so very different between these two. The beings living in the spirit realm are not even physical; to enter a room they walk through the walls, when they want to leave they vanish. To travel in their realm, they think where they want to be and they arrive, at the speed of thought. (This assumption is based on the way Jesus travelled as a spirit after his resurrection and the way angels appear and disappear.) Let's concentrate for a moment on the one who designed and created all this. We are not even in the same book, let alone on the same page. He speaks words and galaxies appear, He is everywhere at the same time (omnipresent) and He is all knowing (omniscient). The list of things about Him is awesome, mind boggling and staggering to any human who has a peanut of a brain. At this point the skeptic may say, "But, I don't believe in this God." If this is true, why write books about someone you don't believe in and try to argue that He doesn't exist?

Let me illustrate how senseless this sounds. Let's suppose you are I are having a serious conversation. In the process I tell you that before sunup this morning, I arose early and flew to Pluto and had breakfast; went from there to Mars and played a game of street hockey with a group of Martians, caught a flight from there and spent the afternoon in a library on Saturn studying for my bar exam. Now, I am reasonably sure that you would conclude that I was either loco, or a blatant liar, or both. I am, also reasonably certain that you would not sit there and argue with me about my journey because it is just too ridiculous to argue about; you would leave it alone. It is similar when arguing about the existence of God. If they really believe that He does not exist, why are they arguing? Trouble is, deep down they *know*; it's just that they refuse to accept Him. Fools don't believe, as the Bible says in Psalm 14:1, but smart, educated men who refuse to accept Him must make a large effort to get Him off their radar.

It is unfortunate that leading scholars, mere men, make rash statements about such lofty subjects which they have no hope of substantiating. Many things in our universe do need a cause. This we observe in our study of the sciences. However, it is impossible for a finite being to study infinite things and draw absolute conclusions. To do so, is to be presumptuous and implies that we know all things.

The last thing a wise, educated man will tell you is that he knows all things. He would be sensible enough to know that the more we study, the more we discover we don't know. We must also conclude that we are in no position to draw absolute conclusions since we are unable to study anything to its absolute end. The more we learn, the more we know there is more to learn. Honest scientists have been known to say the answers leave us with brand new questions.

When an atheist makes a claim that God does not exist, the burden is on him to prove that his statement is true. However, this is a statement that clearly cannot be proven. For example, if someone said there is a fingerprint on a rock somewhere in the Rocky Mountains, no one would be foolish enough to dispute that statement. To start with, the person making the statement could very well have seen it, or put it there. Meanwhile, if someone said there is *no* fingerprint on any rock in the entire Rocky Mountains, we all know that this person is just flapping his jaws. He is making a statement that he has no way of proving. An atheist capable of saying there is no God is akin to one saying there is no fingerprint on any rock in the Rocky Mountains! The best an atheist could conclude about the existence of God, with his limited knowledge and limited wisdom would be, "I do not know." David makes this strong statement about the atheist: **The fool has said in his heart, There is no God! They acted corruptly; they have done abominable works, *there is* none who does good** (Psalm 14:1). It's a fool indeed who concludes in his heart that God does not exist. By such a presumptuous conclusion, he would have us believe that he has visited all places on earth; searched the far reaches of the universe; examined all the forces therein; interviewed every human and every spirit in the entire cosmos, studied and understood it all to perfection. Yeah right! David's description may seem harsh, but it is accurate.

The existence of God does not need a cause as some suggest. Most of us, at some time or another, have wondered where God came from. Since He is omnipresent, as the Bible indicates, He doesn't need to be *from* anywhere. The Bible declares that He does reside in Heaven; He is also present on earth. Our finite mind cannot grasp this because we are all *from* someplace; further, we are from some particular place on earth. Humans are tied to terra firma and know nothing yet as to how spirits relate to terra firma. This alone ought to caution us in drawing conclusions about God's "location."

He has supplied an abundance of information as to how we may get to know Him. Getting to know Him may be possible in three simple steps: One, believe that He exists; two, meet His Son and invite Him into your life; and three, move into His Kingdom. The Kingdom is spiritual but that's OK, you are a spiritual being.

# 57 GOD HAS UNLIMITED POWER

Every book in the Bible displays the power of God in some way or another. In Genesis, His power is demonstrated by the creation of worlds using mere words. God created the entire universe with about 214 spoken words. In Exodus, His words brought national disasters down upon the land of Egypt. Through the rest of the Bible, He demonstrated His power by taking kingdoms from some and giving them to others as He pleased. He gives rain and withholds rain. He shows mercy when He feels like it and He destroys whole nations when He sees fit. The book of Revelation prophetically speaks of unstoppable power that He will unleash on the earth in the near future. It takes real power to speak a prophetic word and then ensure that the word comes to pass. Every ripe prophetic word spoken by Him thus far has come to past.

Humans are always interested in powerful people. We admire those who have power. We like to have friends in high places, with big names that we can drop at appropriate times. We desire to be in the presence of such individuals. As powerful as He is, He gives us opportunity to know Him personally. This ought to catch our attention.

How could there be hope for a relationship between One so mighty and those so weak? What do we have in common? With His spectacular creative ability and our total lack thereof, we are not in the same league. By comparison, we speak nothing physical into being with our words and are challenged when we try to create by assembling things He gave us. We cannot create a building or a car, but by use of our hands and brain we manage to use His raw materials and can assemble a building or a car.

God is obviously cautious in sharing His power with humans. Submissive and meek men like, Moses and Elisha were given a measure of supernatural power and they handled it reasonably well. Moses did allow his emotions get out of hand on one occasion by striking a rock when He was ordered to speak to it and was reprimanded severely (Numbers 20). Think of what James and John would have done with this supernatural power when they passed through Samaria and were rejected by the Samaritans. They would have wiped out the city of Samaria with fire from heaven (Luke 9). God's power, in the hands of carnal men could be extremely dangerous. There are many other examples in the Old and New Testament where God demonstrated a willingness to share His supernatural power but only with men who could be trusted. We may think that as Christians God ought to more readily share His power with us—but if we knew how to handle real power, God would gladly share it.

In our fleshly nature we have a tendency to abuse power and use it for selfish gain. **You ask and receive not, because you ask amiss, that you may spend it upon your lusts** (James 4:3). When we get it right and ask for His power to do His work, He promised to give it. In Mark 16:17, Jesus said: **miraculous signs will follow to those believing these things: in My name they will cast out demons; they will speak new tongues; they will take up serpents; and if they drink any deadly thing, it will not hurt them. They will lay hands on the sick, and they will be well.** We certainly cannot blame God for not sharing this amazing power if our motives are wrong. Even we can see the wisdom of withholding power from those who abuse it. To illustrate, would any wise father give an immature child full access to the family bank account?

Jesus demonstrated the power of God among us and said we should be like Him, as seen in these references:

> **And all the crowd sought to touch Him, for power went out of Him and healed them all . . . And He called His twelve disciples together and <u>gave them power and authority</u> over all demons and to cure diseases** (Luke 6:19; 9:1).

> **And behold, I send the promise of My father on you. But you sit in the city of Jerusalem until you are <u>clothed with power</u> from on high** (Luke 24:49).

As we learn to be more like Him and practice love, God is more likely to share His power with us. We will speak the word and people will be healed. Peter demonstrated this in Acts 3:6 when he met a lame man near the temple: **But Peter said, Silver and gold have I none, but what I have I give you. In the name of Jesus Christ of Nazareth, rise up and walk! And taking him by the right hand, he lifted him up. And immediately his feet and ankle-bones received strength. And leaping up, he stood and walked and entered with them into the temple, walking and leaping and praising God.**

Regarding those He will entrust with a measure of His power, meekness is more important than perfection.

# 58 GOD CREATED MAN AND WOMAN NAKED

In God's eyes, the first man's physical nakedness was not a problem. When we consider the importance we place on being clothed, and how much we shun nakedness, we find it peculiar that God started us out bare naked: **And they were both naked, the man and his wife; and they were not ashamed** (Genesis 2:25). John Wesley (Salem Communications Corporation) makes this observation on this verse:

> *They were both naked, they needed no clothes for defense against cold or heat, for neither could be injurious to them: they needed none for ornament. Solomon in all his glory was not arrayed like one of these. Nay, they needed none for decency, they were naked, and had no reason to be ashamed. They knew not what shame was, so the Chaldee reads it. Blushing is now the color of virtue, but it was not the color of innocence.*

After the Fall, when Adam and Eve disobeyed the voice of God and obeyed the voice of Satan, they looked at each other and felt ashamed, as we still do when naked. True to His great mercy and compassion, God solved their problem by performing the first sacrifice. He killed an animal, shed its blood to temporarily cover their sins, then took the skin of the animal and clothed them: **And for Adam and his wife Jehovah God made coats of skins, and clothed them** (Genesis 3:21). Symbolically, sin is represented by nakedness and the shedding of blood removes sin. Read what Leviticus 17:11 says regarding blood: **For the life of the flesh *is* in the blood, and I have given it to you on the altar, to atone for your souls; for it *is* the blood which makes atonement for the soul.**

Symbolically, all references to the sacrificing of animals and the shedding of their blood pointed to Jesus, God's only Son, who would eventually shed His blood for the forgiveness of all sin: **For this is My blood of the New Covenant which concerning many is being poured out for remission of sins** (Matthew 26:28). The writer to the Hebrews confirms:

**For if the blood of bulls and goats, and ashes of a heifer sprinkling those having been defiled, sanctifies to the purity of the flesh, by how much more the blood of Christ (who through *the* eternal Spirit offered Himself without blemish to God), will purify your conscience from dead works, to serve *the* living God! And almost all things are purified by blood according to the Law; and apart from shedding of blood no remission occurs** (9:13-14, 22).

The nakedness of our forefather symbolized purity and innocence. Covering, or clothing for the body, symbolizes the covering of the blood. We will treat this subject further in the chapter 65, *God is Big on Symbols*.

# 59  GOD IS DEMANDING

In some ways and about some things, God is very demanding. He expects to be obeyed. As soon as He had creation in place He put man in charge of it and immediately started issuing commands. The very first recorded word out of His mouth to Adam was a command to *do* something: **Be fruitful, and multiply and fill the earth, and subdue it. And have dominion over the fish of the sea and over the fowl of the heavens, and all animals that move upon the earth** (Genesis 1:22). Along with the *"do"* command came one *"do not"* command: **And Jehovah God commanded the man, saying, You may freely eat of every tree in the garden, but you shall not eat of the tree of knowledge of good and evil** (Genesis 2:16-17a).

Both commands were very basic and ought to have been easily understood and in all likelihood were. They were simple, but God allowed things to get complicated by allowing Satan access to Adam's garden, approach Adam's wife, lie to her and try to convince her that God was lying and was holding out on them. However, God still demanded obedience of Adam. In fact, Adam was warned in verse 17 that if he disobeyed he would die for his disobedience: . . . **for in the day that you eat of it <u>you shall surely die</u>.**

We see that God issues commands, expects to be obeyed, warns of severe punishment, allows for temptation and still demands absolute obedience. There must be some point to all of this. Why couldn't Jehovah have shielded Adam from the temptation or at least made the consequence of disobedience a little easier? This seems very demanding and the consequences frightful.

Here are several other examples of how God demands allegiance in spite of the fact that there were things that the Lord could have done to make things easier for those He loved dearly:

- He put Job in Satan's hands and watched the fight (Job 1 and 2).

- He told Abraham to kill his only son, stopping him at the last second (Genesis 22).

## What is God Like?

- He preplanned Joseph's slavery and then his jail term (Genesis 37 to 40).

- He sent Israel into Egypt for 400 years of slavery: **And He said to Abram, You must surely know that your seed shall be a stranger in a land not theirs, and shall serve them. And they shall afflict them four hundred years** (Genesis 15:13).

- He commanded Moses to go back to Egypt and face Pharaoh, despite the fact that he could have been charged with murdering an Egyptian (Exodus 3).

- He anointed David to be king then allowed Saul to hunt him like a dog (1 Samuel 18-31).

- He sent His own Son to earth to die (See Matthew, Mark, Luke and John).

The point is this—it is always hard to follow His commands. If it all worked out with ease it would mean very little to us and therefore of no value to God. It is only when we learn to love, trust and serve Him that we become valuable to His kingdom. We will only make it through the fire of adversity by crucifying the desires of our carnal nature. Even then we must have His help. He is constantly teaching us that our strength is of little value. It is of value only when combined with His great strength. The purpose for the high demand that God makes is to teach us that we have no strength on our own to match these challenges but He has made provision to supply what we lack. This is what the Psalmists understood in these verses:

> **Jehovah *is* my strength, and my fortress, and my deliverer; my God, my rock; I will trust in Him; *He is* my shield, and the horn of my salvation, my high tower. I will go in the strength of the Lord Jehovah; I will speak of Your righteousness, of Yours alone. Seek Jehovah and His strength; seek His face evermore** (Psalm 18:2; 71:16; 105:4).

Isaiah also understood that the Lord was his source of strength: **Behold, God *is* my salvation; I will trust and not be afraid for the LORD JEHOVAH is my strength and my song; He also has become my salvation** (Isaiah 12:2).

Jesus put it best with these words which mean total, absolute, dependency on Him: **Abide in Me, and I in you. As the branch cannot bear fruit of itself** unless it remains in the vine, so neither *can* you unless you abide in Me (John 15:4). The painful demands that He has placed on us can only be satisfied by this kind of dependency on Him and His Son. We saw in chapter four that God believes in pain.

Not only does our Heavenly Father require obeying His *Do's and Don'ts*, He goes much further and it gets more demanding. God is also insistent in terms of wanting every scrap of your life. He wants every bit of love that you possess and He wants it lavished on Himself and His other children. In Deuteronomy 10:12-13, Moses put it this way: **And now, Israel, what does Jehovah your God ask of you, but to fear Jehovah your God, to walk in all His ways, and <u>to love Him</u>, and to serve Jehovah your God with <u>all your heart and with all your soul</u>, to keep the commandments of Jehovah, and His statutes, which I command you today for your good?** Jesus, who is God in the flesh, not only demanded our heart and soul, He added our mind also: **Jesus said to him, <u>You shall</u> love the Lord your God with <u>all your heart, and with all your soul, and with all your mind</u> This is the first and great commandment. And the second *is* like it, You shall love your neighbor as yourself** (Matthew 22:37-39).

Are we faced with a God who makes demands of us that we cannot keep? As selfish humans, we love our own egos and our own bodies, probably more than anything else, yet even here we don't lavish that kind of devoted love. For example, if we truly loved our own ego we would seek out the perfect treatment for egos and filter what we allowed in. Our tendency is more of a lazy approach; we allow our fallen nature to lead where it pleases. If we loved our body with the kind of dedicated love that God demands for Himself—with all our heart, soul and mind—we certainly would not be abusing it the way we do by depriving it of exercise and proper diet or abusing it with harmful substances.

So, how can God expect us to love Him with love that requires heart, soul and mind? He teaches how in His Word. The Bible, especially the New Testament, teaches that the key ingredient is obedience. 1 John 5:2-3 gives us one example: **By this we know that we love the children of God, whenever we love God and keep His commandments. For this is the love of God, <u>that we keep His commandments</u>, and His commandments are not burdensome.** God is patient, long suffering, kind, and very merciful toward us. It seems that all we really have to do is make an honest attempt to please Him. He knows we are frail and He knows that we will fail, but He also knows that He has given us a will of formidable power, and this is the ultimate treasure He seeks. He is willing to constantly forgive and covers our corrupt nature by the blood of His Son, Jesus Christ.

## What is God Like?

All any of us can offer God is this inner desire from our heart: "God, I want to know you and follow you." This is all our Creator seeks. He does the rest. He made the difficult demands but He also made the provisions whereby we can meet the demands. Jesus, God in the flesh, offered His own life on the cross to redeem us: **And being found in fashion as a man, He humbled Himself *and* became obedient unto death, even *the* death of the cross** (Philippians 2:8). The impossible demands of God are made possible by the Cross.

# 60  GOD INVENTED FAITH

According to God, you must have faith to truly live. As it relates to Him, this means trusting a Being that we cannot see, hear, or touch. It means trusting words He spoke years ago, written by mere men and by these words we must live. For example, these words spoken by Jehoshaphat in 2 Chronicles 20:20 are echoed throughout the entire Bible: **And as they went out, Jehoshaphat stood and said, Hear me, O Judah, and you people of Jerusalem. Believe in Jehovah your God, and so you shall be established. Believe His prophets, and so you shall be blessed.** Here a mere man is speaking on behalf of God, and the listeners are supposed to obey?

Faith started when God spoke a few words to Adam and expected the man to obey. Up to this time no man had ever had opportunity to live by faith and no one knew the consequences of disobedience; yet shortly after the man heard the words of God, his ultimate decision was to basically say, "I will not place my faith in those words. I will do it my way." As we know, Adam's way brought spiritual death to us all. After he died (spiritualy), God provided a means whereby he could be redeemed, but faith was still the major requirement. Later, the Law was instigated to teach about sin and redemption. In it, through the words of Moses, He made this profound statement about faith in Deuteronomy 8:3 (MSG): **He put you through hard times. He made you go hungry. Then he fed you with manna, something neither you nor your parents knew anything about, so you would learn that men and women don't live by bread only; we live by every word that comes from GOD's mouth.** Moses reminded the Hebrews that a steady job and a full belly under slavery was not real living. Meanwhile, God had no intention of leaving His children as slaves. His intent was to teach them to live by faith in His words. From the time of Adam, to the Hebrews and until now, God is still using hard times and pain of every sort to teach us to trust His words by this thing called faith.

According to the words of Jesus in Matthew 17:20, a tiny bit of faith can go a long way. His Father has set it up so that believing His words can result in a display of supernatural, earth-moving power: **For truly I say to you, If you have faith like a grain of mustard seed, you shall say to this mountain, Move from here to there. And it shall move. And nothing shall be impossible to you.**

## What is God Like?

There are two important things to remember regarding this amazing thing called faith. First, there are rewards for exercising it: **But without faith it is impossible to please Him, for he who comes to God must believe that He is and that He is a rewarder of those who diligently seek Him. He expects us to believe that "He is"** (Hebrews 11:6). Second, we are disciplined for not exercising it. In the case of Adam, because he did not trust the Word of God, he lost his home, the wealth of Paradise and immediately became a slave to Satan. Paul explains in Romans 6:16 how this slavery works: **Know ye not, that to whom ye yield yourselves servants to obey, his servants ye are to whom ye obey; whether of sin unto death, or of obedience unto righteousness?** The human race has experienced hard times at the hand of Satan ever since. Our Father, who exercises compassion, uses faith to rescue us from our misery.

God expects obedience by faith and not by sight or hearing or any other sense, as these Scriptures confirm:

> **I, the LORD, refuse to accept anyone who is proud. Only those who live by faith are acceptable to me** (Habakkuk 2:4 CEV).
>
> **Now, the Just shall live by faith. But if he draws back, My soul shall have no pleasure in him** (Hebrews 10:38).
>
> **For therein is the righteousness of God revealed from faith to faith: as it is written, The just shall live by faith** (Romans 1:17).
>
> **But that no one is justified by the Law in the sight of God** *is* **clear, for, "The just shall live by faith"** (Galatians 3:11).

God places a very high value on the words He spoke to us. He placed His WORD higher than His NAME: **. . . for You have magnified Your Word above all Your name** (Psalm 138:2). We have trouble trusting His words. Satan is always prompting our carnal mind to ask the question: "Can God be trusted?" Meanwhile, God has placed His word as the highest force and the most revered thing in the whole universe. Jesus said this about these words: **Heaven and earth shall pass away, but my words shall not pass away** (Matthew 24:35).

Jesus expects us to live by the WORDS that He spoke. **It is the Spirit that makes alive, the flesh profits nothing. The words that I speak to you are spirit and are life** (John 6:63).

The kingdom of God is a very real kingdom where men will live in good health, prosperity and peace for all eternity. One peculiar fact about this kingdom is that it will be populated totally by volunteers. Those who make the choice of going there will escape hell and gain eternal life. But it is totally based on faith in the word of God.

# 61 GOD IS TO BE FEARED

Some men had sense enough to fear God even without a whole lot of written material about Him. Abraham was one of those: **And He said, Do not lay your hand on the lad, nor do anything to him. For now I know that you fear God, since you have not withheld your son, your only one, from Me** (Genesis 22:12). When Joseph spoke to his brothers in Genesis 42:18, he told them he feared God, even though he was hiding his true identity from them: **Joseph said to them the third day, Do *this* and live. I fear God.**

Some men do not have sense enough to fear God. Pharaoh did not fear Him and paid a horrible price for his arrogance. After the 7th plague of hail in Exodus 9:30, Moses observed: ***as for* you and your servants, I know that you will not yet fear Jehovah God.** God has warned us to fear Him. Our godly fear is often reflected in the way we treat one another. He voices warnings in the following verses:

> **You shall not curse the deaf, nor put a stumbling-block before <u>the blind</u>, but shall fear your God. I *am* Jehovah** (Leviticus 19:14).
>
> **You shall rise up before the gray head and honor the face of <u>the old man</u>, and fear your God. I *am* Jehovah** (Leviticus 19:32).
>
> **Let us hear the <u>conclusion</u> of the whole matter. Fear God, and keep His commandments. For this is the <u>whole duty of man</u>** (Ecclesiastes 12:13).

Jesus gave us good reason to fear God: **And do not fear those who kill the body, but are not able to kill the soul. But rather fear Him who <u>can destroy both soul and body in hell</u>** (Matthew 10:28). Someone put it this way: fear Him who, when you are dead, isn't finished with you yet!

*Ralph H. Matthews*

# 62  GOD IS THE ULTIMATE TERRORIST

God invented punishment and constructed Hell. Satan and the angels who followed him causing war in Heaven were among the first to experience His terror. God banished them from His presence and they will eventually know the everlasting horror of hell.

He destroyed the entire earth and its population during Noah's time. This could have been called the first global cleansing, and God did it: **Every living creature on the face of the earth was wiped out. Humans, domestic animals, crawling creatures, and birds were wiped off the earth. Only Noah and those with him in the ship were left** (Genesis 7:23 GW). Men and women outside that Ark, on the first day of rain, would have known terror. In their last moments they would have known that they had spurned the mercy of God and would never be given another chance. When humans terrorize other humans, there is always a glimmer of hope that someone will come to the rescue or the oppressor will stop, but when men face the wrath of God there is no such hope.

In Ezekiel 30:1-2 (GNB) God gives warning that He is capable of terrorizing: **The LORD spoke to me again. "Mortal man," he said, "prophesy and announce what I, the Sovereign LORD, am saying. You are to shout these words: A day of terror is coming!"** In Joel 1:15 (GNB), the prophet warns of the same: **The day of the LORD is near, the day when the Almighty brings destruction. What terror that day will bring!** We need to heed His words because God, during this Age of Grace, is giving advanced warning as to what the future holds for those who ignore Him.

In Psalm 50, God condemns wicked people and concludes with this warning: **"Consider this, you who forget God, or I will tear you to pieces, with none to rescue you** (v 22 NIV). Jesus sternly warns unbelievers that His Father reserves the right to take body and soul, after we are dead, and send it to hell (Matthew 10:28). Now that's terrifying!

## What is God Like?

Meanwhile, we have no need to dwell on terror if we have accepted His offer of salvation. Instead we can capitalize on His grace. He rewards those who fear him. Here are three references:

**He will <u>fulfill the desire</u> of those who fear Him; He also will <u>hear their cry</u>, and will <u>save them.</u> Jehovah takes <u>pleasure</u> in those who fear Him, who hope in His mercy** (Psalm 145:19; 147:11).

**But without faith** *it is* **impossible to please** *Him,* **for he who comes to God must believe that He is and** *that* **He is a rewarder of those who diligently seek Him** (Hebrews 11:6).

# 63 GOD HAS LIKES AND DISLIKES

God was pleased with His new creation. When He finished making it all, He concluded that it was all good. He liked Adam and wanted to spend time with him. He liked giving Adam good things.

- He gave him a garden, a job, food, and a profession.

- He gave Adam authority to rule the planet.

- He gave him a wife to help him.

- He gave him the best wedding gift ever, sex. **And God blessed them. And God said to them, Be fruitful, and multiply and fill the earth, and subdue it** (Genesis 1:28). Fruitfulness and multiplying involves sex.

God liked what He saw in certain people and was attracted to them: Abel, Abraham, Noah, Moses and David, etc. They were singled out and blessed. He liked what He saw in Enoch. He walked with this man, had fellowship with him and then took him directly from earth into heaven without a funeral. **And Enoch walked with God, and then he *was* not, for God took him** (Genesis 5:24).

His greatest dislike would easily be disobedience. His reaction is drastic: Death! God loves the sinner, but He hates all sin, as noted below:

> **Live in the fear of GOD—be most careful, for GOD hates dishonesty, partiality, and bribery** (2 Chronicles 19:7 MSG).

> **GOD hates cheating in the marketplace; he loves it when business is aboveboard** (Proverbs 11:1 MSG).

> **You must not worship the LORD your God in their way, because in worshiping their gods, they do all kinds of detestable things the LORD hates. They even burn their sons and daughters in the fire as sacrifices to their gods** (Deuteronomy 12:31 NIV).

*What is God Like?*

When His Word so emphatically states that there are things that He dislikes and even hates, how careful we should be to avoid these sins.

*Ralph H. Matthews*

# 64 GOD HAS INCREDIBLE PATIENCE

God waited about sixteen hundred and fifty six years for one man to arrive. Before destroying all of mankind, God needed one righteous man, Noah, to replenish the earth: **But Noah found grace in the eyes of Jehovah. These *are* the generations of Noah. Noah was a just man and perfect in his generations. Noah walked with God** (Genesis 6:8-9). Then, He waited another one hundred and twenty years for mankind to repent before sending the flood: **And Jehovah said, My Spirit shall not always strive with man in their erring; he is flesh. And his days shall be a hundred and twenty years** (Genesis 6:3). God has always waited patiently for righteous men to worship Him. From Noah to Abraham He waited approximately another 400 years. Now that's patience!

From day one His purpose was to have a people to call His own who would fellowship and worship Him. Abraham's descendants were selected to be that people. However, to train them He had to send them into Egypt to learn the basics of obedience and trust. God did this and then waited another four hundred years: **And He said to Abram, You must surely know that your seed shall be a stranger in a land not theirs, and shall serve them. And they shall afflict them four hundred years. And also I will judge that nation whom they shall serve. And afterward they shall come out with great substance** (Genesis 15:13-14).

God loved and cherished the tribe that He had made a covenant with. If you love someone and they are hurting, you hurt too. During Israel's oppression, God felt their pain, but He patiently waited for the right time: **And it happened after many days the king of Egypt died. And the sons of Israel sighed because of the bondage, and they cried, and their cry came up to God because of the bondage. And God heard their groaning, and God remembered His covenant with Abraham, with Isaac, and with Jacob. And God looked upon the sons of Israel, and God knew *them*** (Exodus 2:23-25).

God also waited for the right time when He would solve the sin problem for us, once and for all: **But when the fullness of the time came, God sent forth His Son, coming into being out of a woman, having come under Law, that He might redeem those under Law, so that we might receive the adoption of sons** (Galatians 4:4-5).

He still waits patiently for His people to come back to Him. His warning that he will not always strive with us is as relevant now as it was in Noah's day (Genesis 6:3). What can be done with people who ignore warnings? To date, every conceivable thing that can be done has been done. People were warned; the warnings were ignored; God's patience ran out; then they were destroyed. God still issues warnings and they are still falling on deaf ears. This is one from the writings of Paul in 2 Thessalonians 1:8-9: . . . **in flaming fire taking vengeance on those who do not know God and who do not obey the gospel of our Lord Jesus Christ, who shall be punished with everlasting destruction from the presence of the Lord and from the glory of His power.** The Doomsday Clock is minutes from the midnight hour but our world shows no real concern. The book of Revelation covers tomorrow's news but the majority of people are not reading it. Meanwhile, God patiently waits.

# 65  GOD IS BIG ON SYMBOLS

Merriam-Webster defines symbols as: *something that stands for or suggests something else by reason of relationship, association, convention, or accidental resemblance; especially*: *a visible sign of something invisible* (*the lion is a symbol* of *courage*). We use symbols every day. There are literally thousands of symbols around us that communicate thoughts and teach us how to interact with things and with each other. We use them because they are an efficient means of communicating. Your car dashboard likely uses the symbol of a gas pump to represent the gas in the tank; an hourglass symbolizes time; an arrow on the highway symbolizes direction; the "$" sign means money . . . the list is long and varied.

God uses symbols extensively throughout the Bible. He used symbols for much the same reason we do—to communicate and teach the most profound lessons we will ever learn. For example, in the Old Testament Law, a lamb symbolized His Son, Jesus. From any viewpoint, no greater person existed in Heaven or on earth than God's own Son, and He picked the lowly lamb to symbolize Him. God was, and still is, extremely sensitive about any symbol that represented His Son. He instructed Moses that the lamb picked to represent Jesus had to be absolutely perfect. **Your lamb shall be without blemish, a male of the first year** (Exodus 12:5). Its age symbolized Christ in the prime of His life.

This symbol of Jesus is carried all the way throughout the Old and New Testament to the last chapter in the Bible: **And every curse will no longer be; but the throne of God and of the Lamb will be in it, and His servants will serve Him** (Revelation 22:3). The killing of the lamb symbolized the killing of Jesus. John the Baptist, for the first time in scripture, identifies Jesus as The Lamb: **The next day John saw Jesus coming toward him and said, "Look! The Lamb of God who takes away the sin of the world** (John 1:29 NLT)!

Jesus Himself presented us with two new symbols, the bread which symbolized his broken body, and the wine which symbolized His shed blood. He commanded us to remember Him and celebrate the sacrifice He made for us: **He took some bread and gave thanks to God for it. Then He broke it in pieces and gave it to the disciples, saying, "This is My body, which is given** for you. Do this to remember Me." After supper He took another cup of wine and said, "This cup is the new covenant between God and His people—an agreement confirmed with My blood, which is poured out as a sacrifice for you (Luke 22:19-20 NLT).

In Revelations 5:5, Jesus is also symbolized by a powerful lion: **And one of the elders said to me, Do not weep. Behold, the Lion of the tribe of Judah, the Root of David, has prevailed to open the book and to loose the seven seals of it.** Here He is being introduced not as a gentle, submissive animal but as a conquering victorious lion getting ready to unleash seven seals (global disasters) upon the earth.

Only when we understand the importance that God placed on symbols can we understand Leviticus 21:17-21.

> **Speak to Aaron, saying, No man of your seed in their generations shall draw near to offer the bread of his God if there is a blemish in him. For no man in whom** *there is* **a blemish shall draw near, a blind man, or a lame man, or disfigured, or deformed, or a man that is broken-footed, or broken-handed, or crook-backed, or a crushed one, or who has a blemish in his eye, or a scurvy or scabbed person, or one with crushed testicles. No man of the seed of Aaron, the priest, in whom there is a blemish shall come near to offer the fire offerings of Jehovah. He has a blemish; he shall not come near to offer the bread of his God.**

God was not being harsh or unkind to people with physical flaws. He was simply teaching us that when using ordinary men to represent, or symbolize, Christ they had to be as perfect as could be found. Christ was perfect and the symbol had to be without visible defect in order to represent Him.

The people in the list above were not excluded from his mercy or grace, they just could not be used as a symbol to represent Jesus. They all needed healing and God made provision for them: **And he said, If you will carefully listen to the voice of Jehovah your God, and will do that which is right in His sight, and will give ear to His commandments, and keep all His Laws, I will put none of these diseases upon you; . . . for I** *am* **Jehovah who heals you** (Exodus 15:26). These were the very people that Jesus spent much of His time touching and healing as indicated here:

> **And evening coming on, they brought to Him many who had been possessed with demons. And He cast out the spirits with a word, and healed all who were sick** (Matthew 8:16).
>
> **But when Jesus knew** *it*, **He withdrew Himself from there. And great crowds followed Him, and He healed them all** (Matthew 12:15).

In numerous other ways God used animals, days, trees, and people as symbols to teach the world about their Savior. A study of the Law of Moses will reveal an abundance of symbols that can be studied further. These symbols, in particular, will help in understanding the New Testament.

In 1 John 1:5, the author uses light to symbolize God: **And this is the message which we have heard from Him and declare to you, that God is light, and in Him is no darkness at all.** Darkness is the absence of light and darkness symbolizes sin. When light is removed from an environment we are left with darkness, when God is removed in our world we are left with evil.

Another important symbol would be the tree that Adam and Eve were told not to eat from on pain of death. Since we know the actual fruit was not poisonous, we conclude that the tree symbolized accountability. God had only given one command thus far and it was, "Don't touch that tree." Therefore we can reason that when Adam saw the tree he would have to conclude: "I am required to obey, I am accountable to God. That's what this tree is all about."

The entire book of Leviticus was given to help us understand the meaning of holiness and the holiness of God. This book uses numerous symbols. Spiritual holiness is symbolized by physical perfection; however, it was not just the offering and priests that needed to bodily represent perfection. When an offering was presented in an imperfect manner, God took drastic action: **And Nadab and Abihu, the sons of Aaron, each took his censer and put fire in it, and put incense on it, and offered strange fire before Jehovah, which He had not commanded them. And there went out fire from Jehovah and devoured them, and they died before Jehovah** (Leviticus 10:1-2). Up to this point in time, very few people had been killed by God for a single violation of the Law; however, in His wisdom, Jehovah saw fit on this occasion to demonstrate that symbols are important. Don't tamper with them!

Blemishes on the human body symbolized a lack of perfection and serve as a reminder of our spiritual condition before a Holy God. A woman's hemorrhaging after childbirth; sores; burns; baldness; a man's bodily discharge; all were symbols He used to help us remember to try and keep ourselves spiritually perfect. The people bearing these defects were never a problem themselves in God's sight since His love never changes, and He demands that we love all men as we love ourselves. Remember, He also made provision for their healing. Jesus allowed Himself to be whipped so that their bodies could be healed: He **Himself bore our sins in His own body on the tree, that dying to sins, we might live to righteousness; by whose stripes you were healed** (1 Peter 2:24).

There were a number of things that God selected to represent or symbolize Holiness such as:

| | |
|---|---|
| Holy ground | **And He said, Do not come near here. Pull off your sandals from your feet, for the place on which you stand *is* holy ground** (Exodus 3:5). |
| The Holy of Holies | **And you shall hang up the veil under the clasps, that you may bring the ark of the testimony in there within the veil. And the veil shall divide for you between the holy *place* and the Holy of Holies** (Exodus 26:33). |
| Holy Perfume | **And you shall make it a perfume, an incense according to the art of the perfumer, salted, pure *and* holy. And you shall beat *some* of it very small, and put it before the testimony in the tabernacle of the congregation, where I will meet with you. It shall be most holy to you** (Exodus 30:35-36). |
| Holy Bread | **And the rest of it Aaron and his sons shall eat. It shall be eaten *with* unleavened bread in the holy place. They shall eat it in the court of the tabernacle of the congregation. It shall not be baked with leaven. I have given it *as* their portion of My offerings made by fire. It *is* most holy, as is the sin offering, and as the trespass offering is** (Leviticus 6:16-17). |

His very presence was symbolized by a cloud that would guide the Hebrews on a daily basis: **And Jehovah went before them by day in a pillar of a cloud, to lead them the right away, and by night in a pillar of fire, to give them light, to go by day and night. He did not take away the pillar of the cloud by day, nor the pillar of fire by night, *from* before the people** (Exodus 13:21-22).

He picked eight creeping things in Leviticus 11:29-30 (KJV) to represent uncleanness: the weasel, mouse, tortoise, ferret, chameleon, lizard, snail and mole. Seeing these creatures would be a constant reminder to the Hebrew that he must try and present himself holy before the Lord and obey His commands. He picked twelve unclean persons and things all for the same purpose: to remind man of the Holiness of God (Dake Page 135).

1. A man with a running issue or a bodily discharge (Leviticus 15:2-3).

2. The bed on which he lies (Leviticus 15:4).

3. The chair on which he sits (Leviticus 15:4).

4. Any person who touches such a man's bed (Leviticus 15:5).

5. Any person who sits on the chair on which he sat (Leviticus 15:6).

6. Any person who touches the flesh of such a man (Leviticus 15:7).

7. One who contacts his spittle (Leviticus 15:8).

8. The saddle on which the man rides (Leviticus 15:9).

9. Whoever touches what was underneath him (Leviticus 15:10).

10. Whoever carries any of those things (Leviticus 15:10).

11. Anyone touched by the man without washing his hands (Leviticus 15:11).

12. Any vessel that he touches (Leviticus 15:12).

Water baptism symbolizes our death to an old way of life and the beginning of a new one: **Therefore go and teach all nations, baptizing them in the name of the Father and of the Son and of the Holy Spirit** (Matthew 28:19). You go down into the water a sinner and come up a new creature. **Therefore we are buried with him by baptism into death: that like as Christ was raised up from the dead by the glory of the Father, even so we also should walk in newness of life** (Romans 6:4 KJV).

A command is attached to the use of two New Testament symbols: celebration of the New Covenant in Blood and water baptism. Regarding the first Jesus said, "<u>Do this </u>in remembrance of Me," in the second He said, "<u>Go and baptize </u>them in the name of the Father and of the Son." Let us not forget that He always means what He says.

The cross is a sacred symbol for Christians (but, nowhere are we commanded to make an image of one and wear it around our neck). It reminds us that the love of God surpasses the love of all others and no sacrifice could be greater: **No one has greater love than this, that a man lay down his life for his friends** (John 15:13).

God will continue to use symbols in the future. In Revelation fine linen is symbolic of the righteousness of the Saints: **And to her was granted that she should be arrayed in fine linen, clean and white. For the fine linen is the righteousness of the saints** (Revelation 19:8). In Revelation He also uses the symbol of stars to represent angels, lamps to represent churches and a prostitute to represent Babylon.

If symbols are important to God they ought to be important to us. He uses them in communicating His thoughts and plans to us. We need to study them if we want to more fully understand His Word.

*Ralph H. Matthews*

# 66  GOD DESIRES TO BLESS

God blessed animals, Adam, a day (the Sabbath), Noah, Abraham, Ishmael, Isaac and Jacob. He blessed men in spite of their sins. He is liberal with His blessings and has poured them out on numerous occasions and is still doing so. We are all still enjoying the earthly home He built for us with its blessings of sunshine, rain and food.

Even from the beginning, God showed us he wanted to bless us, and did it with more than words. His first blessing was on the creatures of the sea and birds of the air: **And God blessed them, saying, Be fruitful and multiply, and fill the waters of the seas and let the fowl multiply in the earth** (Genesis 1:22).

His second blessing was on the human race: **And God blessed them. And God said to them, Be fruitful, and multiply and fill the earth, and subdue it. And have dominion over the fish of the sea and over the fowl of the heavens, and all animals that move upon the earth** (Genesis 1:28).

His third blessing was on a Day: **He blessed the seventh day and set it apart as a special day, because by that day he had completed his creation and stopped working** (Genesis 2:3 GNB). Regarding this special day, The Geneva Study Bible adds: *Appointed it to be kept holy, that man might in it consider the excellency of his works and God's goodness toward him* (Salem Communications Corporation).

His fourth blessing was on a particular man: **And God blessed Noah and his sons. And He said to them, Be fruitful and multiply, and fill the earth** (Genesis 9:1).

His fifth blessing was on a very special man, Abraham: **And I will make you a great nation. And I will bless you and make your name great. And you shall be a blessing. And I will bless those that bless you and curse the one who curses you. And in you shall all families of the earth be blessed** (Genesis 12:2-3).

His sixth blessing was on Ishmael: **And as for Ishmael, I have heard you. Behold, I have blessed him, and will make him fruitful, and will multiply him exceedingly. He shall father twelve chiefs, and I will make him a great** nation (Genesis 17:20). In spite of this man's obstinacy, God still poured out a blessing upon him. The angel who visited his mother, Hagar, prophetically spoke this regarding Ishmael: **And the Angel of Jehovah said to her, Behold, you are with child, and shall bear a son. And you shall call his name Ishmael, because Jehovah has heard your affliction. And he will be a wild man. His hand will be against every man, and every man's hand against him. And he shall live in the presence of all his brothers** (Genesis 16:11-12).

The seventh blessing was on Abraham after he passed his difficult test of obedience: **that in blessing I will bless you, and in multiplying I will multiply your seed like the stars of the heavens, and as the sand which is upon the seashore. And your Seed shall possess the gate of His enemies. And in your Seed shall all the nations of the earth be blessed, because you have obeyed My voice** (Genesis 22:17-18).

He blessed Isaac: **And after the death of Abraham, it happened that God blessed his son Isaac** (Genesis 25:11).

Jacob received a blessing by demanding it. He spent a night wrestling with God and refusing to let Him go until he received it: **And He said, Let Me go, for the day breaks. And he said, I will not let You go except You bless me** (Genesis 32:26). In spite of his brashness he got his blessing: **And Jacob asked and said, I pray You, reveal Your name. And He said, Why do you ask after My name? And He blessed him there** (Genesis 32:29). Wrestle with God Almighty? And live? I think God must have enjoyed the uneven match because of what He said here: **And He said, Your name shall no longer be called Jacob, but Israel; for like a prince you have power with God and with men, and have prevailed** (Genesis 32:28).

Here is a very short list from just one chapter of the New Testament (Ephesians 1) where He is still pouring down good gifts upon His children today: In verse one Paul calls them generally, spiritual blessings. He has chosen us (v4); predestinated us (v5 & 11); made us accepted (v6); redeemed us (v7); abounded toward us (v8); made known His mysteries to us (v9); gave us an inheritance (v11 &14) and tops it all off by putting His seal of approval on us (v13). They are there for the taking.

He likes nothing better than a man who believes in Him so much, and is so desperate for His blessing, that the man will risk life and limb to get the blessing. God is like that.

# 67 GOD HAS INTENSE EMOTIONS

We all have emotions contained in the soul department of our being and they rise and fall with our passions. We are not known to be passionate about everything, all of the time. However, the passions of God are never halfhearted or lukewarm. When the Bible speaks of the emotions of God it is most often described with intensity. If His anger is spoken of, it's often as "very" angry, or "hot" anger. His love is referred to as "great" love and "everlasting" love. When speaking of sorrow, it is intense: **The LORD was sorry that he had made humans on the earth, and he was heartbroken** (Genesis 6:6 GW).

Deuteronomy 29:20 (NLT) warns Israel of His intense hatred toward their sin: **The LORD will never pardon such people. Instead His anger and jealousy will burn against them. All the curses written in this book will come down on them, and the LORD will erase their names from under heaven.** Perhaps this was why David recognized and was afraid of God's intense emotions: **O Jehovah, rebuke me not in Your anger, nor chasten me in the heat of Your fury** (Psalm 6:1). He knew of God's intense anger from another perspective. On one occasion David cried out for help during an extremely difficult trial: **In my distress I called on Jehovah, and I cried to my God; He heard my voice out of His temple, and my cry came before Him, into His ears. Then the earth shook and trembled; and the foundations of the hills moved and were shaken, <u>because He was angry</u>. A smoke went up out of His nostrils, and fire devoured out of His mouth; coals were kindled by it. And He bowed the heavens and came down, and darkness was under His feet** (Psalm 18:6-9).

Once His compassion and mercy have been ignored, God is capable of hot anger against even those He loves. In Judges 2:14 (BBE), God was angry with Israel because they were worshipping Baal and other false gods, **and he gave them up into the hands of those who violently took their property, and into the hands of their haters all round them, so that they were forced to give way before them.** He is a God of love, but He is no stranger to anger, and we would do well to keep this in mind. His fury and hot anger can be unleashed at any time on those who ignore Him: **Therefore wait for Me, says Jehovah, for the day I rise up to the prey; for My judgment *is* to gather the nations, for**

**Me to collect the kingdoms, to pour on them My fury, all My hot anger. For all the earth shall be burned up with the fire of My jealousy** (Zephaniah 3:8).

His intense emotions should never be confused with our human behavior of "getting even." Every action of God emerges from His holiness and justice. He did make it clear from the beginning that if we sin, we die (Genesis 2:17). However, in tender mercy He waits and forgives and waits some more: . . . **Jehovah God, merciful and gracious, long-suffering, and abundant in goodness and truth** (Exodus 34:6). When mercy runs out, He unleashes red hot wrath: **Who can stand before His fury? And who can stand up in the heat of His anger? His fury is poured out like fire, and the rocks are broken down because of Him** (Nahum 1:6).

The positive side of God's emotions is equally intense. His mercy is described as rich and His love is described as great and everlasting.

> **But God, who is rich in mercy, for His great love *with* which He loved us** (Ephesians 2:4).

> **Jehovah has appeared to me from afar, *saying,* Yea, I have loved you with an everlasting love; therefore with loving-kindness I have drawn you** (Jeremiah 31:3).

Eight times in the gospels it is said that Jesus had compassion on the people. He made this compassionate plea in Matthew 23:37 as He spoke to the crowd: **O Jerusalem, Jerusalem, the *one* killing the prophets and stoning those who are sent to her, how often would I have gathered your children together, even as a hen gathers her chicks under *her* wings, and you would not!** At the funeral of Lazarus He was stirred with intense emotion to the point of tears: **Then when He saw her weeping, and also the Jews who came with her weeping, Jesus groaned in the spirit and troubled Himself. And *He* said, Where have you laid him? They said to Him, Lord, come and see. Jesus wept** (John 11:33-35).

Imagine getting God riled up to this extent: **But this is what the Sovereign LORD says: When Gog invades the land of Israel, My fury will boil over! In My jealousy and blazing anger, I promise a mighty shaking in the land of Israel on that day. All living things—the fish in the sea, the birds of the sky, the animals of the field, the small animals that scurry along the ground, and all the people on earth—will quake in terror at My presence. Mountains will be thrown down; cliffs will crumble; walls will fall to the earth** (Ezekiel 38:18-20 NLT).

# 68  GOD LIKES ALTARS

Noah built the first altar mentioned in the Bible, as an act of gratitude for having passed through the judgment of a global flood: **Noah built an altar where he could offer sacrifices to the LORD. Then he offered on the altar one of each kind of animal and bird that could be used for a sacrifice. The smell of the burning offering pleased God, and he said: Never again will I punish the earth for the sinful things its people do. All of them have evil thoughts from the time they are young, but I will never destroy everything that breathes, as I did this time** (Genesis 8:20-21 CEV). Up until this time the Lord had not requested any altars as He did later in the Law of Moses. Yet this man knew that taking the life of an animal, spilling its blood and burning it on an altar would please God.

Abraham built the second altar that we know of: **And Jehovah appeared to Abram and said, I will give this land to your seed. And he built an altar there to Jehovah who appeared to him** (Genesis 12:7). He also built another altar: **And he moved from there to a mountain on the east of Bethel. And he pitched his tent *with* Bethel toward the sea and Hai on the east. And he built an altar there to Jehovah, and called upon the name of Jehovah** (Genesis 12:8). Men who found favor with God such as Abel, Noah and Abraham, and others, offered sacrifices and built altars. They took their desire to worship to a serious level.

When He first gave instructions to Moses to build an altar, God also described its purpose: **You shall make an altar of earth to Me, and shall <u>sacrifice on it</u> your burnt offerings and your peace offerings, your sheep and your oxen. In all places where I record My name I will come to you, and I will bless you** (Exodus 20:24). God still likes altars today, ones whereon we climb and offer *ourselves* as living sacrifices: **I beseech you therefore, brothers, by the mercies of God, to present your bodies a living sacrifice, holy, pleasing to God, *which is* your reasonable service** (Romans 12:1). Altars are places where sacrifices are made. God taught that freewill offerings made on an altar was pleasing to Him. It signified an act of love. There isn't much that we can give someone who has everything and owns it all. However, to offer Him a sacrifice of love, which is what the Old Testament altar sacrifices symbolized, is to demonstrate love in the purest sense. When we climb on the altar to offer ourselves, meaning we crucify our flesh or deny our carnal nature, He accepts this as an act of obedience and love. Jesus gave us very practical examples of self-sacrifice that our Father would classify as pure love: **For I was hungry, and you gave me food; I was thirsty, and you gave Me drink; I was a stranger, and you took Me in; I was naked, and you clothed Me; I was sick, and you visited Me; I was in prison, and you came to Me** (Matthew 25:35-36).

The altar was also a place to ask for forgiveness and to be forgiven. Jesus continued to use the symbol of an altar in His Sermon on the Mount: **But I say, if you are even angry with someone [*without cause*], you are subject to judgment! If you call someone an idiot, you are in danger of being brought before the court. And if you curse someone, you are in danger of the fires of hell. So if you are presenting a sacrifice at the altar in the Temple and you suddenly remember that someone has something against you, leave your sacrifice there at the altar. Go and be reconciled to that person. Then come and offer your sacrifice to God** (Matthew 5:22-24 NLT).

To sum up the meaning and necessity for altars we would have to conclude that they are about forgiveness and sacrifice and that God desires both, but not the Old Testament kind. The modern kind is a living, breathing human who has a willingness to submit to His will. To quote from Romans 12:1 above, they are holy and pleasing to God, and from Hebrews 13:15 they **offer praise to God continually, that is,** *the* **fruit of** *our* **lips, confessing His name.**

# 69  GOD WILL TEST YOU

Any human who shows an interest in God has been tested by Him. He tested the faith of Abraham in this manner: **Some time later, God tested Abraham's faith. "Abraham!" God called. "Yes," he replied. "Here I am." "Take your son, your only son—yes, Isaac, whom you love so much—and go to the land of Moriah. Go and sacrifice him as a burnt offering on one of the mountains, which I will show you"** (Genesis 22:1-2 NLT).

God prepared a test for the fledgling nation of Israel by sending them into Egypt where they would be afflicted: **GOD said to Abram, "Know this: your descendants will live as outsiders in a land not theirs; they'll be enslaved and beaten down for 400 years. Then I'll punish their slave masters; your offspring will march out of there loaded with plunder"** (Genesis 15:13-14 MSG).

He tested Job by allowing Satan to take his children and his wealth: **And Jehovah said to Satan, Behold, all that he has is in your power. Only do not lay your hand upon him. And Satan went forth from the presence of Jehovah** (Job 1:12). That was round one in the exam. God allowed Satan another round to complete the exam. This one involved Job's health and this time Satan was allowed to lay his hand on him: **And Jehovah said to Satan, Behold, he is in your hand, but save his life** (Job 2:6). Satan afflicted Job with painful boils—with God's permission.

God loved David. He said David was a lot like Himself: . . . **He raised up David to them to be their king; to whom He also witnessed and said, I have found David the son of Jesse to be a man after My own heart, who shall fulfill all My will** (Acts 13:22). But God tested him too. He selected him from among his brothers and anointed him to be king in Israel. Then the examination started. God placed David under a madman, Saul, who became obsessed with trying to kill him. But since God had given him a heart like Himself, all David was allowed to do was duck and run when Saul threw spears. Although David could have easily thrown the spears back (and he was good at throwing things), he was only permitted to escape. Saul tracked him with an entire army for about 12 years and all during that time David never fought back. (Gene Edwards writes an excellent account of this in his book, *A Tale of Three*

*Kings*.) After the testing and after he "passed," God placed David in charge of His most precious possession on planet Earth, the apple of His eye, the Jewish nation. David ruled his people well and led them in worship, war, peace and prosperity. David excelled in leading his people to worship and trust God better than any other king throughout history. Further, God is not finished with this man yet. **And David My servant *shall be* King over them. And there shall be one Shepherd to all of them. And they shall walk in My judgments, and obey My Laws, and do them** (Ezekiel 37:24). Reference to David's future is also recorded in Jeremiah: **But they shall serve the LORD their God, and David their king, whom I will raise up unto them** (Jeremiah 30:9).

There were many others who were tested by God. Those who passed were always promoted to higher positions. Joseph was tested and ended up being second in command to the most powerful man on earth during that time: **And Pharaoh took off his ring from his hand, and put it upon Joseph's hand, and arrayed him in vestures of fine linen, and put a gold chain about his neck; And he made him to ride in the second chariot which he had; and they cried before him, Bow the knee: and he made him [ruler] over all the land of Egypt. And Pharaoh said unto Joseph, I [am] Pharaoh, and without thee shall no man lift up his hand or foot in all the land of Egypt** (Genesis 41:42- 44).

As we can see from the few examples above the tests are not oral exams or questions with multiple choice answers. They involve life and death; sometimes even our sanity seems to be at stake. On the surface this seems horrifying and scary, to say the least. We know we have an enemy who is out to kill us in any manner he sees fit. That is how Jesus portrays him: **The thief cometh not, but for to steal, and to kill, and to destroy: I am come that they might have life, and that they might have [it] more abundantly** (John 10:10 KJV). So, why is it that our Heavenly Father sometimes hands us over to Satan for a time of testing? We have life and death tests coming at us from Heaven and a lying murderer coming at us from Hell. In the middle of this, Jesus claims He is offering an *abundant* life! Something seems to be missing. There are some important things we need to understand about this abundant life. We need His Word to put things in proper perspective.

First, Paul teaches that our Heavenly Father can be trusted as a tester of men. **There hath no temptation taken you but such as is common to man: but God *[is]* faithful, who will not suffer you to be tempted above that ye are able; but will with the temptation also make a way to escape, that ye may be able to bear it** (1 Corinthians 10:13 KJV). No matter how desperate our test may appear, God is promising that you are either able to pass it or He is going to cut it short before you break. Granted, this is all about trust. We need to be able to answer this very important question: Can God, who is "all-knowing" and "all-powerful," know when a human has reached his limit? We often wonder during our testing if God knows how far He has pushed us. Once we get to know Him we would have to conclude that He does know our limits, and would have to admit that we don't know our own limits. The Designer knows the limits of His design. Any good human designer would know this about the innovations they work on. A designer of cars would know better than to expect his model to achieve 300 mph if he had designed it for only 200 mph. We question God's ability because we have never been stretched this far before. It all boils down to trust, the very thing the test was designed for! It would be sad indeed if the Great Designer created beings in His own image and breathed His own breath into them and they could never learn to trust Him. Trials and tests are His method of overcoming this problem. When we learn to trust Him we pass the test. Meanwhile, for every time we fail, He is nearby, offering gentle mercy, encouragement, teaching and always giving a second chance.

Second, God has provided some supernatural protection to guarantee our success during every test, if we only learn to use it: **Wherefore take unto you the whole armor of God, that ye may be able to withstand in the evil day, and having done all, to stand** (Ephesians 6:13 KJV). This protection is adequate and covers every part of the body except the back. No provision is made for retreat! **Stand therefore, having your loins girt about with truth, and having on the breastplate of righteousness; And your feet shod with the preparation of the gospel of peace; Above all, taking the shield of faith, wherewith ye shall be able to quench all the fiery darts of the wicked** (Ephesians 6:14-16 KJV).

This supernatural protection includes an offensive and powerful weapon. When we normally think of fighting we would like a dependable gun or at least a knife in our hands. God is offering a totally different kind of weapon—one in your Spirit and your mind. According to Him it is more reliable that any gun or knife. To utilize this spiritual weapon you stop what you are doing pick up the Word and speak it. Weird or what! Ephesians 6:17 tells us to **take the helmet of salvation, and the sword of the Spirit, which is the word of God.** This is no ordinary sword when used properly. During His wilderness temptation (Matthew 4: 1-11), Jesus lived out 2 Corinthians 10:4, proving to us that this weapon is very effective against the enemy: **For the weapons of our warfare *are* not fleshly, but mighty through God to the pulling down of strongholds.**

## What is God Like?

The third provision God has given to help us pass the test is two of the mightiest forces in the universe. The first is the Holy Spirit mentioned by Paul in Romans 8:26-27: **Likewise the Spirit also helps our infirmities. For we do not know what we should pray for as we ought, but the Spirit Himself makes intercession for us with groanings which cannot be uttered. And He searching the hearts knows what *is* the mind of the Spirit, because He makes intercession for the saints according to the will of God**. The second is Jesus Himself, who takes our side and prays for us. The writer of Hebrews said this in reference to Jesus: **Therefore He is able also to save to the uttermost those who come unto God by Him,** *since He* **ever lives to make intercession for them** (Hebrews 7:25). So, when God sets an exam we know there is going to be a rough road ahead. However, from the provisions He has made it would certainly seem as if the exam is "rigged" to enable us to pass.

Since tests and trials are so offensive and disruptive (at least to the carnal mind) we need to know their purpose. Why would a kind and gracious God put a man through all this when he has already come over to God's side and surrendered? Why not apply all the suffering associated with testing to sinners? Well, can you see yourself, as a genuine sinner, reacting in any kind of positive manner to having God test you to woo you to His side? Not likely! But Scripture clearly indicates that testing and trials are good for the inner man. The carnal man is still much opposed to anything that disrupts it's comfortable, corrupt nature.

Here is what Paul said about this part of us: **For to be carnally minded** *is* **death, but to be spiritually minded** *is* **life and peace because the carnal mind** *is* **enmity against God, for it is not subject to the Law of God, neither indeed can** *it be* (Romans 8:6-7). We discover that God has a problem with that part of us too because it is not in submission to Him. If we examine ourselves carefully from the stand point of our "Inward Man," we too would have a problem with that other half. The two are constantly at war. Paul describes this battle: **I find then a law: when I will to do the right, evil is present with me. For I delight in the Law of God according to the inward man; but I see another law in my members, warring against the law of my mind, and bringing me into captivity to the law of sin being in my members** (Romans 7:21-23).

We can all identify with this struggle. A part of us wants to do a good thing and another part finds it too much trouble. Our inner man knows we are eating too much but the carnal man says, "But I want more." The inner man knows it should not spend hours in front of a TV looking to be entertained, but the carnal man says, "It's entertaining, and I crave it, now don't bother me with all this moral stuff." As in any battle, there is always a winner. When the carnal man wins, we are in trouble. Its pursuits will eat up our valuable time and may even cause depression or sickness. God looks on and decides we need help. He designs a test specifically to defeat the carnal man and help us become more spiritual. There are numerous Scriptures related to this struggle and the benefits. Here are a few:

> Paul writes: **And not only *this*, but we glory in afflictions also, knowing that afflictions work out patience, and patience *works out* experience, and experience *works out* hope** (Romans 5:3-4).
>
> In this verse Paul makes it clear who must win and who must die: **Therefore, brothers, we are not debtors to the flesh, to live according to the flesh. For if you live according to the flesh, you shall die. But if you through *the* Spirit mortify the deeds of the body, you shall live** (Romans 8:12-13).
>
> The demise of carnal man is not likely to be pleasant: **But those belonging to Christ have with *its* passions and lusts** (Galatians 5:24).
>
> Peter's words encourage us, the test is of great value and comes with a reward: **. . . so that the trial of your faith (being much more precious than that of gold that perishes, but being proven through fire) might be found to praise and honor and glory at the revelation of Jesus Christ** (1 Peter 1:7).
>
> James says it's possible that the inner man can be joyful when the carnal man is being hurting: **My brothers, count *it* all joy when you fall into different kinds of temptations, knowing that the trying of your faith works patience** (James 1:2-3). Testing can never be joyful unless the student is aware of why they are being tested. As students, if we see the goal, we may just be able to see the joy.

We can certainly say, with confidence, that there is value in testing. God uses it to build character, confidence, and strength in our inner man and help us control those parts of us that even we detest. God's exams are designed to answer important questions: Have we accomplished the work that He assigned? Have we used the skills and talents He gave us? Are we using the weapons He provided? Are we advancing His Kingdom by introducing others into it?

God knows that for some, testing will not work. In Exodus 3:19, He planned to test Pharaoh even though He knew Pharaoh would fail. Consider Genesis

**15:13-14: And He said to Abram, You must surely know that your seed shall be a stranger in a land not theirs, and shall serve them. And they shall afflict them four hundred years. And also I will judge that nation whom they shall serve. And afterward they shall come out with great substance.**

If Pharaoh had not failed his test but had let the people go the first time he was ordered, there would be no need for judgment on God's part; however, God knew Pharaoh would fail and knew He would have to judge him. So, why would God test a man knowing the man will fail? The answer is found in David's statement when, in reference to himself, he had sinned by killing one of his own men and committing adultery with the man's wife: **Against you, you only, have I sinned and done what is evil in your sight, so that you are proved right when you speak and justified when you judge** (Psalm 51:4 NIV).

When God gives an order it must be obeyed. Even kings must obey. If no order is given then there is no order to disobey. Paul teaches this in Romans 5:13 when he says, **for until the Law sin was in *the* world, but sin is not imputed *when* there is no law.** In other words, if God had not told Pharaoh to let His people go, there would have been no charge against him. Since God repeatedly ordered Pharaoh to release the Hebrews and Pharaoh disobeyed, there was plenty to charge him with. Therefore, God was justified in what He did to Pharaoh (i.e. testing him knowing he would fail) and could bring clear judgment against him. One other important fact needs to be mentioned relating to Pharaoh (and others like him): his heart was in total rebellion against God to begin with and God in His wisdom knew this. This king was already written off and would be used in the same manner that God uses Satan.

# 70 GOD WILL HURT YOU

It seems strange that the one who created you and made every possible provision for your well-being could end up hurting you. Saint and sinner alike, we are all destined for a bout with pain.

When the big rift occurred between you and Him (you sinned), He fixed the problem by sending His Son to die in your place. Nonetheless, He is going to hurt you. Here is what His Word says about the pain He's got in store for you: **My son, do not make your heart hard against the Lord's teaching; do not be made angry by his training: For to those who are dear to him the Lord says sharp words, and makes the son in whom he has delight undergo pain** (Proverbs 3:11-12 BBE).

The writer of Hebrews 12:5 -10 has the most comprehensive teaching on reasons why God will hurt you. This is the Word of God and is meant to strengthen you during your next bout with pain:

> **And you have forgotten the exhortation which speaks to you as to sons, "My son, despise not the chastening of the Lord, nor faint when you are rebuked by Him; for <u>whom the Lord loves He chastens</u>, and He scourges every son whom He receives." If you endure chastening, God deals with you as with sons, for what son is he whom the father does not chasten?**
>
> **But if you are without chastisement, of which <u>all are partakers</u>, then you are bastards and not sons. Furthermore we have had fathers of our flesh who corrected *us*, and we gave *them* reverence. Shall we not much rather be in subjection to the Father of spirits and live? For truly they chastened *us* for a few days according to their own pleasure, <u>but He for our profit</u>, that *we* might be partakers of His holiness.**

God confirmed in the Old Testament, in many places, that He would use the pain of chastening to keep His people in line. Isaiah spoke for God in this passage: **Behold, I have refined you, but not with silver; I have chosen you in the furnace of affliction** (48:10).

God has been known to test people prior to conversion or children who are established members of His family. Consider the Canaanite woman mentioned in Matthew and Mark. She was outside the family and under a curse pronounced by Noah, on her forefather, Canaan (Genesis 9:25). She really represents all of us because we were all under the cursed of sin. However, she had a problem: her daughter was demon-possessed. No man could help her. She heard that Jesus was in town and from what she heard about Him she knew that He had the power to heal her daughter. This is how Matthew 15:22 recorded it: **And behold, a woman of Canaan coming out of these borders <u>cried to Him</u>, saying, Have mercy on me, O Lord, Son of David! My daughter is grievously vexed with a demon.**

A desperate, loving mother does not mind crying out and being noticed by the crowd when she is sure that the one she cries to can fix her problem. When Matthew called her a Canaanite, he used an archaic Old Testament expression that depicted her as a pagan. She, however, recognized Jesus as the Messiah and addresses Him as, "Lord, Son of David." Not bad for a pagan! Verse 23 tells us that Jesus ignored her: **But <u>He did not answer</u> her a word. And His disciples came and begged Him, saying, Send her away, for she cries after us.**

We will call that slap number one. The disciples did not like her; they found her annoying. We will call that slap number two. Imagine if you or I visited a church and the pastor refused to speak to you when you approached him and the ushers and deacons were requesting to have you thrown out. Most of us would leave in a cloud of dust and give the preacher and the church a bad name, but not this woman. She only had one single thing on her mind, "This Man has the power to heal my daughter and I am not leaving until He does." When He did acknowledge her presence in verse 24, she got slap number three: **But He answered and said, I am not sent except to the lost sheep of the house of Israel.**

It was as if she was too far down under the pile of curses. As a non-Jew she didn't count. What Jesus said was true in that He was sent to the lost sheep of Israel (see Matthew 10:5-6). His disciples would be responsible for taking the gospel to her and the rest of the world—later. At this point we need to remind ourselves of what God is like, and that Jesus is just like Him: He will test people, and this was a perfect test with a perfect student. Jesus knew this woman before she ever showed up and cried out to Him. He knew her heart;

knew that she had tenacity; and knew her need would drive her past the hurt from the insults. He also knew that she represented all sinners under the curse with great needs. He had come to her part of the country knowing she was there, and He knew she could be trusted with a test; a test that was not yet over. Verses 25 and 26 tell us: **Then she came and worshiped Him, saying, Lord, help me! But He answered and said, It is not good to take the children's bread and to throw it to dogs.**

This fourth slap was the hardest. There was a dig in that statement as the Jews often referred to Canaanites as dogs. In spite of what it sounded like, keep in mind that Jesus knew what He was doing because He knew this woman. He knew she would not break; that she would keep coming until she got her answer. This conversation was for all of us who need miracles, because sometimes it's only people with faith and tenacity that get answers. The sad thing for most of us is that we often give up after the first slap. This woman, however, could not be swayed, as verse 27 records: **And she said, True, O Lord; but even the little dogs eat of the crumbs which fall from their masters' tables.**

Her love for her child was so great that she would not be deterred. She knew that Jesus was a healer and she knew that He was the only hope for her demon-possessed daughter. Crumbs would do.

It is possible that the whole angelic population of heaven looking on up to this point may have been in anxious suspense. They may have been wondering if she would break; if Jesus had pushed her too far, slapped her too hard. I am not sure, but as humans if we did not know the outcome we would certainly have questioned His methods. If there are times when the Father and the Son have occasion to have their chest swell with pride over one of their children, verse 28 indicates that this was one: **Then Jesus answered and said to her, <u>O woman, great is your faith</u>! So be it to you even as you wish. And her daughter was healed from that very hour.**

Someday, in Heaven, we will have the opportunity to ask Jesus about this woman. I believe He will tell us that when He left Galilee to go to the region of Tyre and Sidon, His main purpose was to encounter her so He could meet her need. God uses everything and everyone He created. He used this woman to teach the world a lesson about faith with tenacity. The simple solution is to ask, seek and knock. And nobody did it better!

Every prominent man or woman in the Bible endured pain administered by God in various degrees. They all came through it and were better off in the

## What is God Like?

end. Paul was one of them, and he writes in Romans 5:2-5 that the pain He delivers does a marvelous job on our character: **Through Him we also have access by faith into this grace in which we stand, and <u>we rejoice</u> on the hope of the glory of God. And not only this, but <u>we glory in afflictions</u> also, knowing that afflictions work out patience, and patience works out experience, and experience works out hope. And hope does not make us ashamed, because the love of God has been poured out in our hearts through the Holy Spirit given to us.**

By His Spirit He will also supply a measure of grace that will enable you to rejoice through it all. If you are in the midst of a struggle, remember, no struggle last forever—this too shall pass. You have His Word on it.

# 71 GOD LEANS TOWARD MERCY

God hates sin, but because of mercy He provided a very expensive covering for it—lifeblood. It cost an innocent animal its blood to cover the first sin and every sin until the cross. Then it cost God Himself the blood of His very innocent Son. He has done this since Adam and Eve, and is still covering our sins today. When Eve sinned God gave her pain in childbirth and ordained that her husband would rule over her. Adam sinned and God cursed the earth, making it difficult for him to work. Cain sinned and was cursed and the earth was restricted from yielding to him. As much as God hated their sin, He showed them mercy. He even protected Cain from being killed by others (Genesis 4:12-15).

His great dislike for sin is expressed in this verse: **And Jehovah repented that He had made man on the earth, and He *was* angry to His heart. And Jehovah said, I will destroy man whom I have created, from the face of the earth, both man, and beast, and the creeping thing, and the fowls of the air. For I repent that I have made them** (Genesis 6:6-7). Yet, as we see again and again, His mercy is undeniable and He gave these sinners time to repent by allowing them one hundred and twenty more years (Genesis 6:3).

God allowed Moses to live when he complained and did not immediately obey God to go to Pharaoh and order him to release the Hebrews. **Moses said to God, Who *am* I that I should go to Pharaoh, and that I should bring forth the sons of Israel out of Egypt?** (Exodus 3:11). He forgave Moses and extended mercy several times after that.

God allowed Pharaoh to live after he disobeyed Him to let His people go. He forgave Pharaoh's disobedience ten times between Exodus 5 and 11.

God displayed mercy by sending 9 plagues that were *warnings* to Pharaoh:

1. Turned water to blood (Exodus 7:17)

2. Created millions of frogs (Exodus 8:5)

## What is God Like?

3. Turned dust to lice (Exodus 8:17)

4. Created millions of flies (Exodus 8:24)

5. Sent a plague to kill the animals (Exodus 9:6)

6. Brought boils upon the Egyptians (Exodus 9:10)

7. Sent hail storm to kill everything living in the fields (Exodus 9:22)

8. Sent locus to destroyed the barley and flax (Exodus 10:12)

9. Brought 3 days of intense darkness (Exodus 10:22)

This stubborn, Egyptian ruler was extended the mercy nine times before God put to death every first-born male, including the first born of all livestock in Egypt (Exodus 11:1-5). Meanwhile, a clear warning had been given to Pharaoh by Moses during their *first* meeting: **And I say to you, Let My son go, that he may serve Me. And if you refuse to let him go, behold, I *am* going to kill your son, your first-born** (Exodus 4:23). Finally, in Exodus 11:4, God gave Pharaoh one last warning: "You have until midnight before the killing begins."

This instant in time would mark Egypt's greatest misery. It would mean thousands of dead children, adults and animals in a night. No Egyptian home would be spared. The Egyptians worshiped their beasts and considered them sacred. Pharaoh's heir to the throne would die at midnight. This instant in time would also be significant for the Hebrews. It was the beginning of their new calendar, the beginning of time for Israel, the beginning of freedom and it marked their day of escape from misery and oppression. It marked the first Passover, a very special celebration: **And you shall eat of it this way, *with* your loins girded, your sandals on your feet, and your staff in your hand. And you shall eat it in a hurry. It *is* Jehovah's Passover** (Exodus 12:11).

God brought ten plagues against Pharaoh knowing he would disobey each time. Mercy does not work for some. Only then did He get rid of Pharaoh by making him breathe salt water (Psalms 136:15 in the NLT, NIV, TNIV and MSG versions of the Bible supports that Pharaoh was drowned along with his army). We could compare this act of judgment by God with Pharaoh's own judgment against the Hebrews in Exodus 1:22: **And Pharaoh charged all his people, saying, Every son that is born you shall cast into the river, and every daughter you shall save alive**. This harsh command was intended to wipe out approximately half the population of Israel in one generation and thus completely destroy the nation over time with no males to propagate the race. God's sentence on Egypt was more merciful, in that only the firstborn would die. His justice may seem harsh to some but it was still available and still tempered with unmerited mercy.

# 72  GOD WILL ONE DAY SHOW NO MERCY

This warning came early in the Bible and is very clear: **And Jehovah said, My spirit shall not always strive with man** (Genesis 6:3). There were times when He brought immediate justice to a few individuals for their sins as a reminder to the rest of us. The following are individuals for whom God's mercy expired and death was immediate:

> Two sons of Aaron - **And there went out fire from Jehovah and devoured them, and they died before Jehovah** (Leviticus 10:2).

> Nabal, the stingy drunk - **And it happened about ten days afterward Jehovah struck Nabal so that he died** (1 Samuel 25:38). Nabal had ten days wherein He could have repented.

> Jeroboam, the rebellious king of Israel - **And Jeroboam did not recover strength again in the days of Abijah. And Jehovah struck him and he died** (2 Chronicles 13:20).

> One of David's men - **And the anger of Jehovah was kindled against Uzza, and He struck him because he put his hand to the ark. And he died there before Jehovah** (1 Chronicles 13:10).

In the past His mercy expired for entire cities and nations. God used the army of Israel, under the command of Joshua, to wipe out the nations who occupied the Promised Land because of their extreme wickedness: **And Joshua struck all the land, the hills, and the south, and the valley, and the springs, and all their kings. He left none remaining, but destroyed all that breathed, as Jehovah, the God of Israel commanded** (Joshua 10:40). In the New Testament mercy was removed for Herod and he was struck dead by an angel of the Lord (Acts 12:23). Two church members, Ananias and his wife, died immediately in front of Peter when they lied (Acts 5). Elymas the conjurer was extended mercy but was struck blind (by the hand of the Lord), for a season for opposing the Gospel (Acts 13:11).

He has already wiped out the greater population of the earth once with a flood because His mercy was ignored. He promises in Revelation 20:15 that He will once more destroy sinners by fire when the time is right and when mercy has run its full course: **And if anyone was not found having been written in the Book of Life, he was cast into the Lake of Fire.** Throughout the span of our lives mercy is all we have ever known, and it is difficult to picture that it will someday end in this fashion. We should not take mercy for granted.

# 73  GOD IS A GUARDIAN

The Bible describes God as a shield, a refuge, a defense and a hiding place. In some ways He is strict and unmoving regarding His laws, yet Psalm 91:4 compares the tenderness of God with that of a mother hen: **He shall cover you with His feathers, and under His wings you shall trust.** It's been known that a mother hen instinctively sacrificed herself during a fire by covering her chicks, and when the body was moved after the fire, the chicks ran out alive and well. Matthew 23:37 records the words of Jesus who shared the exact same passion over His people as His Father did: **O Jerusalem, Jerusalem, the *one* killing the prophets and stoning those who are sent to her, how often would I have gathered your children together, even as a hen gathers her chicks under *her* wings, and you would not!** His desire to protect His people exists, in spite of the fact that they hated Him and murdered His messengers and they murdered His Son. Israel turned on Him and would not accept the covering of His wings, but He loved them anyway. Our Creator put that instinct in a mother hen to show us that He cares no less. In fact that is exactly what He did at Calvary!

From our earliest beginning, our forefathers came under His protection. Instead of throwing the book at them when they blatantly sinned, He protected Adam and Eve and their descendants from destruction. He had planned a way of redemption for them and He shielded them in that plan. He could have easily wiped them out and started over.

He still affords a measure of Divine protection to all mankind including sinners who will not recognize Him as Lord. This is seen here in the words of Jesus: **He makes His sun to rise on *the* evil and on *the* good, and sends rain on the just and on the unjust** (Matthew 5:45b).

His followers have been given His Word that He will ultimately protect them now and forever. Divine protection does not necessarily mean that there will be no troubles because, as seen elsewhere in Scripture, trials and pain are part of His teaching process. Here are promises you can count on:

His protective eyes are constantly on you: **For the eyes of Jehovah run to and fro in all the whole earth to show Himself strong on behalf of those whose heart** *is* **perfect toward Him** (2 Chronicles 16:9).

He has assigned guardians who hang out close to you: **The Angel of Jehovah camps round about those who fear Him, and delivers them** (Psalm 34:7).

Psalm 46:1 and 11 assures us that He is watchful and ready to help those in trouble: **God is our refuge and strength, a very present help in trouble . . . Jehovah of Hosts is with us; the God of Jacob is our refuge.**

Have you ever felt that there is someone out to get you and the battle you are facing is a bit too much? Here is a promise He makes to you for such a time: **Bring me out of the net that they hid for me, for You** *are* **my strength** (Psalm 31:4). Would it be safe to relax during such a struggle and trust in His strength? Can He be trusted? If you are not sure just remember this promise: **There has never been the slightest doubt in my mind that the God who started this great work in you would keep at it and bring it to a flourishing finish on the very day Christ Jesus appears** (Philippians 1:6 MSG). His Word is powerful during our time of need. All we have to do is to feed on it and fix it into our memory to draw on when troubles come.

# 74 GOD IS LIGHT

God is the originator of all light. In the beginning He set the Earth rotating at exactly the right distance around the Sun to provide us with heat and light, and He did it all with just four words: "Let there be light."

To dispel our spiritual darkness He is also our spiritual light:

> **In Him was life, and the life was the light of men. And the light shines in the darkness, and the darkness did not overtake it** (John 1:4-5).

> **Every good gift and every perfect gift is from above and comes down from the Father of lights, with whom is no variableness nor shadow of turning** (James 1:17).

> **And this is the message which we have heard from Him and declare to you, that God is light, and in Him is no darkness at all** (1 John 1:5). Light is related to truth, it exposes both good and evil. Nothing can hide from this Light.

According to the following, He will also be the only source of light in the New Jerusalem:

> **The sun will no more be your light by day; nor the brightness of the moon give light to you; but Jehovah will be to you for everlasting light, and your God your glory. Your sun will no more go down, nor your moon withdraw; for Jehovah will be your everlasting light, and the days of your mourning will be ended** (Isaiah 60:19-20).

> **And the city had no need of the sun, nor of the moon, that they might shine in it, for the glory of God illuminated it, and its lamp *is* the Lamb** (Revelation 21:23).

> **And there will be no night there. And they need no lamp, or light of the sun; for the Lord God gives them light. And they will reign forever and ever** (Revelation 22:5).

This concept of God replacing our sun and filling the new universe with His own light is hard to comprehend. After all, the only source of natural light we have ever known on earth is our sun that rises in the morning and goes down at night.

Jesus helps us to comprehend the concept of spiritual light in Matthew 5:14 and 16 (KJV), by informing us that we too are a kind of light in a dark world: **Ye are the light of the world. A city that is set on a hill cannot be hid . . . Let your light so shine before men, that they may see your good works, and glorify your Father which is in heaven.**

We understand from these words that one of the significant features of our light is that it will *glorify* our Heavenly Father.

# 75 GOD DELEGATES MEN TO LEAD MEN

It is obvious that men need leadership. It is also obvious that God Himself does not lead men directly in our earthly affairs. So, why did He not select a wise and powerful angel to lead His people? Why not at least endow leaders with the wisdom of Solomon and the physique of Sampson? Instead, in His wisdom, He opted to call ordinary men to lead other men. He delegates His awesome power of authority to mere humans.

Of course the big problems with that is this—men have trouble following other men. This is not difficult to understand when we recognize the fact that leaders, even the ones that God picks, are imperfect. They have warts, holes in their socks, and sin in their lives. Even the great men recorded in the Bible had some serious problems that would cause their followers to question their leadership. Noah got drunk and ended up naked in his tent where his son, Ham, could behold him in all his glory. Yet Noah's sons were still expected to respect their father. Noah was clearly in the wrong by getting stoned out of his mind but this did not change the fact that he was the leader in his home and his position demanded respect as far as God was concerned. When he sobered up and found out what had happened, he issued a curse upon Ham's descendants that God upheld: **And he said, Cursed** *be* **Canaan. He shall be a servant of servants to his brothers** (Genesis 9:25). If we follow that name through the Old Testament we find in Judges 1 they became servants to the Israelites.

David is yet another example. He had sex with another man's wife and then had the man killed to try and cover up his sin, yet God still expected the Israelites to follow him as their leader. He had delegated him to rule over them and nothing could overturn God's decision. Absalom, David's son, had lost all respect for his father and later led a rebellion against him. Even though David was in the wrong in the way he treated Absalom earlier, the Lord ultimately backed David and the rebellious son died hanging from an oak tree (2 Samuel 18:9-14).

In the New Testament Paul acted like a terrorist to the early church and yet later God expected the early church to follow Paul's leadership. This is what makes it especially difficult to follow mere men: even the best of them sin, their sin is known to God, and yet He uses men to lead men.

He used Moses, a mere human, a hot tempered man, to lead His people out of Egypt. If you didn't know about his temper, read how he killed the Egyptian in Exodus 2:12, smashed the 10 commandments in Exodus 32:19, and hit the rock twice instead of speaking to it in Numbers 20, and in Numbers 16:15 he is described as *very* angry while speaking to the Lord. Regardless, God ordained that He would speak to Moses and Moses would speak to the people. Since this man was probably the greatest leader of men that the earth has ever known we will examine his life a little further.

When God picks a man to lead other men He knows more about that man than the man knows about himself. Moses saw no leadership abilities in himself and offered 11 complaints as to why he couldn't lead and thus highlighting his own flaws:

1. Lack of confidence (Exodus 3:11)

2. Lack of knowledge (Exodus 3:13)

3. Lack of faith (Exodus 4:1)

4. Lack of eloquence (Exodus 4:10)

5. Fear and lack of confidence - he asked God to send someone else (Exodus 4:13)

6. Lack of trust in God and he complained that God had sent him (Exodus 5:22)

7. Lack of confidence - complained that his people would not listen to him and then why would Pharaoh (Exodus 6:12)

8. Lack of confidence—"I speak with faltering lips, why would Pharaoh listen to me?" (Exodus 6:30)

9. Fear of being stoned by the people (Exodus 17:4)

10. Complained of being afflicted, "Why have you afflicted me and why lay the burden of this people on me" (Numbers 11:11)

11. Complained that there was not enough food (Numbers 11:21-22)

In each of his complaints, Moses seemed to be expecting God to be using what Moses *had* or what he *was* or what he *could do*. This was his excuse to the Lord: **"Master, please, I don't talk well. I've never been good with words, neither before nor after you spoke to me. I stutter and stammer"** (Exodus 4:10 MSG). What God was really trying to teach him was that He would be present and doing all the real work: **"So, get going. I'll be right there with you–with your mouth! I'll be right there to teach you what to say"** (Exodus 4:12 MSG).

Moses had trouble with those who were supposed to follow him. His brother and sister rebelled against his leadership and the Israelites at one time were going to kill him. However, when God picks a man to lead, He *equips* the man, *backs* the man, and *expects* the rest to follow.

To say that God supports the men that He appoints as leaders may be putting it mildly. Remember when Aaron and Miriam questioned the leadership of Moses, God struck Miriam with leprosy in Numbers 12:10. How about in chapter 14 when the people rebelled against Moses and Aaron? Here, the Lord made it clear in Numbers 14:11 who they were really opposing: **And Jehovah said to Moses, How long will this people provoke Me? And how long will it be before they believe Me, for all the signs which I have shown among them?** Then, to express how serious He considers rebellion against leaders, the Lord makes this statement in verse 12: **I will strike them with the pestilence and will disinherit them, and will make of you a greater nation and mightier than they.** Thankfully, for Israel, God picked a good leader when He called Moses. This man, in spite of his other flaws, is probably the greatest intercessor that has ever lived. After all, Moses passed up on the offer to have Israel destroyed and have himself become a great nation. Instead, he pleaded with God to spare them. In spite of all the blemishes, this man was perfect for the job and this is why God had picked him to lead in the first place. When God's justice demanded punishment for the Israelites' rebellion, death was within His right to demand: **Behold, all souls *are* Mine. As the soul of the father, also the soul of the son, they *are* Mine. The soul that sins, it shall die** (Ezekiel 18:4). By the letter of the Law, Israel had sinned and was worthy of death. Moses knew that law, but he also understood the longsuffering and compassionate heart of God, and interceded to reach the mercy side of God.

Another good example of how God feels about rebelling against His leaders is found in Numbers 16. A man named Korah opposed Moses with a group of 250 Israelites. Not only did the Lord show support for Moses, He ordered a showdown which resulted in the earth opening up and swallowing the entire household of Korah and his followers and then, in verse 35, burned the other 250 men with **fire which came out from the Lord.**

When it comes to the men that God selects to be leaders, we observe that they are not necessarily greater or smarter than the rest of us, but they are given the responsibility of leading and they are also accountable to God for their behavior: **Yield to those leading you, and be submissive, for they watch for your souls,** *as those who must* **give account, that they may do it with joy and not with grief; for that** *is* **unprofitable for you** (Hebrews 13:17). In the end we subject ourselves not just to the leader God has appointed, but to God Himself; He is the one delegating. Paul teaches the Christians in Rome: **Let every soul be subject to the higher authorities. For there is no authority but of God; the authorities that exist are ordained by God. So that the one resisting the authority resists the ordinance of God; and the ones who resist will receive judgment to themselves** (Romans 13:1-2). Here, it is clear that we bring judgment upon ourselves by disobeying those in authority over us: parents, pastors, prime ministers, presidents, kings, bosses, supervisors and foremen, etc. God placed them over us as a covering. If they fail to cover, they answer to Him and not to us: **Obey your leaders and do what they say. They are watching over you, and they must answer to God. So don't make them sad as they do their work. Make them happy. Otherwise, they won't be able to help you at all** (Hebrews 13:17 CEV).

The principal of God-appointed leaders is relevant inside His own kingdom and also in the world. We might say that the kingdom of this world presently belongs to Satan, but ultimately it is God's and He appoints, or allows, various rulers to govern. This is how God explained it to King Nebuchadnezzar through Daniel who was interpreting the king's dream: **They shall drive you from men, and your dwelling shall be with the animals of the field, and they shall make you eat grass like oxen. And they shall wet you** *with* **the dew of heaven, and seven times shall pass over you, until you know that the Most High rules in the kingdom of men, and gives it to whomever He will** (Daniel 4:25). The ungodly need leadership and God provides it as He sees fit. Jeremiah 27:5 confirms this: **I have made the earth, man, and the animals on the face of the earth, by My great power and by My outstretched arm, and have given it to whom it seemed right to Me.**

## What is God Like?

If we questioned why the earth has seen so many evil and despicable leaders, we would have to conclude that nations get the kind of leaders they deserve. A nation composed of righteous people who are filled with a desire toward the things of God will receive a righteous leader to rule over them. If they are bent on sin, He will allow an ungodly man to rule over them so the oppression brought by an evil ruler will cause the people to call out to God for deliverance. This was repeated over and over by the Israelites. God delivered them every time they repented.

When God calls a man to represent Him in a nation, a church or a home, He supports and backs that man, regardless of their behavior. It's not that God ignores the sin in their lives or that they will not reap what they sow. His Word demonstrates that once you are called to a task, you are given the skills and talents to match the job and God will not remove your gifts. Romans 11:29 supports this: **For the free gifts and calling of God *are* without repentance.**

The best leaders in the Bible were disobedient and obstinate toward God at various times, but He continued to keep them in their position of leadership over others. Moses and David, two of the most prominent leaders, were both guilty of murder, and yet God supported and backed them in leadership. In fact, despite his many failures, this is what God had to say of Moses when his leadership was challenged by Miriam and Aaron: **And Jehovah came down in the pillar of the cloud and stood *in* the door of the tabernacle, and called Aaron and Miriam. And they both came forth. And He said, Hear now My words. If there is a prophet among you, *I* Jehovah will make Myself known to him in a vision, and will speak to him in a dream. Not so, My servant Moses. He *is* faithful in all My house** (Numbers 12:5 -7). Acts 13:22 records this regarding David: **He raised up David to them to be their king; to whom He also witnessed and said, I have found David the *son* of Jesse *to be* a man after My own heart, who shall fulfill all My will.**

Saul had been hand-picked and anointed by God to be a leader over Israel. But Saul changed. He sinned and went against God's will and refused to repent. However, he was not immediately removed from his place of leadership even when God had another king (David) ready to take his place. Saul's gifts regarding his kingship were not removed even though he abused his position and power. God kept the same promise to Saul by not removing the gifts (see Romans 11:29 above).

When a leader is chosen and anointed by God to lead His people, that person is given a grave responsibility and is accountable to the One who appointed him. It should also be obvious that the followers have a serious responsibility and are accountable to their leader because God sides with the leader. This is the warning given in Hebrews 13:17 regarding Godly leaders: **Yield to those leading you, and be submissive, for they watch for your souls,** *as those who must* **give account, that they may do it with joy and not with grief; for that** *is* **unprofitable for you.** Romans 13:1-4 (NLT) teaches that even worldly leaders command the same respect and submission:

**Everyone must submit to governing authorities. For <u>all authority comes from God</u>, and those in positions of authority have been placed there by God. So anyone who rebels against authority is <u>rebelling against what God has instituted</u>, and they will be punished . . . The authorities are God's servants, sent for your good. But if you are doing wrong, of course you should be afraid, for they have the power to punish you. <u>They are God's servants</u>, sent for the very purpose of punishing those who do what is wrong.** The only time when this submission it nullified is when rulers go against the will of God as taught by the apostles: **But Peter and the apostles replied, "We must obey God rather than any human authority** (Acts 5:29 NLT).

Nebuchadnezzar, an ungodly king who at one time was leader of the majority of God's creation, was authorized by God as stated in this verse: **O king, the Most High God gave Nebuchadnezzar your father a kingdom, and majesty, and glory, and honor. And for the majesty that He gave him, all people, nations, and languages trembled and feared before him. He killed whom he would, and whom he would he kept alive. And whom he would, he set up; and whom he would, he put down** (Daniel 5:18-19).

We would do well to heed God's teaching on the subject of following leaders. He warns in this verse to refrain from touching anyone that has His anointing: **He did not allow any man to do them wrong. Yea, He reproved kings for their sakes, saying, Touch not My anointed, and do My prophets no harm** (1 Chronicles 16:21-22). This has nothing to do with leaders being perfect, sinless, smarter, or greater in knowledge; it simply has to do with anointing and authority that goes with the gift. In a family of five there is one leader and four followers; in a company of fifty there is one leader and forty nine followers; in a nation of thirty million there is one leader and 29,999,999 followers. This is how He ordained it. When we change what He ordained there is confusion and disorder.

How should Christians treat leaders over them who are behaving like Saul when he was lording it over David? What should we do when they mistreat us and throw spears at us? David set the perfect example for us when he decided that God would have to fix this problem, in His way and in His time.

*What is God Like?*

He allowed himself only to duck and run. This really means he trusted God, but not the man. For us, it means we place ourselves, ultimately, in total submissiveness to God and trust Him with our very lives. To throw the spears back means we are taking on the fight and with our own skills and cunning to try and fix the problem. It also means that the leader God placed over us is no longer our authority. We remove ourselves from the authority God placed over us as if He had no control and was helpless to protect us. We would do well to remember His promise that **He will not fail you nor forsake you** (Deuteronomy 31:8). If we trust Him to take care of a leader who is in error, we will learn that in the meantime He is knocking rough spots off us and developing character in us as He did David. God may even be calling it chastisement!

# 76 GOD IS TOUGH

In spite of the fact that God is Love and shows great mercy and compassion, He is tough. He invented 'tough love.' He is tough on sin and disobedience. He is tough on both sinners and Christians.

In Genesis 2:17, God told Adam he would die if he disobeyed and ate from the tree of knowledge of good and evil. On that day, Adam's spiritual life was taken from him and he and his wife were driven from their home.

In Deuteronomy 1, the Israelites disobeyed God by not going to war when they were told to, then by going to war to try and make up for the disobedience. After their defeat, Moses declared in verse 45: **you returned and wept before Jehovah. But Jehovah would not listen to your voice, nor give ear to you.**

The Lord got tough with wicked King Jehoram, who had murdered his entire family and no repentance could be found in him even after he had been warned: **And after this Jehovah struck him in his bowels with a disease that could not be cured. And it happened as days and as the time went out, at the end of two years, his bowels fell out because of his sickness. And he died of painful diseases . . .** (2 Chronicles 21:18-19).

He can dish out severe punishment when warranted: **And I will set My face against you, and you shall be slain before your enemies. They that hate you shall reign over you. And you shall flee when none pursues you. And if you will not yet listen to Me for all this, then I will punish you seven times more for your sins** (Leviticus 26:17-18).

God was tough on Joseph. He allowed Joseph to be sold into slavery, allowing him to be accused of a crime he didn't commit and be jailed for it, all to test him for a leadership role. Joseph understood this and explained it to his brothers: **But as for you, you thought evil against me,** *but* **God meant it for good, to bring to pass, as** *it is* **this day, to save a great many people alive** (Genesis 50:20).

## What is God Like?

God was tough on David. He picked this man and had him anointed to rule over His people, but allowed Saul to remain on the throne. Saul was jealous of the young king-to-be and tried to kill him. It seemed God did nothing to protect him. When David fled for his life, Saul hunted him with an army for about 12 years. God noticed that David had a good heart, but allowed him only two options: duck and run. All this was to train him in leadership, recorded in the two books of Samuel. (I encourage you again to read *A Tale of Three Kings*.)

God is tough on lazy people. In 2 Thessalonians 3:10, Paul teaches: **For even when we were with you, we commanded you this, that if anyone would not work, neither should he eat.** One wonders what might happen to lazy people if we and our government practiced God's kind of toughness. Would it solve the problems of street people if they were offered work in exchange for food? If we offered them work and they refused what would we do? Would we wait until they were willing to work and watch them go hungry? Or would we take pity and give them food? From the verse above Paul indicated: no work, no food. (Of course this does not include those who cannot work, such as orphans and the elderly, etc. God takes care of them in other ways as specified through His Word, see Exodus 23:11; Leviticus 19:10; and Galatians 2:10.)

We can conclude that God is right about this for the following reasons: One, a man or woman will work when they are hungry enough. It teaches them that others have to work for their food and so should they. Two, it is right for a man to work. It is good for him, physically, spiritually and mentally. An idle mind and an idle body is a setup for poor health and poor wealth. Three, work gives a man dignity, a sense of self-worth and a sense of belonging to the human race. A man who depends on others to feed him cannot experience this. Four, when God says a man must work in order to eat, it means God believes in the man. God believes the man is capable, that he is not without skills, strength and energy. God believes in work. Genesis 2:15 records the very first thing He gave to man was a job as a gardener. **And Jehovah God took the man and put him into the Garden of Eden to work it and keep it.** This was not a form of punishment or chastisement, because it was given before Adam had sinned. It was only after he had sinned in Genesis 3:17-19 that work was made hard:

> And to Adam He said, Because you have listened to the voice of your wife and have eaten of the tree, of which I commanded you, saying, You shall not eat *of* it! The <u>ground *is* cursed for your sake</u>. In pain shall you eat of it all the days of your life. It shall also bring forth

> thorns and thistles to you, and you shall eat the herb of the field. In the <u>**sweat of your face you shall eat bread**</u> until you return to the ground, for out of it you were taken. For dust you *are*, and to dust you shall return.

Every man and woman with a healthy mind and body likes to work. When we feed a lazy man, we commit a crime against him by treating him opposite to how God would treat him. We treat him as though he is incapable and believe he is less than ourselves—we can do it but he can't. We unwittingly label them as useless and helpless. Since we know that God is neither mean nor cruel, we must conclude that letting a man who refuses to work go hungry is good for the man.

We should use wisdom and listen to what God says in His Word. This is where we ought to use compassion and wisdom: when work is offered to the poor, see to it that the man or woman is up to the task. Take the time to encourage them and get them to a work site if necessary. For someone starting over, training and patience may be needed, with some coaching along the way. Unhealthy people should be nursed back to health. Discouraged people who are down need to be counseled and helped back up. However, healthy people who will not work should be left that way until they get hungry enough to work. God is tough but wise.

It is interesting to note that there are others in the secular world who also believe in being tough but wise with the poor. Lester Thurow, a New York Times bestselling author, writes a book on the global economy, *Fortune Favors The Bold* (Page 224):

> "How should people in the wealthy developed world help people in the poor developing world? The answer is to help those who have the necessary social organization. Foreign aid is not a matter of giving money regardless of outcomes or of giving money to the poorest countries. Not all poor countries should be helped. Aid should go to those who can efficiently use it. If foreign aid doesn't go to the right countries, it simply ends up in corrupt hands.

> "For proof that aid without social organization does not work, look at Nigeria. It has received over $250 billion in oil revenues since its independence, yet its per capita GDP is only one-third of what it was then. Outside aid is important, but it is not the starting point of economic development. The real starting point is found in social organization."

## What is God Like?

When nations give aid to other nations without using wisdom, their money is wasted. When we give to individuals who are not "socially organized" enough to work, we could be squandering our money. There are lots of deserving people such as those in industrious nations or a poor family down the street who could use the help.

God is tough on Christians, even when they surrender their lives to Him. Apparently, we will not learn any other way. It seems as if when things are going well for us we tend to wander further away from Him. The writer of Proverbs agrees and gives us this advice: **My son, do not despise the chastening of Jehovah; nor be weary with His correction; for whom Jehovah loves He corrects, even as a father** *corrects* **the son** *in whom* **he delights** (Proverbs 3:11-12). Hebrews 12:6 suggests that chastisement is inevitable and necessary: . . . **for whom the Lord loves He chastens.**

Often we lose sight of why God is tough on us. We get caught up in the pain and we forget the purpose. This passage in Hebrews 12:11 (MSG) is worth remembering: **At the time, discipline isn't much fun. It always feels like it's going against the grain. Later, of course, it pays off handsomely, for it's the well-trained who find themselves mature in their relationship with God.**

God was very tough on His only Son. Jesus was required to leave the comforts of heaven and come to live on our planet. God knew that even His chosen people, the Jews, would refuse to accept His Son. He knew the Romans would have no respect for Him and would treat Him as a common troublemaker. They would mock and ridicule Him and without the slightest mercy, whip Him and finally hang Him on a cross to die. God also knew that in His hour of greatest need, every disciple would run for the sake of their own safety. At the end of His torture on the cross, the ultimate pain was administered when the Father turned is back toward His Son. Sensing this, Jesus spoke these words recorded in Matthew 27:46: **And about the ninth hour, Jesus cried with a loud voice, saying, Eli, Eli, lama sabachthani? That is, My God, My God, why have You forsaken me?** No one knows better than God that it is not easy to be tough. When He considered the cost, He decided it was worth it: your life for His Son's!

In every example above, God's display of toughness was for our sake. We just don't seem to be able to have the blessings of God bestowed on us and earnestly seek His face at the same time. If that is not true then God is tough on us for no good reason. The average Christian sins, wanders away, is complacent, careless and prays less when left to him or herself. In His mercy and tenderness, God knows that the pain accompanied by His tough love is the only remedy for our wanderings. When He got tough with Job, the man complained but in his spirit he knew that God knew what was best. This is how Job put it: **Behold, blessed *is* the man whom God corrects. Therefore do not despise the chastening of the Almighty** (Job 5:17).

It is interesting to note the conversation God had with Job at the end of his ordeal. There was no apology from God for giving Job over to Satan who persecuted him mercilessly. There is not a trace of pity in the entire conversation. There is nothing to suggest that it was a mild mannered, low keyed, casual conversation. God spoke to Job out of a whirlwind: **Then the LORD answered Job from the whirlwind: "Who is this that questions My wisdom with such ignorant words? Brace yourself like a man, because I have some questions for you, and you must answer them** (Job 38:1-3 NLT).

During this long conversation between God and Job (about 122 verses - possibly the longest discourse between God and any man in the Bible), God demands answers to a barrage of questions that Job could not answer and the only other important command was that he act like a man. I personally believe this means, "Act like the man I created you to be." Job accepted the chastening and God was pleased. The toughness, in every respect, had been worth it and Job had proven himself to be a man in the eyes of God. This should give us hope that we can too.

When God shows His tough side there is always a purpose. He is never tough just because He is Almighty. Tough love sometimes succeeds in turning rebellious hearts back to Him as it did with King Manasseh. This is a man, who among other things, desecrated the Lord's temple in Jerusalem, worshiped the stars, practiced witchcraft and burned his children alive (See 2 Chronicles 33: 4-6).

> First, the man was warned: **And Jehovah spoke to Manasseh and to His people, but they would not listen** (2 Chronicles 33:10).
>
> Then God got tough: **And Jehovah brought on them the commanders of the army of the king of Assyria, who took Manasseh among the thorns and bound him with chains and carried him to Babylon. And when he was in affliction, he sought Jehovah his God, and humbled himself greatly before the God of his fathers** (2 Chronicles 33:11-12).

## What is God Like?

Then the tough love paid off: **And he prayed to Him, and He was entreated of him, and heard his prayer, and brought him again to Jerusalem into his kingdom. And Manasseh knew that Jehovah is God** (2 Chronicles 33:13).

True to His loving nature, God will always try the easy way first to teach us His ways. When that doesn't work, He warns us. Ignore that and He gets tough.

# 77 GOD BELIEVES IN CAPITAL PUNISHMENT

God has been known to apply the death penalty when justice demands it. Regardless of what you or I, or the politicians believe, this is what God believes. Here are some sins, punishable by death, as listed from Genesis to Deuteronomy:

| Offence | Reference(s) |
|---|---|
| Adultery | Leviticus 20:10; Deuteronomy 22:22-30 |
| Backsliding | Deuteronomy 17:2-7 |
| Bestiality | Exodus 22:19; Leviticus 20:15-16 |
| Blasphemy | Leviticus 24:11-16 |
| Sacrificing of children to idols | Leviticus 20:1-5 NLT |
| Cursing parents | Exodus 21:17; Leviticus 20:9 |
| False prophecy | Deuteronomy 13:1-18; 18:20 |
| Gathering firewood on the Sabbath | Numbers 15:32-36 |
| Idolatry | Exodus 22:20 |
| Kidnaping | Exodus 21:16; Deuteronomy 24:7 |
| Murder | Genesis 9:6; Exodus 21:12; Leviticus 24:17; Numbers 35:16-31; Deuteronomy 19:11-12 |
| Negligence with animals that kill | Exodus 21:28-32 |
| Smiting parents | Exodus 21:15 |
| Sodomy/homosexuality | Leviticus 20:13 |
| Stubbornness and rebellion | Deuteronomy 21:18-23 |
| Whoredom | Leviticus 21:9; Deuteronomy 22:20-21 |
| Witchcraft | Exodus 22:18 |

## What is God Like?

| Working on the Sabbath | Exodus 35:2 |
| Working on day of atonement | Leviticus 23:27-30 |

In the beginning God set one law in place and instigated the death penalty for anyone who broke that law: **And Jehovah God commanded the man, saying, You may freely eat of every tree in the garden, but you shall not eat of the tree of knowledge of good and evil. For in the day that you eat of it you shall surely die** (Genesis 2:16-17). It is obvious from the long list of death penalty sins that eating the fruit from the tree of knowledge of good and evil was not the only sin that could bring death. When God spoke to Ezekiel (18:4) the cause for death was more aptly described: **Behold, all souls *are* Mine. As the soul of the father, also the soul of the son, they *are* Mine. The soul that sins, it shall die.** The reason for death under this law was simply, "If you sin, you die." God cannot tolerate sin and the message being sent to us by this law is quite clear: we must not sin. He cannot tolerate sin because He is holy. He would not be a good judge if He ignored the breaking of laws. The only reason any of us are still alive is that He also has great compassion and mercy. We live because He also made a provision to cover our sin—if we want it covered.

With regard to the death penalty law—if you sin you die—it is obvious that they continued to live after sinning and enjoyed His mercy. Cain murdered his brother but was allowed to live; Moses murdered an Egyptian and God did not kill him; David had one of his soldiers killed and God allowed him to live. In at least these three examples the taking of a human life was involved by another and God showed mercy instead of justice.

However, there were seemingly less heinous sins where He did enforce the death penalty:

Two sons of Judah were killed by God, one for being wicked and the other for spilling his seed on the ground when asked by his father to raise up children unto his dead brother: **But Er was a wicked man in the LORD's sight, so the LORD took his life. Then Judah said to Er's brother Onan, "Go and marry Tamar, as our law requires of the brother of a man who has died. You must produce an heir for your brother." But Onan was not willing to have a child who would not be his own heir. So whenever he had intercourse with his brother's wife, he spilled the semen on the ground. This prevented her from having a child who would belong to his brother. But the LORD considered it evil for Onan to deny a child to his dead brother. So the LORD took Onan's life, too** (Genesis 38:7-10 NLT).

Leviticus 10:1-2 records that God killed two sons of Aaron for disrespecting the offering. Instead of taking fire from the brazen altar as instructed, they used common fire: **And Nadab and Abihu, the sons of Aaron, each took his censer and put fire in it, and put incense on it, and offered strange fire before Jehovah, which He had not commanded them. And there went out fire from Jehovah and devoured them, and they died before Jehovah.**

According to Numbers 14:36-37, the ten spies that Moses sent into the Promised Land who brought back a bad report were killed by God: **And the men whom Moses sent to spy out the land, who returned and made all the congregation to murmur against him, by bringing up an evil report upon the land, even those men that brought up the evil report upon the land died by the plague before Jehovah.**

Very clear instructions as to how the ark was to be transported had been given in Exodus chapters 25 and 37. David, the Levites and Uzza had ignored those instructions. Uzza reached out to steady the Ark of Covenant when the oxen stumbled and 1 Chronicles 13:10 records he was killed by God: **And the anger of Jehovah was kindled against Uzza, and He struck him because he put his hand to the ark. And he died there before Jehovah.**

In the New Testament (Acts 5:5-10), two church members, Ananias and Sapphira, lost their lives for lying to the Holy Spirit.

As a society, what do we learn from God as to when we should enforce the death penalty? We should be obedient to the words of Jesus when He said we have no right to judge others and He ordered us not to judge and issued this stern warning: **Judge not, that you may not be judged. For with whatever judgment you judge, you shall be judged; and with whatever measure you measure out, it shall be measured to you again** (Matthew 7:1-2). There are those in society who have the responsibility of deciding when a man should be executed or whether he should live. We call them judges and they have a grave responsibility. While many of them may not recognize it, their responsibility is to God. It's His creation that they are making decisions about regarding life and death and He made this very clear in many places in the Bible including this one: **Behold, all souls *are* Mine** (Ezekiel 18:4). In the verse above we know that Jesus did not mean that no one could ever be judged because judgment is a necessary part of any society. What He meant was for those of us who are not judges, and have no authority to judge, to stop judging others when it's not our business. Judging is authorized by Him to keep law and order. **Let every soul be subject to the higher authorities. For**

**there is no authority but of God; the authorities that exist are ordained by God** (Romans 13:1).

There are times when a company president or the pastor of a church must pass judgment on an individual under their authority and God would uphold them as they attempt to bring true justice. It is assumed that such judges are only interested in the truth and diligently dig for it. It is also assumed that they base their final judgments on facts and nothing else. When Jesus commanded us not to judge He knew that we have a tendency to judge others based on flimsy evidence or no evidence at all. We rarely dig for all the facts before delivering such judgments. That kind of judging is forbidden.

We see that there is a proper place for judging. According to God's own actions we understand that He believes there are some who deserve to die for certain sins. Regarding our involvement in judging my personal belief is this: First, when an accused person is brought before the courts to determine their guilt, the majority of us should not judge them because that is what Jesus ordered. Second, we refrain from judging because we are not party to all the facts in order to make proper judgment. For those whose job it is to judge (you may sit on a board or as a juror someday) we should diligently seek to find all the facts, search our hearts as to our every motive and seek God's face for wisdom. It is an extremely important decision that is about to be made because the life He has placed in our hands belongs to Him.

There were certain people that God killed and others He set free. He knew their hearts and He was the only one who knew their hearts. We can be sure that He killed no one who did not deserve to die and set no one free that did not deserve to be set free. In making our decisions as to who goes free or who should die, we need to find out what He thinks about that individual. This is one important time to seek His face. If you are ever put into a situation where the decision must be made as to whether a criminal lives or dies, be sure you know what God is saying. Will He answer your request for such wisdom? Here is the answer: **Call to me and I will answer you. I'll tell you marvelous and wondrous things that you could never figure out on your own** (Jeremiah 33:3 MSG). Is it always that simple? No! Sometimes we have to add asking, seeking and knocking.

# 78 GOD IS A MIRACLE WORKER

God has been known to display miracles to build faith in His children. Sometimes these displays are for the benefit of a leader like Moses to authenticate the divine commission of the leader. Other times, miracles demonstrate the power of God to unbelievers like Pharaoh. As Moses and the Hebrews looked on, their faith in God would be strengthened. The following is a list of the first 7 miracles performed by God:

| REFERENCE | MIRACLE |
| --- | --- |
| Genesis 1 | Creation of the earth by the spoken Word |
| Genesis 7 | The flood that destroyed the entire earth except those on Noah's ark |
| Genesis 11:7-9 | Multiplication of languages at the Tower of Babel to defeat wrong ambition |
| Genesis 19:11 | Sodomites smitten with blindness to punish them for evil intent |
| Genesis 19:24-25 | Destruction of Sodom and Gomorrah as punishment for wickedness |
| Genesis 19:26 | Lot's wife turned into a pillar of salt as punishment for disobedience |
| Exodus 3:2 | The burning bush not consumed designating the call of Moses |

When God planned the deliverance of His children who were slaves in Egypt He put on an awesome display of supernatural power. At the end of the plagues that were rained down on Egypt, God had determined to perform an amazing miracle in the hearts and minds of the Egyptian population. Exodus 11:3 records: **the LORD gave the people favor in the sight of the Egyptians. Moreover the man Moses was very great in the land of Egypt, in the sight of Pharaoh's servants, and in the sight of the people.** Could this be the greatest miracle of all? Consider what these people had just gone through:

1. The Egyptians had endured 3 to 7 weeks of absolute misery because of the Israelites (26 days can actually be totaled).

2. They were about to lose the best work force they ever had. Slaves worked for free and the Jews were possibly the best builders they ever had.

3. They had just suffered 9 plagues, each precisely foretold by Moses and each came to pass exactly as predicted (the 10$^{th}$ plague hadn't happened yet). The Egyptian people would know who to blame.

4. Their land and their economy were almost totally destroyed.

After all this destruction, the Egyptians showed the Israelites . . . *favor?* This was no natural occurrence! God orchestrated this miracle. He had planned from the beginning to have Israel compensated for their labors and suffering in Egypt: **And I will give this people favor in the sight of the Egyptians. And it shall be that when you go, you shall not go empty. But every woman shall ask of her neighbor, and of her that stays in her house, jewels of silver and jewels of gold and clothing. And you shall put *them* upon your sons and upon your daughters. And you shall plunder the Egyptians** (Exodus 3:21-22). When they left, the Hebrews had enough material goods given to them by the Egyptians to last them for forty years.

In the New Testament Jesus did many signs and wonders. He turned water into delicious wine; walked on the surface of a lake, at night, terrifying His disciples (Mark 6:49); and He spoke three words to raise a man from the dead to comfort two sisters: **When he had said this, Jesus called in a loud voice, "Lazarus, come out!" The dead man came out, his hands and feet wrapped with strips of linen, and a cloth around his face. Jesus said to them, "Take off the grave clothes and let him go"** (John 11:43-44 NIV). He healed numerous sick people and set many possessed people free from the bondage of demons.

Miracles still happen today. However, the unbelieving, carnal minded often try to explain away a miracle, or refuse to believe that it happened at all. This occurred many times with the children of Israel. And remember we are just like them. They had just seen the mightiest miracles ever displayed on the earth. They saw themselves protected from the plagues that were rained down upon the Egyptians; they saw the Red Sea part allowing them to escape on dry ground; they saw the Egyptian army drown. But even so, a short time later they manufactured their own god from gold and started to worship it.

In John 9, the people of Jesus day saw a blind man who had been healed by Jesus and refused to believe that a miracle had just taken place. Today there are TV evangelists and others who pray for people and many receive supernatural miracles but there are lots of skeptics. Even some Christians refuse to believe when the supernatural occurs right in front of them. We need to be careful. If God shows up with miracle working power, it would be wise of us to believe because only believers receive miracles: **Jesus said to him, If you can believe, all things *are* possible to him who believes** (Mark 9:23).

However, we need to note that miracles <u>could</u> be a waste of time for unbelievers. All the miracles that God performed were for His Glory (Exodus 14:4 NLT; Numbers 14:22, John 11:4). These miracles did nothing for the stiff-necked Israelites. This was God's assessment of them after all the marvelous things they had just witnessed: **And Jehovah said to Moses, I have seen this people, and behold, it *is* a stiff-necked people** (Exodus 32:9). It was similar in the New Testament. Jesus healed the multitudes, cast out demons, raised the dead, and fed thousands with a boy's lunch. His disciples saw all of these miracles and yet had doubts about this mighty miracle worker until after His death. On the night of His arrest they all deserted Him. Only after His resurrection when they accepted the help of God's Holy Spirit and believed His Word did they become changed, powerful men. What do we learn from this? Miracles don't seem to change us much. We like seeing them but they don't change us. Only His word changes us. He made that clear in this verse: . . . **man does not live on bread alone but on every word that comes from the mouth of the LORD** (Deuteronomy 8:3 NIV). We live by His Word. If you see a miracle today you need another one tomorrow. John confirms: **But despite all the miraculous signs Jesus had done, most of the people still did not believe in Him** (John 12:37 NLT). We tend to forget yesterdays' miracles and focus instead on the need for a new miracle. And that list is endless. Jesus confirms His Fathers words: **"Very truly I tell you, whoever hears my word and believes him who sent me has eternal life and will not be judged but has crossed over from death to life** (John 5:24 NIV). To live, that is <u>really live,</u> you must have God's word in you.

# 79 GOD CAN CREATE MASS CONFUSION

The first language God developed for communication between Himself and man was the one used in the Garden of Eden. That language remained untouched for possibly 2,000 years, at which time God found it necessary to interrupt the communication among men: **Come, let Us go down and there confuse their language, so that they cannot understand one another's speech. So Jehovah scattered them abroad from that place upon the face of all the earth. And they quit building the city. Therefore the name of it is called Babel; because Jehovah confused the language of all the earth there** (Genesis 11:7-8). He created confusion for a purpose and He used it to His advantage. Due to the extreme wickedness of mankind during this period they could have been wiped out, but He simply brought confusion to stop man from continuing with the tower. Mercy, rather than judgment, ruled that day and man was spared and given more time to repent.

On the day of Pentecost, the Holy Spirit did the opposite of what God did at Babel when He brought mass confusion. Men understood each other by the power of the Gift from Heaven; God bridged the gap created by the different languages (and the resulting confusion) with the gift of tongues. Understandable tongues: **And dwelling at Jerusalem there were Jews, devout men out of every nation under heaven. But this sound occurring, the multitude came together and were confounded, because they each heard them speaking in his own dialect. And they were all amazed and marveled, saying to one another, Behold, are not these who speak all Galileans? And how do we each hear in our own dialect in which we were born? Parthians, and Medes, and Elamites, and the dwellers in Mesopotamia, and in Judea, and Cappadocia, in Pontus, and Asia, Phrygia, and Pamphylia, in Egypt, and in the parts of Libya around Cyrene, and strangers of Rome, Jews and proselytes, Cretans and Arabians, we hear them speaking the great things of God in our own languages** (Acts 2:5-11).

God used mass confusion on two other occasions to help Gideon and Saul to defeat their enemies:

> **When the 300 Israelites blew their rams' horns, the LORD caused the warriors in the camp to fight against each other with their swords. Those who were not killed fled to places as far away as Beth-shittah near Zererah and to the border of Abel-meholah near Tabbath** (Judges 7:22 NLT).
>
> **Then Saul and all his men rushed out to the battle and found the Philistines killing each other. There was terrible confusion everywhere** (1 Samuel 14:20 NLT). Verse 23 indicated that this was God's doing.

In a future battle He will, once again use confusion to defeat His enemies:

> **I will summon the sword against you on all the hills of Israel, says the Sovereign LORD. Your men will turn their swords against each other** (Ezekiel 38:21 NLT).
>
> **On that day men will be stricken by the LORD with great panic. Each man will seize each other by the hand, and they will attack one another** (Zechariah 14:13 NIV).

Our merciful Heavenly Father has total and absolute control over all things. He first tries love to woo us. When that doesn't work, He issues warnings. If that doesn't work, He may try confusion. His aim, ultimately, is to win us to Himself for eternity.

# 80 GOD HAND PICKED THE JEWS

First, He handpicked their father, Abraham. Then He made promises to Abraham that related to his offspring, and to every seed that came from their bodies, that He would bless them abundantly.

One might say that hand picking one race over others could be interpreted as being a "respecter of persons." But we know God does not show favoritism. Deuteronomy 10:17 records these words of Moses: **Jehovah your God *is* God of gods, and Lord of lords, a great God, the mighty, and a terrible God, who does not respect persons nor take a bribe.** Before making an assumption that God was frivolously playing favorites by blessing the offspring of Abraham, we must look at the whole picture.

Something very special took place regarding Abraham's "only son" (this is how God referred to Isaac in spite of the fact that Abraham had also fathered Ishmael): **And He said, Take now your son, <u>your only one</u>, Isaac, whom you love. And go into the land of Moriah, and offer him there for a burnt offering upon one of the mountains which I will name to you** (Genesis 22:2). In this same verse, God is telling Abraham to offer Isaac as a living sacrifice. No other human had ever been commanded to do this by God that we know of. He is instructed to take a three day journey. Three days of torture; three days to think it over—obey or disobey; three days to find the answer to the question, "Do I love God this much?" By the time he reaches Mount Moriah in Genesis 22:9-10, he has decided He loves God that much: **And they came to the place which God had told him of. And Abraham built an altar there and laid the wood in order. And he bound his son Isaac and laid him on the altar, on the wood. And Abraham stretched out his hand and <u>took the knife to slay his son</u>.** The Heavenly hosts looking on at this moment were in for the most dramatic, genuine, award winning, cliff hanger ever beamed up from earth. This would be the one to outdo all others. As you know, God stopped him at that instant.

Jehovah did not really require human sacrifices. After the incident with Abraham, God specifically commanded the Hebrews not to offer any humans as sacrifices (see Leviticus 18:21 and Deuteronomy 12:31). This trip to Moriah (in Jerusalem) was used by God to test Abraham's heart. The significance of this event is that in that moment, with the knife above his son's chest, as far as Abraham was concerned, his son was dead. Isaac had been offered. But just as important, also, as far as God was concerned, Isaac had been offered, simply because Abraham's will had been set to obey God and God knew his heart. The sacrifice was given by Abraham and accepted by God. Done deal! So, when Isaac, was *willingly* given back to God as a living sacrifice, the boy now became God's. If Isaac truly belonged to God it meant God could do with him whatever He pleased. No boy had ever been given back to God by a father in such a manner. However, instead of accepting a dead sacrifice, God spared Isaac's life, and now God owned not only Isaac, but all the seed that would come from his body. The "seed" from his body is the nation of Israel.

As legal owner of all the offspring of the "sacrificed" child, God had big plans for them. His first part of the plan had been revealed to Abraham in this passage: **And I will make you a great nation. And I will bless you and make your name great. And you shall be a blessing. And I will bless those that bless you and curse the one who curses you. And in you shall all families of the earth be blessed** (Genesis 12:2-3). This was the good part that would cause any father to get excited. It may even sound like favoritism to some, but later Abraham would hear words that would terrify him: **And it happened as the sun was setting, and a deep sleep fell upon Abram. And, behold, a horror of great darkness fell upon him! And He said to Abram, You must surely know that your seed shall be a stranger in a land not theirs, and shall serve them. And they shall afflict them four hundred years** (Genesis 15:12-13). This was the second part of the plan. God had many plans for this chosen nation to make them a blessing to the whole earth. He had many lessons to teach the whole population of earth using Israel as example, and judgment would be brought to many nations because of the Jews. The greatest blessing Jehovah gave us through this nation was Jesus, who would save any who simply called upon His name. John 4:22 records the words of Jesus to the woman from Samaria: **You worship what you do not know, we know what we worship, for <u>salvation is of the Jews</u>**.

They are a blessing to the world in numerous other ways. Consider these statistics: *Jews make up only 2% of the total U.S. population yet 45% of the top 40 of the Forbes 400 richest Americans are Jewish; One-third of all American multimillionaires*

## What is God Like?

*are Jewish; 25% of all American Noble Prize winners are Jewish.*[6] Men with money spend money. They build things and to do so they hire people who in turn make money. The Jews are responsible for providing jobs to millions of families. God has blessed them with resourceful minds. They discovered vitamins and the vaccines for hepatitis B, polio and cholera. They invented the electrocardiogram; discovered the human blood groups A, B, and O. Dell computers was the brainchild of Michael Dell; Larry Ellison started Oracle Corporation; Robert Pritzker founded Hyatt Hotels; Bernard Marcus gave us Home Depot, to name just a few. The Jews have always been blessed and often their neighbors look on with jealously, and sometimes that turns into hate.

The Jew is no different than the rest of us except for one obvious fact: God has blessed them. They make all the same mistakes and have the same weaknesses we do; have just as many sins; hurt just as easily. God did not make them superior, but He gave them a measure of prosperity that is remarkable. With that, however, they have endured more pain and persecution than any other nation on earth. Jesus taught His disciples: **For to whomever much is given, of him much shall be required.** This is about accountability and responsibility and applies to the Jew and to you and me (Luke 12:48).

Hand picking the Jews to bless them was easy. He is a God of Love and the Bible is full of promises whereby He demonstrated His love toward them. But sending someone you love down into Egypt to become slaves must have been difficult. A couple of days maybe, but 400 years? Oh, the lessons the world would learn from them! Only an obstinate people would do. This is how God Himself described them: **Jehovah said to Moses, I have seen this people, and behold, it *is* a stiff-necked people** (Exodus 32:9). God handpicked them because they are the perfect example for the rest of us. Every negative characteristic they had is a perfect example of us. They were stubborn just like us. They murmured, lusted, rebelled and were unfaithful, just like us. In spite of all this, God still loved them, just like He loves us. It is as if God wanted to show us what we look like and the nation of Israel became an archetype for the whole of humanity. Here is what Paul taught the Christians at Corinth about the Jews:

> **But with many of them God was not well pleased: for they were overthrown in the wilderness. Now these things were our examples, to the intent we should not lust after evil things, as they also lusted . . . Now all these things happened unto them for examples:**

---

[6] The Jewish Phenomenon by Steven Silbiger, back cover.

**and they are written for our admonition, upon whom the ends of the world are come** (1 Corinthians 10:5-6, 11).

His chosen people are very special to God, but that is exactly the message He has tried to teach us through them—we are all special. He really does not place one child above another. The Jew was blessed abundantly and still is, but with the great blessings come great responsibility. God knew they would fail as He knows we all fail. They only learned through suffering, so it is with us.

When our Heavenly Father picked our brother, the Jew, He blessed them and then sent them into slavery. Why slavery? Why not go past Jail, down Mediterranean Ave., board the Pennsylvania Railway and straight into the Promised Land? Unfortunately, it doesn't work that way for any of us. The fact that Israel was the seed of Abraham did not mean that they had bypassed the sinful traits of the seed of Adam. They still sinned like Adam, and all sinners must either die or be redeemed. So, the important purposes that God had for the handpicked "Chosen People," was to demonstrate in them how sinners get redeemed as Paul teaches in 1 Corinthians 10. This demonstration, in which the Jew was used as an example, had to do with four basic steps:

1. They committed lots of sin, which was easy and came natural because they were born that way. Just like us. This was David's confession: **Indeed, I was born guilty. I was a sinner when my mother conceived me** (Psalm 51:5 GW).

2. God gave them the Law to bear witness to their sin. This is what Paul taught the Roman Christians: **But we know that whatever things the Law says, it says to those who are under the Law; so that every mouth may be stopped and all the world may be under judgment before God, because by the works of the Law none of all flesh will be justified in His sight; for through the Law is the knowledge of sin. What shall we say then?** *Is* **the law sin? Let it not be said! But I did not know sin except through the law. For also I did not know lust except the law said, You shall not lust** (Romans 3:19-20; 7:7).

3. Then God *abolished* the law to show them, and us, that we cannot be saved or redeemed by keeping laws:

## What is God Like?

> **Having abolished in His flesh the enmity (the Law of commandments contained in ordinances) so that in Himself He might make the two into one new man, making peace between them;** (Ephesians 2:15).

> The Contemporary English Version puts it this way: **God wiped out the charges that were against us for disobeying the Law of Moses. He took them away and nailed them to the cross** (Colossians 2:14).

> **The Law of Moses is like a shadow of the good things to come. This shadow isn't the good things themselves, because it cannot free people from sin by the sacrifices that are offered year after year** (Hebrews 10:1 CEV).

4. As soon as the Law was fulfilled by Christ, God abolished it since Christ had satisfied all the requirements of the Law and in doing so He became our Redeemer. Abraham's only son was spared from being offered as a human sacrifice, but God did not spare His only Son. He went all the way to the cross (on Mount Moriah in Jerusalem). There are numerous Scriptures to support this. In Matthew 5:18 Jesus assures us that the Law will be fulfilled: **For truly I say to you, Till the heaven and the earth pass away, not one jot or one tittle shall in any way pass from the Law until all is fulfilled.**

Paul explains to the Galatians that *it is faith*, not keeping the Law that justifies us:

> **But we know that God accepts <u>only those who have faith in Jesus Christ</u>. No one can please God by simply obeying the Law. So we put our faith in Christ Jesus, and God accepted us because of our faith** (Galatians 2:16 CEV).

> **But Christ <u>rescued us from the Law's curse</u>, when he became a curse in our place. This is because the Scriptures say that anyone who is nailed to a tree is under a curse** (Galatians 3:13 CEV).

> **So that the Law has become a trainer of us until Christ, <u>that we might be justified by faith</u>. But faith coming, we are no longer under a trainer** (Galatians 3:24-25 CEV).

Jehovah used the Jews to teach the world that we all have a sin problem. He gave them The Law through Moses and we learn that The Law condemns us but it is also our teacher, informing us that we have broken the law of God.

When He was finished with The Law, and in the fullness of time, He sent us our Redeemer, who was a Jew.

But what about all the suffering the Chosen People endured? What purpose did it serve? Satan set up evil nations to persecute them, and God let him. The Egyptians, the Moabites, the Philistines, the Canaanites, the Midianites, the Assyrians, the Babylonians, and many others tormented and plundered Israel. Apparently, as far as God is concerned, there is only one solution to a sinful, stiff-neck: pain and sorrow! (See Psalms 89:32). Rewards, cuddling, and coaxing do not work on humans in their natural sin mode. But pain works, as we discussed in chapter four. God applies it because we are much too precious to Him to be left in our sins.

Meanwhile, the handpicked Jew will continue to suffer for a while longer yet. Jehovah made a promise to their father, Abraham, that He will bring them back into fellowship with Himself and He will. But woe betide those who have persecuted them.

# 81 GOD IS ROLLING IN WEALTH

**P**salm 50:9-12 makes it clear that all wealth belongs to God: **I will take no bull out of your house, nor he-goats out of your folds. For every beast of the forest is Mine, and the cattle on a thousand hills. I know all the birds of the mountains; and the wild beasts of the field are Mine. If I were hungry, I would not tell you, for the world is Mine, and the fullness of it.**

The title deed of all the wealth on earth was originally given to Adam by God to administer, according to Genesis 1:28-30 NLT: **God blessed them and said, "Be fruitful and multiply. Fill the earth and govern it. Reign over the fish in the sea, the birds in the sky, and all the animals that scurry along the ground." Then God said, "Look! I have given you every seed-bearing plant throughout the earth and all the fruit trees for your food. And I have given every green plant as food for all the wild animals, the birds in the sky, and the small animals that scurry along the ground—everything that has life." And that is what happened.**

When Adam sinned and obeyed Satan, he forfeited his right to the kingdom and Satan became his master and the temporary owner of the earth. The claim of ownership made by Satan in Matthew 4:8-9 is undisputed: **Again, the Devil took Him up into a very high mountain and showed Him all the kingdoms of the world and their glory. And *he* said to Him, All these things I will give You if You will fall down and worship me.** Jesus confirms that Satan is the temporary prince and ruler of this world: **I shall no longer speak many things with you, for the ruler of this world comes, and he has nothing in Me** (John 14:30).

As ruler of this earthly kingdom Satan is also temporary owner of its wealth. Jesus made a promise that the wealth of this world would eventually be given to its rightful owners, God's children, if they obeyed His commands. It is interesting and ironic that Satan offered to give "all these things" to Jesus if Jesus would bow and worship him (Matthew 4:9). However, Jesus, the ultimate owner, used the exact same words—*all these things*—in presenting the wealth of this world to His followers: **For the nations seek after <u>all these things</u>. For your heavenly Father knows that you have need of <u>all these things</u>.**

**But seek first the kingdom of God and His righteousness; and <u>all these things</u> shall be added to you** (Matthew 6:32-33).

Jesus was proclaiming the end of Satan's spiritual reign on earth over man with these words: **Now is *the* judgment of this world. Now shall the prince of this world be cast out** (John 12:31). This is confirmed in this statement by John: **He who practices sin is of the Devil, for the Devil sins from the beginning. For this purpose the Son of God was revealed, that He might undo the works of the Devil** (1 John 3:8). In taking back the Kingdom, Jesus gave His followers the authority to back up their claim: **Behold, I give to you authority to tread on serpents and scorpions, and over all the authority of the enemy. And nothing shall by any means hurt you** (Luke 10:19). So, by believing, obeying, and putting Kingdom values first, God has transferred the wealth of this world, which rightfully belongs to Him, back into the hands of His children, to whom He gave it in the first place. All sealed by the blood of Jesus.

# 82 GOD IS INTO THE ARTS

God is into poetry. Much of the original Old Testament, which was inspired by God, is in poetic form. Meanwhile, every ability and skill within the nature of man was fashioned and put there by God. He created the ability for man to write poetry and has Himself been the inspiration of many poets. Every characteristic and attribute that God has, He has distributed in some measure to men and women throughout the human race. After all, it was God who said, **Let Us make man in Our image, after Our likeness** (Genesis 1:26). No one person has all of His attributes and character but all of us have some. Those with the skills of a poet are simply exhibiting their Creator's poetic skills.

God created music and obviously enjoys good music. To create anything it would be obvious that He was also its master. King David was a man who pleased God. One of the most significant things David taught the rest of us was to create music and offer it to God. David considered it appropriate to worship with the help of musical instruments, believing that good music would be pleasant to God:

> **And David spake to the chief of the Levites to appoint their brethren the singers, with instruments of music, psalteries and harps and cymbals, sounding aloud and lifting up the voice with joy** (1 Chronicles 15:16 ASV).

> **Praise Jehovah with lyre; sing to Him with a harp of ten strings. Sing to Him a new song; play skillfully with shouts of joy** (Psalm 33:2-3).

> **I will also praise You with a harp. O my God, I will sing Your truth; to You I will sing with the lyre, O Holy One of Israel** (Psalm 71:22).

> **It is good to give thanks to Jehovah, and to sing praises to Your name, O Most High; to show forth Your loving-kindness in the morning, and Your faithfulness every night; on the ten *strings*, and on the harp, with sounding music on the lyre** (Psalm 92:1-3).

Satan seems to be connected with music in Heaven as indicated by this passage: **You have been in Eden the garden of God; every precious stone** *was* **your covering, the ruby, topaz, and the diamond, the beryl, the onyx, and the jasper, the sapphire, the turquoise, and the emerald, and gold. The workmanship of your <u>tambourines and of your flutes was prepared in you in the day that you were created</u>** (Ezekiel 28:13).

Regardless of his expertise in Heaven in his past life, Satan is awesome with music here on earth. He is still inspiring his followers with his style and substance of music. There is such a thing as music from hell. Listening to some of todays' most popular music and lyrics it's not difficult to associate many of the artist with drugs, the occult, witchcraft, immorality, violence, rebellion and Satan worship. These are all tools he uses to entrap people. His fingerprints are all over this type of music.

Songs and music will be an important part of the scene in Heaven. The following verses describe a little about how music will be used in Heaven:

- Revelation 5:8 describes the use of a particular instrument: **And when He had taken the book, the four living creatures and the twenty-four elders fell down before the Lamb, <u>each one having harps</u> and golden vials full of incense, which are the prayers of the saints.**

- Revelation 5:9 tells us new songs will be written for special occasions: **And they sang a new song, saying, You are worthy to take the book and to open its seals, for You were slain and have redeemed us to God by Your blood out of every kindred and tongue and people and nation.**

- Revelation 14:3 tells us about one song that will be written for a select group of Jews: **And they sang as it were a new song before the throne and before the four living creatures and the elders. And no one could learn that song except the hundred** *and* **forty-four thousands who were redeemed from the earth.**

- Revelation 15:3 describes the use of songs presumably written on earth. I wonder if Heaven's praise and worship leader is thinking of the senior saints when he picks out an oldie from the hymnal of Moses: **And they sing the song of Moses the servant of God, and the song of the Lamb, saying, Great and marvelous** *are* **Your works, Lord God Almighty, just and true** *are* **Your ways, O King of saints.**

## What is God Like?

God is a writer. He has been known to write Himself, dictate to others who wrote for Him and by His Holy Spirit inspired others to write. He uses books much like we do—to record things.

- Exodus 34:1 describes how He wrote the Ten Commandments on stone: **And Jehovah said to Moses, Cut out two tablets of stone like the first. And <u>I will write</u> upon the tablets the words that were in the first tablets which you broke.**

- Exodus 24:4 declares that God dictated a Book of the Covenant to Moses: **And Moses wrote all the Words of Jehovah, and rose up early in the morning, and built an altar below the mountain and twelve pillars according to the twelve tribes of Israel.**

- Exodus 32:32-33 tells us He is presently working on one book in Heaven as alluded to by Moses: **And now will You forgive their sin! And if not, I pray You, blot me out of Your book <u>which You have written</u>. And Jehovah said to Moses, Whoever has sinned against Me, I will blot him out of My book.**

This last book is obviously a very great undertaking since it contains the complete biography of every human ever created. Your name is in this book. At the very least it contains details of every good and bad deed you have ever committed. It even records your very thoughts. Jesus warned us: **For there is <u>nothing covered</u> that shall not be revealed, <u>nor anything hidden</u> that shall not be known. Therefore whatever you have spoken in darkness shall be heard in the light. And that which you have spoken in the ear in secret rooms shall be proclaimed on the housetops** (Luke 12:2-3). This volume is being constantly updated, names are entered and names are blotted out. It is without a doubt the most important book in the entire universe since its contents govern whether we live or die, or go to Heaven or Hell.

Reference is made to The Book of Life many times through the Bible. It is mentioned in Exodus 32:32, 33; Psalms 69:28; 109:13 and Daniel 12:1. Jesus mentions it in Luke 10:20; Paul mentions it in Philippians 4:3; and God refers to it in Revelation 13:8; 17:8; 20:12; 20:15; 21:27; 22:19. The most important event in the book of Revelation, involves the two groups of people mentioned in the Book of Life as indicated in these verses:

> Believers: **The one who overcomes, this one will be clothed in white clothing. And I will not blot out his name out of the Book of Life,**

but I will confess his name before My Father and before His angels** (Revelation 3:5).

And Non-believers: **And all dwelling on the earth will worship it, those whose names have not been written in the Book of Life of the Lamb slain, from the foundation of the world** (Revelation 13:8). The "it" referred to here is the Dragon.

There are other books referred to in the Bible. Here are some of them.

- One Heavenly book, spoken of in Revelation 5:1-5, is sealed with seven seals, and will be presented for reading on a particular day. Its contents are so very sacred that only Jesus will be allowed to open it: **And I saw a book on the right of Him sitting on the throne, written inside and on the back, sealed with seven seals. And I saw a mighty angel proclaiming with a loud voice, Who is worthy to open the book and to loosen its seals? And no one in Heaven, nor on the earth, nor under the earth, was able to open the book or to look at it. And I wept very much, because no one was found worthy to open and to read the book, nor to look at it. And one of the elders said to me, Do not weep. Behold, the Lion of the tribe of Judah, the Root of David, has prevailed to open the book and to loose the seven seals of it.**

- There is a book described in Revelation 10:2, 9-10, heralded by a mighty angel. This book contained the Word of God with blessings (sweet as honey in his mouth) and judgment (bitter in his belly). It was small and was made to be eaten: **And he had a little book open in his hand. And he set his right foot on the sea and his left foot on the earth . . . And I went to the angel and said to him, Give me the little book. And he said to me, Take it and eat it up, and it will make your belly bitter, but it will be sweet as honey in your mouth. And I took the little book out of the angel's hand and ate it up. And it was sweet as honey in my mouth, and as soon as I had eaten it, my belly was made bitter.**

- God records for all of our afflictions in a book: **You number my wandering; O put my tears into Your bottle; are they not in Your Book?** (Psalm 56:8).

- Before you were born your specifications, characteristics and DNA, were all written and recorded in another book: **You saw me before I was born. Every day of my life was recorded in Your book. Every** moment was laid out before a single day had passed (Psalm 139:16 NLT).

- He had Isaiah write a book regarding the rebellious nation of Israel. This book was authorized and commissioned by God and would be kept by God since its contents would be, "for the time to come forever and ever." **Now go, write it before them in a tablet, and note it in a book, so that it may be for the time to come forever and ever, that this is a rebellious people, lying sons. They are sons who will not hear the Law of Jehovah** (Isaiah 30:8-9).

- He dictated another book to Jeremiah for the sake of His people Israel: **The Word that came to Jeremiah from Jehovah, saying, So speaks Jehovah, the God of Israel, saying, Write all the Words that I have spoken to you in a book** (Jeremiah 30:1-2).

- Some have wondered how the lost tribes of Israel will be accounted for during the last days. Also the Jews, due to their dispersion, have lost their valuable tribal records. However, this will not be a problem for God since His written records are up to date. Daniel mentions a book where God is keeping track of the names of His people: **And at that time Michael shall stand up, the great ruler who stands for the sons of your people. And there shall be a time of trouble, such as never was since there was a nation; until that time. And at that time your people shall be delivered, every one that <u>shall be found written in the book</u> . . . But you, O Daniel, shut up the words and seal the book, even to the time of the end. Many shall run to and fro, and knowledge shall be increased** (Daniel 12:1-4).

- Malachi mentions this special book that seems to record conversations between His children : **Then those fearing Jehovah <u>spoke together</u>, each man to his neighbor. And Jehovah <u>listened and heard</u>. And a book of remembrance was written before Him for those who feared Jehovah, and for those esteeming His name** (Malachi 3:16).

- God authorized and commissioned John to write the book we call Revelation: **I am the Alpha and Omega, the First and the Last. Also, What you see, write in a book and send it to the seven churches which are in Asia: to Ephesus, and to Smyrna, and to Pergamos,**

**and to Thyatira, and to Sardis, and to Philadelphia, and to Laodicea** (Revelation 1:11).

Our Bible, which He inspired men to write for us, is the world's bestselling book. According to Wikipedia, it has sold possibly 6 billion copies. Encyclopedia Britannica says: The all-time best seller in the English-speaking world—said to be unequaled in sales—is the Bible.[7] (Bagnall)

God is artistic. Everything that has beauty was created by Him. The glory of a sunset has often been captured by human artists but there it sits, on a canvas, never changing except to look drab with age. God's sunsets change by the minute and return the next day with new splendor. He directs His artistic skills toward a mountain scene and it slowly changes through the day and then drastically changes during the four seasons of the year. The sky may be light blue one minute and pink and grey the next. In the south He may display low, black clouds and in the north there may be clear blue sky, but it is constantly changing. His mountain scene may be white with snow in winter, red in autumn and green in summer. He painted colorful fish and birds and flowers in deep, bright, colors and even breathes life into them. **He has made everything beautiful in His time** (Ecclesiastes 3:11). As if that were not enough, when He crafts a flower it comes with an attractive fragrance. All created with the sole purpose of bringing pleasure to His masterpiece. And that's you!

When God ordered a wardrobe for Aaron, His High Priest, He was concerned that it would look magnificent: **And you shall make holy garments for Aaron your brother, for glory and for beauty** (Exodus 28:2).

Psalm 145:11-12 declares that His present Kingdom is not just very well done and beautiful, it's glorious and majestic: **They shall speak of the glory of Your kingdom and talk of Your power, to make known to the sons of men His mighty acts, and the glorious majesty of His kingdom.**

Jesus told us he was going to prepare a magnificent stately home for us, a place *of many mansions* (John 14:2). The new palace He is designing for His Bride is smashing, out of this world! It is described in Revelation 21:2, 10-21 by John:

---

[7]  http://www.britannica.com/EBchecked/topic/63105/best-seller

## What is God Like?

> And I, John, saw the holy city, New Jerusalem, coming down from God out of Heaven, prepared as a bride adorned for her Husband . . . And he carried me away in the Spirit to a great and high mountain and showed me that great city, the holy Jerusalem, descending out of Heaven from God, having the glory of God. And its light *was* like a stone most precious, even like a jasper stone, clear as crystal. And *it* had a great and high wall, with twelve gates. And on the gates were twelve angels, and having names inscribed, which are *the names* of the twelve tribes of the sons of Israel: From the east three gates, from the north three gates, from the south three gates, and from the west three gates. And the wall of the city had twelve foundations, and in them were the names of the twelve apostles of the Lamb. And he who talked with me had a golden reed to measure the city and its gates and its wall. And the city lies four-square, and the length is as large as the breadth. And he measured the city with the reed, twelve thousand stadia. The length and the breadth and the height of it are equal. And he measured its wall, a hundred *and* forty-four cubits, according to the measure of a man, that is, of an angel. And the foundation of its wall was jasper; and the city *was* pure gold, like clear glass. And the foundations of the wall of the city had been adorned with every precious stone. The first foundation, jasper; the second, sapphire; the third, chalcedony; the fourth, emerald; the fifth, sardonyx; the sixth, sardius; the seventh, chrysolite; the eighth, beryl; the ninth, topaz; the tenth, chrysoprasus; the eleventh, hyacinth; the twelfth, amethyst. And the twelve gates *were* twelve pearls. Respectively, each one of the gates was one pearl . . .

The lighting in this place will be spectacular, like nothing we have ever seen. The best source of light we have at the moment is our sun with 3.83 H 1026 watts of light power (an ordinary incandescent lamp emits about 100 watts of power) (Bagnall Page 6). In Heaven we won't need the sun for light, it will be replaced with a better source of light: **And the city had no need of the sun, nor of the moon, that they might shine in it, for the glory of God illuminated it, and its lamp *is* the Lamb** (Revelation 21:23).

The trees in Heaven serve a dual purpose of being aesthetically beautiful and for the healing of bodies: **And he showed me a pure river of Water of Life, clear as crystal, proceeding out of the throne of God and of the Lamb. In the midst of its street, and of the river, from here and from there, *was* the Tree of Life, which bore twelve fruits, each yielding its fruit according to one month.**

**And the leaves of the tree were for the healing of the nations** (Revelation 22:1-2).

Can you imagine this place?! Designed by the One who is the ultimate artist and architect, He builds this fabulous place with you in mind! Your particular mansion will be to your specifications because He knows you, your likes and dislikes. The first day you arrive to take possession, you will realize, possibly for the first time in your life, that you are the center of His attention. I wonder if we will be able to do anything at all for a while but fall on our knees, at His feet, and weep in gratitude. The costly architecture will not be the reason for your tears, but the price He paid to get you into heaven will take on a whole new meaning. We were created for His pleasure but everything He created was to bring pleasure to us. It may take a while for that to sink in.

# 83 GOD CANNOT DO SOME THINGS

**I**n Luke 1:37(NLT) the Bible teaches this regarding God's unlimited power: **For nothing is impossible with God**. Yet, His Word also states that there are some things that God cannot do. Scripture actually records these five things:

> He cannot lie: **. . . on hope of eternal life, which God, who cannot lie, promised before** *the* **eternal time** (Titus 1:2).

> He cannot stop being compassionate: *It is of* **the LORD's mercies that we are not consumed, because his compassions fail not** (Lamentations 3:22).

> He cannot forsake His children: Isaiah 41:17 **The poor and needy seek water, and** *there is* **none; their tongue fails for thirst, I Jehovah will hear them, I the God of Israel will not leave them.**

> He cannot change: **For I** *am* **Jehovah,** *I* **change not** . . . (Malachi 3:6).

> He cannot tempt you and He cannot be tempted: **Let no man say when he is tempted, I am tempted of God: for God cannot be tempted with evil, neither tempteth he any man:** (James 1:13 KJV).

It is obvious that these restrictions are self-imposed by God. His Cannot-Do-List has nothing to do with a lack of power or wisdom but is due to His own principals.

Another thing that God cannot do is to act irrationally. For example, even though He can do anything He cannot create a rock too heavy for Him to lift as some atheists have alluded.

# 84 GOD WANTS YOUR MONEY

God's desire for our money has nothing to do with His own cash flow. He didn't ask Adam for anything back in return for the humongous wealth He gave him in Eden, but by the time the Hebrews arrived on the scene, He obviously felt the need to demand of them a portion of their wealth and actually made it a requirement of the Law. Two big items, their firstborn child and the firstborn animal, are listed in this verse: **Sanctify all the first-born to Me, whatever opens the womb among the sons of Israel, of man and of beast. It *is* Mine** (Exodus 13:2). He also laid claim to the most perfect lamb in their flock, one tenth of all their income plus offerings on top of that, and much more.

He didn't keep any of their wealth—it was all used for their own benefit: salaries for the Levites and maintenance for the tabernacle. He had no need for their wealth. He demanded that they give to force the greed and selfishness out of their lives, because these cannot be part of a loving heart. For them, and us, it is a test of obedience and trust: If you give in obedience to God, can He be trusted to look after your needs? Numerous scriptures through His Word indicate that He will take care of us, here are three:

> **But my God shall <u>supply all your need</u> according to His riches in glory by Christ Jesus (Philippians 4:19).**

> **Bring all the tithe into the storehouse, so that there may be food in My house. And test Me now with this, says Jehovah of Hosts, to see if I will not open the windows of Heaven for you, and <u>pour out a blessing for you</u>, until *there is* not enough *room* (Malachi 3:10).**

> **Give, and it shall be given to you, good measure pressed down and shaken together and running over, <u>they shall give into your bosom</u>. For with the same measure that you measure, it shall be measured to you again (Luke 6:38).**

If we disobey, we obviously do not trust Him. As followers of Christ, He loves us too much to leave us in that condition. He has a course lined up for us on giving, it's called TRUST 101. He puts us through it, over and over if necessary, until we get it right. He's like that.

# 85  GOD CAN FOOL YOU

A common method by God in dealing with humans is to inform them as to what they should or should not do. If that doesn't work, He issues warnings. What might He do after that? Could God engineer a ruse to get their attention or to even trap them in their blatant stubbornness? It is my personal belief, based on the Scriptures, He could.

For example, He used a lying demon to fool Ahab to bring judgment upon him. Consider this situation recorded in the Old Testament. Ahab was a despicable ruler. Judgment had already been pronounced on him; and he was slated for destruction. At one time Ahab repented (1 Kings 21:27), and God forgave him. But, later he continued to practice in his evil ways and then God called (supernaturally arranged) a meeting. In 1 Kings 22:19-22, Micaiah the prophet, speaking for God, records: **And he said, Hear therefore the Word of Jehovah: I saw Jehovah sitting on His throne, and all the host of heaven standing by Him on His right hand and on His left. And Jehovah said, Who shall entice Ahab that he may go up and fall at Ramoth in Gilead? And one said this way, and another said that way. And there came forth a spirit and stood before Jehovah and said, I will entice him. And Jehovah said to him, With what? And he said, I will go forth and will be a lying spirit in the mouth of all his prophets. And He said, You shall entice *him* and succeed also. Go forth and do so.**

The story goes on to say that the demonic lying spirit was successfully used by God and Ahab fell for the lie and was killed in battle. Micaiah told Ahab the truth, but he refused to listen. His heart was too hard and his neck too stiff.

There are other such stories. In 2 Kings 3, God fooled the king of Moab into thinking that water in ditches was blood and through this, brought disaster upon him and his entire army. God told the leaders of Israel to communicate to Pharaoh that they needed a three day journey into the wilderness when really it was more—they would not be coming back (Exodus 3:18). He instructed Joshua to fool the king of Ai into thinking the Israeli army would be approaching from the front of the city when God had instructed them to ambush them from the rear (Joshua 8:2). The result of the deception of both

## What is God Like?

Pharaoh and the king of Ai was freedom and victory for His people. In 2 Samuel 5, God instructed David to trick the Philistines in the same manner. He could have used thunder and lightning or hornets but His choice for this occasion was a ruse. In 2 Kings 7:6-7 (NIV), God fooled an entire army with a noise that caused them to run for their lives: **. . . the Lord had caused the Arameans to hear the sound of chariots and horses and a great army, so that they said to one another, "Look, the king of Israel has hired the Hittite and Egyptian kings to attack us!" So they got up and fled in the dusk and abandoned their tents and their horses and donkeys. They left the camp as it was and ran for their lives.**

2 Thessalonians 2:8-12 explains the fact that God will use the lies of Satan to fool those who have been written off due to their own stubbornness and wickedness: **And then the lawless one will be revealed, whom the Lord shall consume with the breath of His mouth and shall destroy with the brightness of His coming, whose coming is according to the working of Satan with all power and signs and <u>lying wonders</u>, and with all deceit of unrighteousness in those who perish, because they did not receive the love of the truth, so that they might be saved. And for this cause <u>God shall send them strong delusion, that they should believe a lie</u>, so that all those who do not believe the truth, but delight in unrighteousness, might be condemned.**

When the Scripture states that God sent them a strong delusion it simply means they were handed over to Satan, the father of lies and delusions. Then God withdrew, allowing them to believe what they had preferred to believe to start with.

The Lord cannot lie, but He does stop providing truth and He will allow men to pursue evil if that's what they desire. This is made clear in Romans 1:24-28 by Paul:

> **Therefore <u>God also gave them up</u> to uncleanness through the lusts of *their* hearts, to dishonor their own bodies between themselves. For they changed the truth of God into a lie, and they worshiped and served the created thing more than the Creator, who is blessed forever. Amen. For this cause, <u>God gave them up</u> to dishonorable affections. For even their women changed the natural use into that which is against nature . . . And even as they did not think fit to have God in *their* knowledge, <u>God gave them over</u> to a reprobate mind . . .**

# 86  GOD USES EVERYTHING HE CREATED

It would be unlike a wise Creator to create anything that had no purpose. So we have to assume that everything He made has a purpose, animate, inanimate and humans. In Genesis 2, He used two trees to teach Adam right from wrong. He used a bush and a fire in Exodus 3:2 to get the attention of Moses. He used an ass in Numbers 22:28 to speak to a stubborn man: **And Jehovah opened the mouth of the ass, and she said to Balaam, What have I done to you, that you have beaten me these three times?** Jesus used a fish to transport tax money to Peter in Matthew 17:27 (MSG). He told Peter to go fishing: **But so we don't upset them needlessly, go down to the lake, cast a hook, and pull in the first fish that bites. Open its mouth and you'll find a coin. Take it and give it to the tax men. It will be enough for both of us.** In Joshua 24:12, He commanded insects to put two entire nations to flight: **And I sent the hornet before you, which drove them out from before you, the two kings of the Amorites, not with your sword, nor with your bow.**

In Exodus, God turned a stick into a snake for Aaron and Moses. He commanded water to turn into blood and called in frogs, gnats, locusts and flies by the millions to cover Egypt. He used hail to ruin every tree and destroy everything growing in the fields, all to demonstrate His power. He used kings and rulers like Pharaoh and Nebuchadnezzar to demonstrate His power over men and the earth. This is how He explains Himself to Pharaoh: **You know that by now I could have struck you and your people with deadly disease and there would be nothing left of you, not a trace. But for one reason only I've kept you on your feet: To make you recognize my power so that my reputation spreads in all the Earth** (Exodus 9:15-16 MSG).

Jesus used water to walk on (Matthew 14:25). He used water to make wine (John 2:8-10). He used His spit and soil to heal blind eyes (John 9:6). He used five loaves of bread and two small fish in Matthew 14:19-21 to feed 5000 people. On many occasions He used a mere word to heal or drive out demons. Imagine the power of God when He is capable of using even a shadow to heal people (Acts 5:15). He can use the hands of a man to transfer the gift of the Holy Spirit to another person (Acts 8:17). Even pieces of cloth can be used by God when faith is present: **And God was doing extraordinary miracles by the hands of Paul, so that even handkerchiefs or aprons that had touched his skin were carried away to the sick, and their diseases left them and the evil spirits came out of them** (Acts 19:11-12).

Elijah and Elisha were amazing prophets who were used to demonstrate the mighty power of God. He used ravens in 1 Kings 17:4 to find and deliver food to Elijah and engineered an amazing mode of transportation, horses and a chariot of fire to deliver Elijah straight from earth to heaven: **And it came to pass, as they still went on, and talked, that, behold, *there appeared* a chariot of fire, and horses of fire, and parted them both asunder; and Elijah went up by a whirlwind into heaven** (2 Kings 2:11).

God used a bowl of salt to heal polluted water (2 Kings 2:21); stretched a little oil belonging to a widow to continue flowing until all her debts were paid (2 Kings 4); used flour to make poisonous stew edible (2 Kings 4:38-41). He caused an iron axe head to defy gravity and float when Elisha threw a stick into the water (2 Kings 6:5-7). His abilities are awesome and unlimited but He obviously cares when you lose something as simple as a tool.

You and I were created for His purpose. Whether we choose to serve good or evil, He can still use us for any purpose at any moment of time. It is always best if we volunteer.

# 87 GOD DOES NOT LIKE WIMPS

**M**ore correctly put, God does not like wimpish behavior. This is made abundantly clear from a number of Scriptures throughout the Bible. He does not like people who sit on the fence; who are fearful; halfhearted; and lack passion. Wimps follow the crowd and they don't like going it alone. The dictionary defines them as weak and cowardly. This is what God said to people of an end time church: **And to the angel of the church of the Laodicea write: The Amen, the faithful and true Witness, the Head of the creation of God, says these things: I know your works, that you are neither cold nor hot. I would that you were cold or hot. So because you are lukewarm, and neither cold nor hot, I will vomit you out of My mouth** (Revelation 3:14-16). God clearly states that His preference is for people to be either hot or cold but half-hearted and uncommitted people are repulsive.

Paul likens immature saints to wimps who have no backbone and no stability: **Then we will no longer be infants, tossed back and forth by the waves, and blown here and there by every wind of teaching and by the cunning and craftiness of people in their deceitful scheming** (Ephesians 4:14 NIV).

James warns that wimps have trouble believing God and, as a result, cannot be trusted: **If any of you lacks wisdom, you should ask God, who gives generously to all without finding fault, and it will be given to you. But when you asks, you <u>must believe</u> and not doubt, because the one who doubts is like a wave of the sea, blown and tossed by the wind. That person should not expect to receive anything from the Lord; Such a person is <u>double-minded and unstable in all they do</u>** (James 1:5-8 NIV).

Jesus left no room for wimpish behavior when He made this demand: **Then Jesus said to His disciples, If anyone desires to come after Me, let him deny himself and take up his cross and follow Me** (Matthew 16:24). The cross He was referring to was not two pieces of wood. It was tough times, hard knocks and a willingness to fight spiritual wars. We know that fear is a very real problem for Christian and sinner alike. So He teaches us how to handle it: **Jesus said to his disciples, "Don't be worried! Have faith in God and have faith in me** (John 14:1 CEV). Basically, He is saying, "Stop worrying." We should conclude that if He said stop worrying we must be able to *do it*. Jesus would never have commanded us to do something we were *unable* to do. When we worry we have fear of something and fear is tormenting. The cause of our fears, lack of love, is revealed in this verse: **There is no room in love for fear. Well-formed love banishes fear. Since fear is crippling, a fearful life–fear of death, fear of judgment–is one not yet fully formed in love** (1 John 4: 18 MSG).

In Revelation 12:11 (MSG), men of faith are marked by their willingness to stand up for Christ even at the cost of their own lives: **They defeated him through the blood of the Lamb and the bold word of their witness. They weren't in love with themselves; they were willing to die for Christ.** In death, they defeated their worst enemy, the fear of dying, and won the toughest battle of their lives. Consider these tough, no-nonsense words: **And Jesus said to him, No one, having put his hand to the plow and looking back, is fit for the kingdom of God** (Luke 9:62). The Message Bible puts it this way: **Jesus said, "No procrastination. No backward looks. You can't put God's kingdom off till tomorrow. Seize the day."**

Jesus didn't like wimpish behavior, yet He called twelve men with such behavior to follow Him during His earthly ministry. They failed miserably: They squabbled over the best position in His kingdom, they started crying during a storm on the lake one night while He was walking toward them on the water (see Mark 6:49 MSG); failed to cast out a single demon due to their unbelief (Matthew 17:16). On the night He was taken to be crucified, they all abandoned Him. One cursed and swore that he didn't even know Him and another turned Him over to His enemies for about four months' pay. Prior to His trial, He had requested that they watch with Him for one hour while He prayed. His request for their help was certainly clear enough: **Then he said to them, "My anguish is so great that I feel as if I'm dying. Wait here, and stay awake with me"** (Matthew 26:38 GW). But they couldn't. They fell asleep in less than an hour. They were powerless and performed like wimps.

Thank God, their story didn't end there. Jesus taught them many things about self-sacrifice, speaking the truth, and about laying down their lives, but it had very little effect, since up to this time they were still hesitating and doubting. Nonetheless, He had given them one command that they did obey. He told them to go to Jerusalem and wait for *power*. . . . **I send the promise of my Father upon you: but tarry ye in the city of Jerusalem, until ye be endued with power from on high** (Luke 24:49 KJV). After He arose from the dead He appeared to them again instructing them what they would do with the Power: **But you will receive power when the Holy Spirit comes on you; and you will be**

**my witnesses in Jerusalem, and in all Judea and Samaria, and to the ends of the earth** (Acts 1:8 NIV). During a prayer meeting on the Day of Pentecost, power fell on them and they were immediately changed from wimps to mighty men of God. They went out in obedience to His command and did what He told them to do. Their obedience cost them their lives. Wimps can't do that, but men or women filled with the power of the Holy Spirit can. We can, too, if we follow His instructions: ask, but don't stop there, seek, but don't stop there, knock and keep on knocking until the door opens or it is shattered from your knocking. God loves that kind of tenacity. He's like that.

An excellent example of a wimp being transformed into a real man is that of Jacob. He was a cheat and a coward, but God saw his potential. This man was maneuvered by God into a situation so desperate that he was willing to take on God Himself in a wrestling match. Can you imagine taking on the Heavyweight Champion of the Universe! Literally! Jacob may have had many shortcomings but on that day he became the man God wanted him to be. Genesis 32:24 (NIV) indicates that the wrestler who took him on seemed to be a man: **So Jacob was left alone, and a man wrestled with him till daybreak.** However, God acknowledged in verse 28 that He was the one whom Jacob had prevailed against. Also, in verse 30 Jacob recognized that it was God. Jacob was a desperate man, and desperate men do desperate things. He needed a blessing so bad that when he encountered God, he decided to advance toward Him, the Almighty One, take a hold of Him physically, and hold on—be it life or death. Any sane man would know that a mere human would not be able to force God to do anything especially by wrestling with Him. However, deep inside the heart and soul of this cowardly man there was enough knowledge about God to know that He was good, that He was approachable. There also had to be some hope that God would not simply destroy him for his brashness. Jacob represents all of us. He was either too desperate to care anymore as to whether this Almighty Wrestler would kill him or maybe he knew that the Wrestler might just take pity on him. God loves it when one of His creatures is desperate enough to take Him on. It means they *believe in Him*, that they have faith in Him that He can meet their need. Wimps will not do this because they do not believe and they are too afraid to try anything out of the ordinary.

There are different ways of wrestling with God. The Canaanite woman mentioned in Matthew 15 (and in chapter 70, *God Will Hurt You*) took Jesus on in a kind of wrestling match. By sheer tenacity, she too won and walked away with a blessing. Jesus set her daughter free from demons. Consider others who were faced with the same predicament: Abraham behaved like a wimp when he allowed another man to take Sarah from him to protect his own skin (Genesis 20). His son, Isaac, did exactly the same with his wife, Rebekah, and yet God worked on both men until they were changed.

Isaiah was a wimp until he willingly allowed hot coals to be placed on his lips. He knew he did not measure up when he was called into the presence of the Lord Almighty. Wimps live dangerously and often, they don't even know it. God warns us:

> . . . **If you do not stand <u>firm</u> in your faith, you will not stand at all** (Isaiah 7:9 NIV).
>
> **Whoever remains stiff-necked after many rebukes will suddenly be destroyed–without remedy** (Proverbs 29:1 NIV).
>
> **Moreover, no man knows when his hour will come: As fish are caught in a cruel net, or birds are taken in a snare, so men are trapped by evil times that fall unexpectedly upon them** (Ecclesiastes 9:12 NIV).

God did not create wimps. Such behavior is developed by listening to the wrong voices. Here God describes such behavior as stubbornness: **But no, My people wouldn't listen. Israel did not want Me around. So I let them follow their own stubborn desires, living according to their own ideas** (Psalm 81:11-12 NLT). Here Jesus labels weak ones as those who are easily offended: **And these are those likewise being sown on stony places; who, when they hear the Word, immediately receive it with gladness. But they have no root in themselves, but are temporary. Afterward when affliction or persecution arises for the Word's sake, they are immediately offended** (Mark 4:16-17). If you fear the wimpish behavior in your life may be displeasing to God, and you are still breathing, be encouraged. He hates the behavior but oh, how He loves the wimp: **But God, who is rich in mercy, for his great love wherewith he loved us, Even when we were dead in sins, hath quickened us together with Christ, (by grace ye are saved;) And hath raised us up together, and made us sit together in heavenly places in Christ Jesus** (Ephesians 2:4-6 KJV).

The disciples received power when the Holy Ghost fell on them and they became men of courage and strength. However, that power was not some sort of magical fix or some kind of spiritual brainwashing or a replacement of faulty genes with good ones. The men still had the same body, soul and spirit that they were born with. What changed was the power of the Almighty that entered them and they surrendered to His will. This led them into a life of discipline where the will of their spirit was in charge and not the will of their flesh. This is how Paul describes the change that had taken place in his life and in the lives of the other followers:

> **That means you must not give sin a vote in the way you conduct your lives. Don't give it the time of day** (Romans 6:12 MSG).
>
> **Therefore I do not run like someone running aimlessly; I do not fight like a boxer beating the air. No, I strike a blow to my body and make it my slave so that after I have preached to others, I myself will not be disqualified for the prize** (1 Corinthians 9:26-27 NIV).
>
> **I have been crucified with Christ and I no longer live, but Christ lives in me. The life I live in the body, I live by faith in the Son of God, who loved me and gave himself for me** (Galatians 2:20 NIV).

A wimp's greatest enemy is fear. He is afraid of pain, failure and the unknown. Paul encouraged Timothy with these words: **For the Spirit God gave us does not make us timid, but gives us power, love and self-discipline** (2 Timothy 1:7 NIV). Chuck Holton writes:

As we have seen, a good soldier learns how to overcome fear through the Spirit. As Christians, we've been given the Holy Spirit—who is the Spirit of truth (see John 15:26) and when the truth resides in us, it sets us free from fear as we tap into the limitless inner enabling of the Spirit. Then we will be able to say with David, "Though an army besiege me, my heart will not fear; though war break out against me, even then will I be confident (Psalm 27:3)" (Page 148).

Be encouraged, as long as we are still breathing there is hope. When you pray for any wimpish behavior you may have in your life remember to pray for the author of this book too.

# 88 GOD IS LIKE JESUS

So, what is God like? Jesus is the most glorious, powerful and awesome example of what God is like! As stated in the introduction, it is impossible for any book to fully answer that question. However, Jesus gives us a good image of God, as he is just like His Father. Jesus is our best source of information as to the likeness of God because He is God. The writer to the Hebrews describes Jesus this way: **The Son radiates God's own glory and expresses the very character of God, and he sustains everything by the mighty power of his command. When he had cleansed us from our sins, he sat down in the place of honor at the right hand of the majestic God in heaven** (Hebrews 1:3 NLT).

What makes Jesus so unique in helping us in comprehending the little we do know is that He lived with us for 33 years. He became a man, just like us. He demonstrated the power of God on our planet. But more than anything, Jesus brought the love of His Father from Heaven to earth and shared it with us. Like His Father, Jesus was and is perfect in every way. He is the perfect example of holiness and justice. Neither He nor His Father can tolerate sin because of their Holiness, which creates a serious dilemma for sinful humans: **For everyone has sinned; we all fall short of God's glorious standard** (Romans 3:23 NLT). Indeed, the Scripture says that: **the whole world is under the power of sin** (Galatians 3:22 GNB). Jesus shares the same interests in justice as His Father: **But to the Son he says, "Your throne, O God, endures forever and ever. You rule with a scepter of justice. You love justice and hate evil. Therefore, O God, your God has anointed you, pouring out the oil of joy on you more than on anyone else"** (Hebrews 1:8-9).

God's need for perfect justice created a serious dilemma for sinful man. However, they worked out this solution: If a perfect man died, then Heaven's Justice Department would be satisfied and those who accept that sacrifice could be redeemed. So Jesus, full of the Father's love, agreed that He would give His life in exchange for ours. Here is the written record of this agreement:

> **For God so loved the world that He gave His only-begotten Son, that whoever believes in Him should not perish but have everlasting life** (John 3:16).

**But God demonstrates his own love for us in this: While we were still sinners, Christ died for us** (Romans 5:8 NIV).

If anything in the Bible and this book is going to be helpful to us as individuals, we must challenge ourselves with a life and death question: Will we accept what Jesus did for us? You may decide that you don't really care that Jesus died in your place. You may believe this is your life and decide to live it as you please. You may as well sing along with O'l Blue Eyes, Frank Sinatra, "I Did It My Way." This, of course, is your choice. God will allow it and He won't bug you about your decision. However, you will inevitably have to account for that decision, at which point it may be too late to have second thoughts. Let's say you refuse God's offer and one day you face Him in His courtroom and should He ask you, "Why should I allow you into my Kingdom?" What will you say? You can't defend yourself by saying you knew nothing about His offer of free salvation. His reply will simply negate your defense: **For ever since the world was created, people have seen the earth and sky. Through everything God made, they can clearly see His invisible qualities—His eternal power and divine nature. <u>So they have no excuse for not knowing God</u>** (Romans 1:20 NLT). You will not be able to say you lived a good life and should be allowed entrance into His kingdom on the basis of your good works. **For by grace are ye saved through faith; and that not of yourselves: it is the gift of God: Not of works, lest any man should boast** (Ephesians 2:8-9 KJV). You may consider yourself to be the most educated and refined atheist in the world, yet you cannot be sure that you will not be asked these questions.

If you are struggling with the question as to why God should allow you into His Kingdom you may want to weigh these facts: Jesus paid the price for your life. On His way to be offered up as the ultimate sacrifice, He had you in mind. When He was sweating drops of blood in prayer, you were in His thoughts. You were on His mind when they hit Him in the face and when they plucked out His beard. He was thinking of you when they bound Him then mocked Him and beat Him some more. When they lied at His trial and He refused to defend Himself, He did this for your sake. He endured the scorn while on His way to the Cross to take your place. Although He had the power to call an army of angels to His defense, He did not call them because it would have meant your doom. Jesus endured the mockery of possibly six trials for you, in which no man could find Him guilty of anything. They decided to scourge Him anyway. On the cross Jesus put up with the suffering when He could have stopped it as easily as He had walked on water and turned water into wine. But, He had left the comforts of Heaven and His Father for one extremely important purpose. It was, and still is, all about you. God loves you.

# EPILOGUE

So, to answer the original question, "what is God like?" is He the ultimate lover of 1 John 4:8 or is He the ultimate terrorist of Matthew 10:28? Yes and yes. He is both! To those who respond to His love He is the ultimate Lover. No price is too high to pay when He goes courting a mortal. This is a quote from one of His "love letters:" **For I am persuaded that neither death, nor life, nor angels, nor principalities, nor powers, nor things present, nor things to come, nor height, nor depth, nor any other creature, shall be able to separate us from the love of God which is in Christ Jesus our Lord** (Romans 8:38 -39).

It seems that you and I are very important to God. He went through a lot of trouble to bring us into a physical life and even more to give us a new spiritual, eternal life. Consider carefully these words from Ephesians 1:4-5 in the Message Bible: **Long before he laid down earth's foundations, he had us in mind, had settled on us as the focus of his love, to be made whole and holy by his love. Long, long ago he decided to adopt us into his family through Jesus Christ. (What pleasure he took in planning this!)** You are on His Facebook page, He is texting you every day, He follows you on Twitter, He's got your phone number and you are always on His mind. In his book on Grace, Max Lucado says: "There is something in you that God loves. Not just appreciates or approves but loves. You cause His eyes to widen and His heart to beat faster. He loves you." (Page 118).

Seeing the love that exudes from just the two scriptures above how could anyone dare suggest that God is a terrorist? Jesus, His Son did! Here are His exact words: . . . **And do not fear those who kill the body, but are not able to kill the soul. But rather fear Him who can destroy both soul and body in hell** (Matthew 10:28). Surely this *is* the ultimate terror: to think you are safely dead and then find out that Someone has dug you up to judge you and send you to everlasting punishment. Matthew 10:28 is a warning by Jesus, about His Fathers wrath and this warning, if you are still breathing, is an act of kindness. However, because of the love of Christ we don't have to face the Fathers wrath. He took care of that when He took our sin and died in our place. . . . **No one has greater love than this, that a man lay down his life for his friends** (John 15:13).

And this is what is amazing: It is all yours! You accept His offer of love and He will accept you. Paul explains how to do this: **But what does it say? "The Word is near you,** *even* **in your mouth and in your heart"; that is, the Word of Faith which we proclaim; <u>Because if you confess the Lord Jesus, and believe in your heart that God has raised Him from** *the* **dead, you shall be saved.</u> For with** *the* **heart one believes unto righteousness, and with** *the* **mouth** *one* **confesses unto salvation** (Romans 10:8-10).

# WORKS CITED

Alcorn, Randy. *Safely Home.* Ed. Curtis H. C. Lundgren. Tyndale, 2001.

Bagnall, Philip M. *Star Atlas Companion: What You Need to Know about the Constellations.* New York, NY: Springer Science and Business Media, 2012. Hardcover.

Balcombe, Jonathan. *Second Nature: the Inner Lives of Animals.* New York, NY: Palgrave MacMillan, 2011.

BibleClassics.com. *John Gill's Exposition of the Entire Bible.* 2000 - 2009. Website. 1 January 2013. <http://www.ewordtoday.com/comments/exodus/gill/exodus20.htm>.

Billheimer, Paul E. *Destined for the Throne: How Spiritual Warfare Prepares the Bride of Christ for Her Eternal Destiny.* Bloomington, MN: Bethany House Publishers, 1975. Paperback.

Buchanan, Mark. *The Rest of God.* Nashville, TN: W. Publishing Group, 2006. Paperback.

Dake, Finis Jennings. *Dake Annotated Reference Bible, KJV.* Lawrenceville, GA: Dake Publishing, 1963. Hardcover.

Dwight, J. *Things To Come.* Grand Rapids: Zondervan Publishing House, 1964. Print.

GodRules.net. *The Adam Clarke Commentary.* 2001-2013. 7 January 2013. <http://www.studylight.org/com/acc/view.cgi?book=ge&chapter=002>.

Henry, Matthew. *Matthew Henry's Commentary on the Whole Bible.* Nashville, TN: Thomas Nelson, Inc., 1977. Hardcover.

Holton, Chuck. *Bulletproof: the Making of an Invincible Mind.* Colorado Springs, CO: Multnomah Publishers, Inc., 2005. Paperback.

Kelfer, Russell. *The Transformation of Jacob.* 5 August 2002. Electronic. 1 2013.

Lehman, Frederick M. "The Love of God." *Songs That Are Different, Volume 2.* Pasadena, 1919.

Lewis, C. S. *The Lion, the Witch and the Wardrobe.* New York, NY: Harper Collins Children's Books, 1950. Paperback.

Lucado, Max. *Grace: More Than We Deserve, Greater Than We Imagine.* Nashville, TN: Thomas Nelson Inc., 2012. Paperback.

McCasland, David. *Oswald Chambers: Abandoned to God.* Grand Rapids: Oswald Chambers Publications Association, Ltd., 1993.

Meyers, Rick. "Adam Clarke's Commentary." *E-Sword add-on.* Updated 2013.

Oxford University Press. *Dictionary.* 2012. Entry. 3 January 2013. <http://oxforddictionaries.com/definition/english/oath?q=oath>.

Salem Communications Corporation. *Geneva Study Bible, Genesis 2.* 2012. webpage. 2013. <http://www.biblestudytools.com/commentaries/geneva-study-bible/genesis/genesis-2.html>.

Silbiger, Steven. *The Jewish Phenomenon.* Marietta, GA: Longstreet Press Inc., 2000. Paperback.

Thurow, Lester. *Fortune Favors the Bold.* New York, NY: Harper Collins Publishers, 2003. Hardcover.

Unger, Merrill F. *The New Unger's Bible Dictionary.* Ed. R. K. Harrison. Chicago: The Moody Bible Institue of Chicago, 1957, Revised and Updated, 1988. Hardcover.

Wesley, Rev. John. *Chapter 11 Reflections.* Ed. Ernest O'Neill. n.d. Christian Corps International. Electronic. January 2013. <http://www.worldinvisible.com/library/wesley/8317/831711.htm>.

Young, Robert L. *Understanding Misunderstanding.* Austin, TX: University of Texas Press, 1999. Paperback.

Edwards Brothers Malloy
Thorofare, NJ USA
June 19, 2013